The Florida Gardener's

Book of Lists

Published by Taylor Trade Publishing
An Imprint of the Rowman & Littlefield Publishing Group
4501 Forbes Blvd., Suite 200
Lanham, Maryland 20706

Designed by David Timmons

Library of Congress Cataloging-in-Publication Data

Chaplin, Lois Trigg.
  The Florida gardener's book of lists : a guide to gardening in the
 Sunshine State / written by Lois Trigg Chaplin and Monica Brandies.
   p. cm.
  Includes index.
  ISBN 0-87833-908-6
  1. Landscape plants—Florida. 2. Landscape gardening—Florida.
 I. Brandies, Monica Moran, 1938– . II. Title.
 SB408.C48 1998
 635.9'09759—dc21   98–5072
 CIP

Printed in the United States of America

Distributed by National Book Network

CONTENTS

ACKNOWLEDGMENTS

We would like to thank all the gardeners and plant professionals with whom we've talked or visited for sharing your knowledge with us. Many of you are listed throughout the pages of this text. Others were not directly involved with this project, but yet have shared information, opinion, and research over the years to help form the current body of Florida gardening knowledge. We would especially like to thank all the wonderful professors and researchers at IFAS, and all of the Extension Agents and Master Gardeners who continually work to promote gardening throughout the state.

Thanks to you all.

TWO LETTERS TO OUR READERS

Dear Floridians,

Gardening in Florida is not like gardening anywhere else in the country. We have different plants, different time tables, and definitely different soil. It seemed I had to learn everything from scratch eleven years ago when we moved here. The first year was full of frustration, but even at first there were some fantastic successes. I found that if you don't give up, you learn much faster in Florida because of the year-round growing season. The possibilities are wondrous and the excitement only grows and grows.

Every gardening book I own that has lists in it has those pages marked on the cover and worn on the edges from use. I hope this entire book will be like that for you. Use it as a starting point to a landscape that makes your private world, the outdoor living area of your home, a great place to be.

May you have flowers, fruits, and vegetables to pick, see, and enjoy every day of your life.

Great Growing,
Monica Moran Brandies

Dear Gardeners,

Since early in my career I've wanted to produce a book about gardening in Florida. Although I now live in Alabama, my first garden experiences were in Jacksonville's sand and hardpan. Today, my work keeps me in touch with Florida gardeners, which is how I've come to know Monica. Monica gardens in Tampa. I know frosty north Florida and studied horticulture there (Go, Gators!). By combining our experience, we trust that we're giving you a better book than either of us could by working alone. We hope that you will use this book so much that you will add your own notes in it. No single book can give details on every plant, so we recommend several books, listed in the introduction, as companions to this one. We hope our efforts will bring you many ideas and plant the seeds of enjoyment in your garden.

Happy Gardening,
Lois Trigg Chaplin

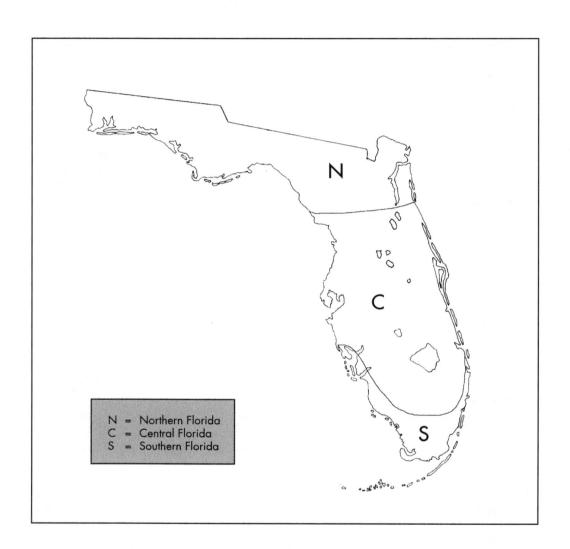

N = Northern Florida
C = Central Florida
S = Southern Florida

DON'T SKIP THIS INTRODUCTION

An introduction seems like the very first thing an author would write, but in reality it is the last. This is where we tell you a little bit about the philosophy of the book and give you a road map for going through it. And that is best done when every detail is known. So please read on and you'll know how to approach the information in the book.

You will see our initials (MB and LC) in the text from time to time; they have been used to indicate which one of us is speaking when a personal experience is being described.

HOW TO USE THIS BOOK

It's a notebook. We want you to write in this book, adding plants (or striking them) over time. Keep it as a sort of garden index that will help guide you from project to project, year to year. Some of the scientific names listed might not be the latest ones, for plant taxonomists continually rename and recategorize plants. All this renaming is necessary to taxonomy, but it sure makes for a lot of frustration on our end. The staff at your local nursery may know some of the plants you're asking about by a different name. Such is the world of horticulture.

We've used the terms *variety*, *cultivar*, and *selection* interchangeably in this book, although scientifically there are differences.

One of the impossibilities in a book such as this is to do a thorough job of listing the many selections of a plant. When you're shopping for a species mentioned on a list, you may find many selections that vary in size and other qualities. When we've chosen to list a specific selection, it's because it has particularly outstanding qualities fitted to that list.

All the plants in this book (except the annuals) are followed by the letters N, C, or S or some combination of them to indicate in which portion of Florida they grow. N is for north Florida, C for central Florida, and S for south Florida. These are not definite boundaries but serve as guidelines. See the map at left for a general idea of how we divided the state.

Folks in the panhandle may feel that our book is heavy on plants that aren't cold hardy enough for the panhandle, but the rest of Florida is so often omitted from books that we wanted to concentrate on sure-enough Florida species. Panhandle gardeners may also want to consult *The Southern Gardener's Book of Lists*, which includes many plants hardy in USDA zones 7, 8, and 9. We apologize to gardeners in the Keys, because some plants that are indicated with an "S" may not grow in your marl soil and salty environs.

FOR TRANSPLANTED GARDENERS

We asked Camille Hunter, a northern transplant like Monica, what advice she gives gardeners concerning climate and considerations of gardening in Florida. She responded with such a great letter that we've included it here almost in its entirety:

> Growing up in the western New York snow belt meant long winters, snowfall measured in feet instead of inches, and sub-zero temperatures that came with depressing regularity. It also meant living in USDA hardiness zone 5—a great source of distress when looking through garden catalogs. Everything desirable, it seemed, grew only in the warm South.
>
> Fixated as I was on zones, I thought moving to Florida was my ticket to paradise. No more worries about cold! You can grow anything in Florida, right?
>
> Well, almost. But hardiness zones, even in the Sunshine State, should never be ignored. Ours is a state that spans zones 8, 9, and 10. Average minimum temperatures range from 20 to 30 degrees in the north to 40 to 50 degrees in the south. Hardiness information is important when selecting plants, but it doesn't tell the whole story. . . .
>
> Soon I learned that there are also diverse microclimates, soil conditions, and rainfall patterns to be concerned about. Coastal areas of Florida are moderated and are warmer in winter as well as cooler in summer (than inland). Large inland waterways and lakes also create moderated microclimates. This is particularly true on eastern shores because prevailing winds are from the west and so are tempered by passing over water (unless you're on the Atlantic Coast and get a Nor'easter).
>
> Soils are as diverse as microclimates. Get too close to the ocean, and you better start checking the salt tolerance and pH requirements of whatever you plant. Sandy beach soils can be very alkaline, and that is a limiting factor with many plants. In contrast to alkaline soils at the beach, inland hammocks can have very acid soil, which is great for blueberries and azaleas but a problem for many other plants. Heavy clay soil or hardpan layers, common in sections of Florida, are a problem for plants because of poor drainage. Even worse, some of us live on reclaimed wetlands that suffer from occasional flooding.
>
> To thrive in Florida, a plant also has to endure a blistering summer sun with temperature and humidity in the nineties; nights offer little relief.
>
> Rainfall is another consideration. We get reasonable amounts of rain but in legendary downpours that drive tourists off the highways and into the rest stops. Often a rainy season is followed by drought, a real one-two punch to any plant. Add to that the astounding diversity of insects and diseases that are spawned by the climate, and we begin to appreciate what a plant has to put up with.

It is still Eden to me, but with an edge. I grow all those wondrous plants I used to moon over in the catalogs: allamanda, bougainvillea, hibiscus, fig trees, and many more. We can grow an amazing variety of plants here, but we need to understand our own micro-paradises to be successful. We also need to ask many questions about a plant and the conditions it will grow in. Is it cold hardy? Is it tolerant of summer heat and humidity? Can it take full sun? What about water, drainage, and soil pH?

And don't expect to grow everything. It's just too warm for the peonies, bearded iris, crisp New England apples, lilacs, perennial tulips, and Kentucky bluegrass that were so well loved back home. Learning this can be a letdown, but the lists of what can be grown are great consolation. Sweet-smelling lemon trees, cassias that cover themselves with golden flowers, fragrant tea olive, and stately palms—they all make Florida seem pretty heavenly after all.

The words of a Florida gardener who is well broken-in. Thanks, Camille.

WHAT A DIFFERENCE THE SOIL MAKES

As Camille noted, soil makes as much difference in whether or not a plant can grow in your locale as climate does. For example, azaleas are fine in areas with acid soil but will not grow near the beaches or in areas with alkaline soil, even though the climate is perfectly suitable. So always use the regions in this book and elsewhere only as a general guideline. Ask questions locally about the plant that interests you. Neighboring gardeners are often your best and most reliable source of information on plant growth requirements.

BOOKS YOU SHOULD KNOW ABOUT

These books will cost you a few dollars, but even if you buy them all, you'll more than get your money back over time by avoiding costly mistakes. These are titles that we refer to often.

Must Have

Bell, C. Ritchie, and Taylor, Bryan J. *Florida Wild Flowers and Roadside Plants*. Chapel Hill, NC: Laurel Hill Press, 1982.

Brandies, Monica Moran. *Xeriscaping for Florida Homes*. St. Petersburg, FL: Great Outdoors Publishing, 1994.

Brookwell, Joan, and Haehle, Robert. *Landscaping with Native Florida Plants*. Houston, TX: Gulf Publishing, in press.

Broschat, Timothy K., and Meerow, Alan W. *Betrock's Reference Guide to Florida Landscape Plants*. Hollywood, FL: Betrock Information Systems, 1994. (MB: Can't live without this one.)

DeFreitas, Stan. *The Complete Guide to Florida Gardening*. Dallas, TX: Taylor Publishing, 1987.

MacCubbin, Tom, and Tasker, Georgia B. *Florida Gardener's Guide*. Cool Springs Press, 1997. (MB: I also have three of Tom's older books.)

Mackey, Betty Barr, and Brandies, Monica Moran. A *Cutting Garden for Florida*. Wayne, PA: B.B. Mackey Books, 1992.

Maxwell, Lewis. *Florida Fruit*, *Florida Vegetables*, and *Florida Flowers*. Tampa, FL: Lewis Maxwell, Publisher. Complete series, constantly updated.

Odenwald, Neil, and Turner, James. *Southern Plants for Landscape Design*. Baton Rouge, LA:

Claitor's Publishing, 1996. (LC: One of my favorites.)

Siedenberg, Charlotte. *The New Orleans Garden: Gardening in the Gulf South.* Jackson: University Press of Mississippi, 1993. (LC: Another of my favorites.)

Tasker, Georgia B. *Enchanted Ground.* Kansas City: Andrews and McMeel, 1994.

Trustees Garden Club of Savannah. *Garden Guide to the Lower South.* Savannah, GA: Trustees Garden Club, 1991. (Look for the lastest edition available.)

Welch, William C. *Perennial Garden Color.* Dallas, TX: Taylor Publishing, 1989.

Others for Special Needs

Ajilvsgi, Geyata. *Butterfly Gardening for the South.* Dallas, TX: Taylor Publishing, 1990.

Brandies, Monica Moran. *Herbs and Spices for Florida Gardens.* Wayne, PA: B.B. Mackey Books, 1996.

———. *Florida Gardening: The Newcomer's Survival Manual.* Wayne, PA: B.B. Mackey Books, 1993.

Creasy, Rosalind. *The Complete Book of Edible Landscaping.* San Francisco, CA: Sierra Club, 1982.

Druitt, Liz. *The Organic Rose Garden.* Dallas, TX: Taylor Publishing, 1996.

Ogden, Scott. *Garden Bulbs for the South.* Dallas, TX: Taylor Publishing, 1994.

Stevens, Ted. *Roses Under the Sun: A Guide for Growing Roses in Florida.* Lakeland, FL: Bread and Butter Press, 1994.

Van Atta, Marian. *Growing and Using Exotic Foods.* Sarasota, FL: Pineapple Press, 1991.

Welch, William C. *Antique Roses for the South.* Dallas, TX: Taylor Publishing, 1990.

Welch, William C., and Grant, Greg. *Southern Heirloom Plants.* Dallas, TX: Taylor Publishing, 1996.

General Reference

DeFreitas, Stan. *The Stan DeFreitas Garden Answer Book.* Dallas, TX: Taylor Publishing, 1998.

Dirr, Michael. *Manual of Woody Landscape Plants.* Champaign, IL: Stipes Publishing, 1975 (rev. 1990). (Especially helpful for the upper and middle South.)

Garden Section of the Woman's Club of Havana. *Flowering Plants from Cuban Gardens.* New York, NY: Criterion Books, 1958. (LC: This is out of print, but you may be able to find a secondhand copy.)

Sunset Books & Magazine. *The Western Garden Book.* Menlo Park, CA: Sunset Publishing, 1995.

"One of the most rewarding things about gardening in Florida is the vast diversity of plants we have available. We can choose natives, exotics, or mix them up as we please. And if you take the kid-in-the-candystore approach ('I want one of those, and one of those, and . . .'), don't apologize. It may not lead to an award-winning landscape, but it does make for a great gardening experience. And after all, that's what it's really about, isn't it?" —Joan Brookwell, horticulture writer; former home and garden editor, *Fort Lauderdale Sun-Sentinel*; and coauthor with Robert Haehle of *Landscaping with Native Florida Plants.*

Note that the following lists are in alphabetical order according to botanical name.

TREES

Traveling down the highway toward Pompano Beach one day, my husband and I (MB) passed a trailer park baking in the sun. "How would you like to live there? It looks like a piece of hell," he said. But before I could answer we passed another trailer park. "Look at that one," I said. "Anyone would like to live there. It looks like a piece of paradise. You know what makes the difference?"

"Trees," we said together.

As Steve Graham, forester for the city of Tampa, puts it, "For all their importance, trees are largely taken for granted. It is the absence of shade that gets our attention." But shade is easier to grow in Florida than anywhere else in the continental United States. Even oaks will grow 5 feet a year here.

There are more native trees listed in this book than any other kind of native plant. Add all the imported species that do well here, and you'll end up with more trees than you probably want to know about.

More deciduous trees thrive in northern Florida than do evergreens. That balance changes until there are mostly evergreen trees, both broadleaved and needled, farther south. Some plants that are trees in south Florida, such as the sea grape and the grumichama, may grow only to shrub size in central Florida. Because we expect some replacement of shrubs in the landscape but expect trees, especially the larger ones, to be relatively permanent, we have been stricter with district notations in this chapter than elsewhere in this book.

Some trees become weeds if allowed to reseed. The worst, such as melaleuca, are not recommended anywhere in this book. Others, such as goldenrain tree, simply need to be planted in an area where you will be mowing or digging often enough to control seedlings.

Where improved varieties are recommended, we put in at least one and indicated with a + if there are several cultivars from which you might choose. We have also listed some trees, like hickory, that you may not find in a nursery but may find in the wild.

Before you purchase and place a tree, ask about its ultimate height and width and plan accordingly. We have not included that information in the following lists because expectations vary so greatly depending on locale and conditions. Consult a local source and know the size, sun, and soil of your site to get an idea of what a specific tree should do for you.

To Do List for Trees

- Select trees for year-round interest to keep the garden lively. This should include evergreens as well as flowering trees for every season. Many trees also have attractive and delicious fruit.
- Trees have many forms: reaching, oval, pyramidal, round, columnar, weeping, vase-shaped, irregular, and palm. Each communicates a different feeling, and a particular form may be better suited than another to practical limitations such as power lines and overhangs.
- Whether you are building a house or paving a driveway, get expert advice on protecting trees from construction before you begin. Tree roots spread great distances; compacting the soil, cutting the roots, or changing the level of the soil that covers their roots can kill trees.
- If you need shade, buy two of the largest trees you can afford and place them to the south and west of the house to provide cooling shadows. Do not put shade trees too close to the house, however. This is a common mistake. Leave at least 30 feet for that expected spread.
- When you plant, *always* leave a circle of mulch around the tree that measures at least the diameter of the rootball. It will keep you from hitting the trunk with the mower or string trimmer—injuries that can kill the tree—and it encourages faster growth by conserving moisture and keeping grass roots at a distance.
- Water and fertilize young trees. *This is an absolute must*, especially in Florida's poor soil. If you have to skip lunch to budget for fertilizer, do it. Even the slowest growing tree should grow at least 1 to 5 feet a year *if* you feed and water it. Fertilize in the fall (after frost, never before), in early spring (as leaf buds break), and again two months later. Water every week during dry weather for the first two years. Water slowly and deeply—at least 5 gallons for a 5-foot-tall tree.
- Even in Florida, the time involved in the growth of a tree demands respect. Never cut one down unless you know what it is and what it will do. Seasons vary widely from year to year, and you may have something choice that will take three years or more after a frost to bloom and bear again. Or you may have a weedy tree that can take over the yard in that length of time. If your city does not have a forester to give you this information, hire one. It will be money well spent.

Trees That Tolerate (or Prefer) Wet Places

Red mangrove

Some trees need a constant source of moisture. If they are near enough to a pond or stream for their roots to reach water, they will thrive. Others on this list are just very adaptable and will do well in wet or dry places. And some, like the mangrove, will stand in water. If you have a spot that is mostly moist or sometimes soggy, there is a wide choice of trees on this list, even including fruits like persimmon and nuts like hickory and pecan. LC: If you like sweet gum for its color and leaves, you'll be pleased to know there is a ball-less cultivar called 'Rotundiloba'. The first time I ever saw it was fifteen years ago in Orlando at the home of nurseryman Randy Knight. I have seen it in nurseries but not very often. Ask for it.

Red maple (*Acer rubrum* 'Armstrong'+)	N, C, S
Paurotis palm (*Acoelorrhaphe wrightii*)	C, S
Black mangrove (*Avicennia germinans*)	C, S

River birch (*Betula nigra* 'Heritage')	N
American hornbeam or musclewood (*Carpinus caroliniana*)	N, C
Water hickory (*Carya aquatica*)	N, C
Hackberry, sugarberry (*Celtis laevigata* 'All Seasons')	N, C, S
Atlantic white cedar (*Chamaecyparis thyoides*)	N, C, S
Persimmon (*Diospyros virginiana*)	N, C, S
Water ash (*Fraxinus caroliniana*)	N, C, S
White ash (*Fraxinus americana* 'Rosehill'+)	N, C
Loblolly bay (*Gordonia lasianthus*)	N, C, S
Dahoon holly (*Ilex cassine*)	N, C, S
American holly (*Ilex opaca*)	N, C, S
American sweet gum (*Liquidambar styraciflua* 'Rotundiloba'+)	N, C
Tulip poplar (*Liriodendron tulipifera*)	N, C, S
Southern magnolia (*Magnolia grandiflora*)	N, C, S
Sweet bay magnolia (*Magnolia virginiana* 'Henry Hicks')	N, C, S
California bayberry (*Myrica californica*)	N, C, S
Southern bayberry (*Myrica cerifera*)	N, C, S
Water tupelo (*Nyssa aquatica*)	N, C, S
Ogeechee tupelo (*Nyssa ogeche*)	N, C
Blackgum (*Nyssa sylvatica*)	N, C
Screwpine (*Pandanus* spp.)	S
Red bay (*Persea borbonia*)	N, C, S
Fevertree (*Pinckneya pubens*)	N, C
Spruce pine (*Pinus glabra*)	N, C
Pond pine (*Pinus serotina*)	N
Loblolly pine (*Pinus taeda*)	N, C
London plane tree (*Platanus* × *acerifolia* 'Bloodgood'+)	N, C
Sycamore (*Platanus occidentalis*)	N, C, S
Overcup oak (*Quercus lyrata*)	N, C
Swamp white oak (*Quercus michauxii*)	N, C
Willow oak (*Quercus phellos*)	N, C
Shumard oak (*Quercus shumardii*)	N, C, S
Live oak (*Quercus virginiana*)	N, C, S
Red mangrove (*Rhizophora mangle*)	C, S
Cabbage palm (*Sabal palmetto*)	N, C, S
Weeping willow (*Salix babylonica*)	N, C
Coastal plain willow (*Salix caroliniana*)	N, C, S
Bald cypress (*Taxodium distichum* 'Pendens')	N, C, S
Winged elm (*Ulmus alata*)	N, C
American elm (*Ulmus americana* 'Princeton')	N, C
Hybrid elm (*Ulmus* × *hybrida* 'Frontier'+)	N, C

 "River birch is the tree for all places. This deciduous native displays attractive structure and form. I have a personal preference for them planted in groupings as an accent to shrub and groundcover designs. River birch speaks to the connoisseur." —Kathy Beck, Tampa Parks Department.

TREES THAT ARE DROUGHT RESISTANT

Trees are generally more drought resistant than many other kinds of plants simply because of their greater size. The root system of a tree can extend three times the reach of the canopy of leaves. While most of the feeder roots stay near the surface, deeper roots draw moisture from far down in the earth. The following trees are highly drought resistant and should not need watering at all once established. Still, remember that it can take two years or more for a young tree to establish a good root system, and you can expect much faster and firmer growth from any tree that does not suffer stress. Mulch makes a significant difference, especially for Florida gardeners who are only here in the winter. A few fruit trees, such as citrus and figs, are remarkably drought tolerant, but we omitted them because they need ample water for a good harvest.

Neem (*Azadirachta indica*)	C, S
Black olive (*Bucida* spp.)	S
Gumbo limbo (*Bursera simaruba*)	S
Golden shower (*Cassia fistula*)	S
Silk cotton tree (*Ceiba pentandra*)	S
Hackberry, sugarberry (*Celtis laevigata* 'All Seasons')	N, C, S
Redbud (*Cercis canadensis*)	N, C
Floss silk tree (*Chorisia speciosa*)	C, S
Pitch apple (*Clusia rosea*)	S
Sea-grape (*Coccoloba uvifera*)	C, S
Geiger tree (*Cordia sebestena*)	S
Parsley hawthorn (*Crataegus Marshallii*)	N, C
Mexican calabash (*Crescentia alata*)	S
Royal poinciana (*Delonix regia*)	S
Persimmon (*Diospyros virginiana*)	N, C, S
Loquat (*Eriobotrya japonica*)	N, C, S
Cockspur coral tree (*Erythrina crista-gallii*)	C, S
Eucalyptus (*Eucalyptus* spp.)	C, S
Green ash (*Fraxinus pennsylvanica*)	N, C
Lignum vitae (*Guaiacum santum*)	S
Blolly (*Guaparia discolor*)	S
Mahoe or sea hibiscus (*Hibiscus tiliacaeus*)	C, S
White ironwood (*Hypelate trifoliata*)	S
American holly (*Ilex opaca*)	N, C, S
Yaupon holly (*Ilex vomitoria*)	N, C, S
Jacaranda (*Jacaranda mimosifolia*)	C, S
Southern red cedar (*Juniperus silicicola*)	N, C, S
Black ironwood (*Krugiodendron ferreum*)	S
Crape myrtle (*Lagerstroemia indica*)	N, C, S
Queen's crape myrtle (*Lagerstroemia speciosa*)	C, S
Southern magnolia (*Magnolia grandiflora*)	N, C, S
Spanish lime (*Melicocca bijugatus*)	S
Horseradish tree (*Moringa oleifera*)	C, S
Palm, many species	N, C, S
Screwpine (*Pandanus* spp.)	S
Copperpod (*Peltophorum pterocarpum*)	C, S
Allspice (*Pimenta dioica*)	S
Pine (*Pinus* spp.)	N, C, S

Chinese pistache (*Pistacia chinensis*)	N, C, S
Frangipani (*Plumeria rubra*)	C, S
Cherry laurel (*Prunus caroliniana*)	N, C
Sawtooth oak (*Quercus acutissima*)	N
Bluejack oak (*Quercus incana*)	N, C, S
Myrtle oak (*Quercus myrtifolia*)	N, C, S
Live oak (*Quercus virginiana*)	N, C, S
Shining sumac (*Rhus copallina*)	N, C, S
Mahogany (*Swietenia mahogani*)	S
Tabebuia (*Tabebuia* spp.)	C, S
Bald cypress (*Taxodium distichum*)	N, C, S
Yellow elder (*Tecoma stans*)	C, S
Tropical almond (*Terminalia catappa*)	S
Chaste tree (*Vitex agnus-castus*)	N, C, S
Jujube (*Ziziphus jujuba*)	N

TREES WITH MULTIPLE TRUNKS

Multitrunked trees have a quality that often makes them as much sculpture as tree, particularly in intimate spaces where the bark and branch patterns are highlighted. If you choose to train a tree thus, select a young one that has already been started in a multitrunked form. Some trees tend to naturally grow with three or more leaders that become multiple trunks as the tree ages. Where this is not the case, you can get the same effect by planting three trees in the same hole. This works well where male and female are separate and you need both, such as with the hollies and osage orange.

Cornus florida

Acacia (*Acacia* spp.)	N, C, S
Japanese maple (*Acer palmatum*)	N, C
Orchid tree (*Bauhinia* spp.)	N, C, S
River birch (*Betula nigra*)	N
American hornbeam (*Carpinus caroliniana*)	N, C
Blue palo verde (*Cercidium floridum*)	N, C, S
Desert willow (*Chilopsis linearis*)	N, C, S
Flowering dogwood (*Cornus florida*)	N, C
Poinciana (*Delonix regia*)	S
Carolina silverbell (*Halesia carolina*)	N, C
Possumhaw (*Ilex decidua*)	N
Crape myrtle (*Lagerstroemia indica*)	N, C, S
Osage orange (*Maclura pomifera*)	N, C
Oriental magnolia (*Magnolia* hybrids)	N
Star Magnolia (*Magnolia stellata*)	N
Sumac (*Rhus* spp.)	N, C, S
Snowbell (*Styrax grandifolius*)	N, C
Prickly ash (*Zanthoxylum* spp.)	N, C, S

A Few Palms with Multiple Trunks

Paurotis palm (*Acoelorrhaphe wrightii*)	C, S
European fan palm (*Chamaerops humilis*)	N, C, S
Areca, yellow-butterfly palm (*Chrysalidocarpus lutescens*)	C, S
Pinangua palm (*Pinangua kuhii*)	S
Reinhardt palm (*Reinhardtia gracilis*)	S

PALMS FOR CONTAINERS

Some palms do very well as container specimens. They have no tap root and will simply grow slower in a container, where they can be maintained for years. Jim Reiners, a member of the International Palm Society, writing in *Florida Gardening* magazine, says, "When transplanting a palm, always go up only one container size—two if the plant is severely root bound. If transplanted into a container that is too large, the palm will spend more time developing roots than fronds or trunk."

Bamboo palm (*Chamaedorea* spp.)	S
Acera, yellow-butterfly palm (*Chrysalidocarpus lutescens*)	S
Beguine palm (*Drymophloeus bequinii*)	S
Kentia palm (*Howea Forsterana*)	N, C, S
Licuala palm (*Licuala grandis*)	S
Pygmy date palm (*Phoenix roebelenii*)	C, S
Pinangua palm (*Pinangua kuhii*)	S
Reinhardt palm (*Reinhardtia gracilis*)	S
Lady palm (*Rhapis excelsa*)	N, C, S

"The most critical factor in caring for potted palms is watering. Water two or three times a week; give enough each time so that water drains out the bottom of the pot. Soils for potted plants should be light and porous or even sandy. Humus, leaf mold, or peat may be mixed with it. Feed with balanced, inorganic, and organic fertilizers. In cold climates, do not fertilize during the winter." —George B. Stevenson, author of *Palms of South Florida*.

FAVORITE PALMS FOR FLORIDA HOMES

Palm trees are the symbol of a climate with warm winters, and many northerners transplanted here love them for that alone. Palms are also among the easiest trees to move even when large (with special equipment), so landscapers love them for that. Your choice of palms increases from about a dozen in north Florida to nearly eighty at the southern tip and in the Keys. Some palms are so broad or towering that they do not fit the scale of a residential lot. We've limited this list to palms best suited to home landscapes. Most palms have a fair degree of salt tolerance; those with asterisks are extremely salt tolerant.

Paurotis palm (*Acoelorrhaphe wrightii*)*	C, S
Alexandra palm (*Archontophoenix alexandrae*)	S
Piccabeen palm (*Archontophoenix cunninghamiana*)	S
Bismark palm (*Bismarckia nobilis*)*	C, S
Guadeloupe palm (*Brahea edulis*)	N, C, S
Hesper palm (*Brahea aculeata*)	N, C, S
Mexican blue palm (*Brahea armata*)	C, S
Pindo palm (*Butia capitata*)*	N, C, S
Fishtail palm (*Caryotas* spp.)	C, S
European fan (*Chamaerops humilis*)	N, C, S
Areca, yellow-butterfly palm (*Chrysalidocarpus lutescens*)	C, S
Silver palm (*Coccothrinax* spp.)*	S
Coconut palm (*Cocos nucifera* 'Malayan Dwarf')*	S

Wax palm, carnauba (*Copernicia* spp.)*	S
Kentia palm (*Howea Forsterana*)	N, C, S
Sentry palm (*Howea* spp.)	C, S
Kaffir palm (*Jubaeopsis caffra*)	N, C, S
Latan palm (*Latania* spp.)*	S
Fan palm (*Livistona* spp.)	C, S
Double coconut palm (*Lodoicea maldivica*)	S
Date palm (*Phoenix* spp.)*	N, C, S
Fan palm (*Pritchardia* spp.)*	S
Needle palm (*Rhapidophyllum hystrix*)	N, C, S
Lady palm (*Rhapis excelsa*)	C, S
Royal palm (*Roystonea* spp.)*	S
Cabbage palm (*Sabal palmetto*)	N, C, S
Queen palm (*Syagrus romanzoffiana*)*	C, S
Thatch palm (*Thrinax* spp.)*	S
Windmill palm (*Trachycarpus fortunei*)*	N, C, S
Christmas, manila palm (*Veitchia merrillii*)*	S

Phoenix dactylifera

"As a palm tree grows, it sheds its fronds at the bottom of the trunk. When you observe fronds turning yellow, remove them using a palm saw. (This tool has a large curved blade on a long extension pole.) Trim when the fronds are still tender. Once they turn brown, they become hard and are difficult to cut. *Never* try to trim the center of a palm. This is the bud from which new fronds emerge. Trimming the bud will kill a palm tree." —Stan DeFreitas, author of *The Complete Guide to Florida Gardening* and *The Stan DeFreitas Garden Answer Book*.

WEEPING TREES

Our love of weeping trees may come from memories of playing as children in a "house" hidden under branches that draped almost to the ground. Their appeal may also come from the feeling of letting go and relaxing that the sight of a weeping tree inspires. In any case, they are eye-catching, powerful forms in the landscape, to be used as specimens or accents. Many, but not all of them, tend to grow in wet places, and sometimes they can give the feeling of a pond where there is none. The evergreens, such as weeping yaupon holly, can be used as a screen. You will find weeping forms of many upright trees. Generally, they are specialty items, but the ones below are among the most common and should be the easiest to find.

Weeping bottlebrush (*Callistemon viminalis*)	C, S
Australian willow (*Geijera parviflora*)	N, C, S
Weeping ginkgo (*Ginkgo biloba* 'Pendula')	N
Weeping yaupon holly (*Ilex vomitoria* 'Pendula')	N, C, S
Colorado red cedar (*Juniperus scopulorum* 'Rependens', 'Tolleson's Green Weeping')	N, C
Wild tamarind (*Lysiloma bahamensis*)	S
Weeping podocarpus (*Podocarpus gracilior*)	C, S
Cork oak (*Quercus suber*)	N, C, S
Weeping willow (*Salix babylonica*)	N, C
Drake elm (*Ulmus parvifolia* 'Drake')	N, C

BEST PLUMERIAS FOR FLORIDA

"The plumeria has truly become the flower of the decade. As people travel more and visit tropical areas of the world, they cannot help but be enchanted by the beauty of this unique and exotic plant," say Richard and Mary Helen Eggenberger in their *Handbook on Plumeria Culture*.

When Alan Bunch first visited Hawaii, he was intrigued by the plumeria, or frangipani, trees and their delicately scented flowers. When he returned, he was even more amazed to find they would grow in parts of Florida where there is little or no frost, and even survive a few frosty nights with socks over their buds. People farther north than the St. Petersburg area must take more drastic steps to keep them through the winter, like growing the dwarf varieties in large pots they can bring inside or cover. Bunch has since made several more trips to Hawaii, done thorough research, and started the largest plumeria nursery in the country in Seffner with the help of his 85-year-young mother, Ruby. As Ruby shows customers photos of their 150 or so varieties, she says, "They're all my favorites, just like children." All are cultivars of *Plumeria alba*, *rubra*, or *obtusa*.

The cultivars listed here are all robust, thickly branched, and less prone to the various pests and fungi that can afflict plumeria in Florida.

	Color	Fragrance	Form
'Costa Pink'	Pink, yellow throat	Slight	Well branched
'Dean Conklin'	Pink and shrimp	Plumeria	Well branched
'Dwarf Singapore'	Pinkish white	Citrusy	Compact/dense
'Hausten White'	White, yellow throat	Plumeria	Well branched
'Hot Pink'	Fuschia, yellow throat	Fruity	Upright
'Irma Bryan'	Dark red	Pleasant	Well branched
'Nebel's Rainbow'	Golden yellow and red	Plumeria	Well branched
'Plastic Pink'	Medium to dark pink	Fruity	Well branched
'Polynesian Red'	Red, yellow throat	Cinnamon	Well branched
'Samoan Fluff'	White, yellow throat	Plumeria	Well branched
'Singapore'	White, yellow throat	Citrusy	Well branched
'Sunset'	Pinkish white, yellow throat	Fruity	Well branched

"Plumeria, or frangipani, have gotten a bum rap in Florida in the past. Unknowing or uncaring nurserymen years back and some even today have taken the cheapest route and grown plumeria from seed rather than from quality cuttings. In other cases inferior cuttings have been used because they could be purchased cheaply. The trees that grow from seeds and inferior cuttings are rather gangly and ugly. I've heard and read supposed horticulture experts make the statement that plumerias are 'ugly trees.' It is obvious they have not seen trees grown from quality root stock. I have made it my mission to try to change this misconception by providing high-quality plants with many specimen samples growing right in my nursery." —Alan W. Bunch, owner, The Exotic Plumeria Nursery, Seffner.

SMALL TREES (30 FEET OR SHORTER)

This may be the most important tree list in this book. Nothing is more discouraging to us or frustrating for the utility company than trees growing into electrical wires. Always look up and envision the mature size of any tree you are considering planting. We have seen streets with fine trees along one side and nothing along the other because of electric lines; that is never necessary, certainly not in Florida, where there is such a wide choice of good small trees. For this list we eliminated all that didn't have attractive flowers as well. In north Florida most of these are deciduous; in south Florida most are evergreen. Also check the lists in "Shrubs" for shrubs that are large enough to train as small trees.

Evergreens

Acacia (*Acacia* spp.)	C, S
Mexican caesalpinia (*Caesalpinia mexicana*)	S
Weeping bottlebrush (*Callistemon viminalis*)	N, C, S
Wild cinnamon (*Canella winterana*)	S
Senna (*Cassia spectabilis*)	S
Citrus (*Citrus* spp.)	C, S
Buttonwood (*Conocarpus erectus*)	S
Texas wild olive (*Cordia boissieri*)	N, C, S
Geiger tree (*Cordia sebestena*)	S
Loquat (*Eriobotrya japonica*)	N, C, S
Spindle palm (*Hyophorbe verschaffeltii*)	S
Holly (*Ilex × attenuata* 'East Palatka', 'Savannah')	N, C, S
Dahoon holly (*Ilex cassine*)	N, C, S
Yaupon holly (*Ilex vomitoria*)	N, C, S
Jaboticaba (*Myriacia cauliflora*)	C, S
Florida yew (*Podocarpus macrophyllus*)	N, C, S
African sumac (*Rhus lancea*)	N, C, S
Arikury palm (*Syagrus schizophylla*)	S
Pink trumpet tree (*Tabebuia heterophylla*)	C, S
Cuban pink trumpet (*Tabebuia pallida*)	C, S
Yellow elder (*Tecoma stans*)	C, S
Tibouchina (*Tibouchina granulosa*)	S

Deciduous

Japanese maple (*Acer palmatum*)	N, C
Cassia (*Cassia surattensis*)	S
Blue palo verde (*Cercidium floridum*)	N, C, S
Redbud (*Cercis canadensis*)	N, C
Desert willow (*Chilopsis linearis*)	N, C, S
Fringe tree (*Chionanthus virginicus*)	N, C, S
Dogwood (*Cornus florida*)	N, C
Parsley hawthorn (*Crataegus Marshallii*)	N
Coral tree (*Erythrina crista-gallii*)	N, C, S
Possumhaw (*Ilex decidua*)	N
Crape myrtle (*Lagerstroemia indica* and hybrids)	N, C, S
Ashe magnolia (*Magnolia asheii*)	N
Chinese pistache (*Pistacia chinensis*)	N, C, S
Frangipani (*Plumeria* spp.)	C, S
Chickasaw plum (*Prunus angustifolia*)	N
Taiwan cherry (*Prunus campanulata*)	N
Shaving brush tree (*Pseudobombax ellipticum*)	S
Purple tabebuia (*Tabebuia impetiginosa*)	C, S
Sparkleberry (*Vaccinium arboreum*)	N, C, S
Chaste tree (*Vitex agnus-castus*)	N, C
Chinese jujube (*Ziziphus jujuba*)	N

TREES FOR THE BEACH

The few trees that will tolerate the wind, sun, and salt at the edge of the sea are important not only for shade and landscaping but also for holding the sandy soil in place. Will and Sally Collins of Osprey, near Sarasota, had fourteen large palms, which are salt tolerant but shallow rooted, on their beach property. They sadly watched one after another wash away, eight at once in a bad storm (but not a hurricane), along with the land beneath them.

Every few feet and every obstacle—building, berm, fence, taller plants—between a beach planting and the water creates a slightly different microclimate in which a few more plants will do well. The leeward side of the house offers enough protection that you can sometimes grow trees that are usually grown farther inland. Also check the list of palms for salt-tolerant varieties.

Highly Tolerant of Salt and Wind

Black mangrove (*Avicennia germinans*)	C, S
Yaupon holly (*Ilex vomitoria*)	N, C, S
Eastern red cedar (*Juniperus virginiana*)	N, C
Southern magnolia (*Magnolia grandiflora*)	N, C, S
Jerusalem thorn (*Parkinsonia aculeata*)	N, C, S
Japanese black pine (*Pinus thunbergiana*)	N, C
Live oak (*Quercus virginiana*)	N, C, S
Red mangrove (*Rhizophora mangle*)	C, S
Cabbage palm (*Sabal palmetto*)	N, C, S

Moderately Tolerant, Requires a Thicket

Red maple (*Acer rubrum*)	N, C
Australian tea tree (*Leptospermum laevigatum*)	C, S
Black tupelo (*Nyssa sylvatica*)	N, C
Sand pine (*Pinus clausa*)	N, C, S
Slash pine (*Pinus elliottii*)	N, C, S
London plane tree (*Platanus* × *acerifolia*)	N, C

Slightly Tolerant, Not for Direct Ocean Front

American hornbeam or musclewood (*Carpinus caroliniana*)	N, C
Leyland cypress (*Cupressus* × *Cupressocyparis leylandii*)	N, C
Eucalyptus (*Eucalyptus* spp., some)	N, C, S
Rusty fig (*Ficus rubiginosa*)	S
Crape myrtle (*Lagerstroemia indica*, hybrids)	N, C, S
Spruce pine (*Pinus glabra*)	N, C
Longleaf pine (*Pinus palustris*)	N, C, S

 "Try to imitate nature and plant in groves when planting trees on the beach side of the property. One tree planted singlely will be buffeted by the wind and never do much. But many trees together, just as they occur naturally in the forests behind the dunes, will help shield one another from the wind. I plant live oaks 5 feet apart. Facing the water, I find that live oak, black pine, and cabbage palm are the toughest of these trees, and you can get by with a 'grove' of three."—Bob Hartwig, Hartwig and Associates, landscape architects, Jacksonville.

TREES WITH FRAGRANT FLOWERS

MB: When the weather is good, you can smell orange blossoms from a block away during the entire month of March. Most crape myrtles have little or no fragrance, but mine wafts its almost lilaclike sweetness up the front walk through much of the summer.

Try to plant some plants for fragrance at every season in every section of the landscape. Because many flowering trees are deciduous, we marked the evergreen ones with asterisks.

Southern magnolia

Sweet acacia (*Acacia farnesiana*)*	C, S
Ylang-ylang (*Cananga odorata*)*	S
Desert willow (*Chilopsis linearis*)	S
Fringe tree (*Chionanthus virginicus*)	N, C, S
Sweet or loblolly bay (*Gordonia lasianthus*)	N, C, S
Japanese raisin tree (*Hovenia dulcis*)	N, C, S
Jacaranda (*Jacaranda mimosifolia*)	C, S
Sausage tree (*Kigelia pinnata*)*	S
Apalachee crape myrtle (*Lagerstroemia* × 'Apalachee'+)	N, C, S
Southern magnolia (*Magnolia grandiflora*)*	N, C, S
Sweet bay magnolia (*Magnolia virginiana*)	N, C, S
Kopsia (*Ochrosia elliptica*)*	S
Copperpod (*Peltophorum dubium*)*	S
Yellow poinciana, copperpod (*Peltophorum pterocarpum*)*	N, C, S
Frangipani (*Plumeria* spp.)	C, S
Karum tree (*Pongamia pinnata*)*	S
Chickasaw plum (*Prunus angustifolia*)	N, C
Snowbell (*Styrax grandifolius*)	N, C

Fragrant but not Showy

Alligator apple (*Annona glabra*)*	C, S
Mastwood (*Calophyllum inophyllum*)*	S
Citrus (*Citrus* spp.)*	N, C, S
Loquat (*Eriobotrya japonica*)*	N, C, S
White mangrove (*Laguncularia racemosa*)*	S
Screwpine (*Pandanus* spp.)*	S
Macarthur palm (*Ptychosperma Macarthurii*)*	S
Royal palm (*Roystonea* spp.)*	S
Windmill palm (*Trachycarpus fortunei*)*	N, C, S

"People don't realize that the best time to plant cold-hardy trees is fall and winter when the sap is down. Then the root system gets established so the tree can be ready for top growth by spring and summer. Of course, with container-grown stock, you can plant any time of the year, but fall and winter planting will give the best results." —Mary Smude, owner, A & A Growers, Plant City.

TREES FOR ALKALINE SOIL

Sometimes a yard with neutral to acid soil in most of its area will have pockets of alkaline soil near the house or walk where stone has been buried or lime washes off a wall. Fill soils tend to be alkaline. A soil test by your local Extension Office costs little and is well worth it before you make a big investment of work, time, and money on trees.

Podocarpus macrophyllus

Gumbo limbo (*Bursera simaruba*)	S
Hackberry, sugarberry (*Celtis laevigata*)	N, C, S
Redbud (*Cercis canadensis*)	N, C
Satin leaf (*Chrysophyllum oliviforme*)	S
Pigeon plum (*Coccoloba diversifolia*)	S
Sea-grape (*Coccoloba uvifera*)	C, S
Buttonwood (*Conocarpus erectus*)	S
Loquat (*Eriobotrya japonica*)	N, C, S
White ash (*Fraxinus americana*, 'Autumn Purple', 'Rosehill')	N, C
Ash (*Fraxinus* spp.)	N, C
Ginkgo (*Ginkgo biloba* 'Autumn Gold')	N, C
Yaupon holly (*Ilex vomitoria*)	N, C, S
Southern red cedar (*Juniperus silicicola*)	N, C, S
White mulberry (*Morus alba*)	N, C, S
Red bay (*Persea borbonia*)	N, C, S
London plane tree (*Platanus* × *acerifolia* 'Bloodgood')	N, C
Florida yew (*Podocarpus macrophyllus*)	N, C, S
Sand live oak (*Quercus geminata*)	N, C, S
Chinquapin oak (*Quercus muehlenbergii*)	N
Myrtle oak (*Quercus myrtifolia*)	N, C, S
Live oak (*Quercus virginiana*)	N, C, S
Cabbage palm (*Sabal palmetto*)	N, C, S
Texas mountain laurel (*Sophora secundiflorum*)	N, C, S
Lavender tabebuia (*Tabebuia impetiginosa*)	C, S
Wild lime (*Zanthoxylum fagara*)	S

TREES WITH ORNAMENTAL FRUIT

Trees with berries, pods, cones, and other ornamental fruits will add interest to your landscape during their fruiting season. It is especially nice to add some with winter berries (such as the hollies) to gardens in north Florida, where winter brings fewer flowers and less color to the landscape. Some of these ornamental fruits will attract birds and other wildlife to your yard.

Purple, Blue, or Lavender Fruit

Golden shower (*Cassia fistula*)	S
Southern red cedar (*Juniperus silicicola*)	N, C, S
Eastern red cedar (*Juniperus virginiana*)	N, C
Glossy privet, glossy (*Ligustrum lucidum*)	S
Yellow poinciana, copperpod (*Peltophorum* spp.)	S
Red bay (*Persea borbonia*)	N, C, S
Royal palm (*Roystonia venezualensis*)	S

White Fruit

Floss silk tree (*Chorisia speciosa*)	C, S
Geiger (*Cordia sebestena*)	S
Mexican elder (*Sambucus mexicana*)	N, C
Chinese tallow tree (*Sapium sebiferum*)	N, C, S
Texas mountain laurel (*Sophora secundiflorum*)	N, C, S
Cuban pink trumpet (*Tabebuia pallida*)	C, S

Red Fruit

Serviceberry (*Amelanchier arborea*)	N
Flowering dogwood (*Cornus florida*)	N, C
Parsley hawthorn (*Crataegus marshallii*)	N
Japanese raisin tree (*Hovenia dulcis*)	N, C, S
Hollies (*Ilex* 'Savannah', 'Foster'+)	N, C, S
Possumhaw (*Ilex decidua*)	N
Yaupon holly (*Ilex vomitoria*)	N, C, S
Southern magnolia (*Magnolia grandiflora*)	N, C, S
Southern crabapple (*Malus angustifolia*)	N
Ogeechee tupelo (*Nyssa ogeche*)	N, C
Yellow poinciana (*Peltophorum* spp.)	S
Sumac (*Rhus* spp.)	N, C
Texan mountain laurel (*Sophora secundiflora*)	N, C, S
Christmas palm (*Veitchia* spp.)	S
Sweet viburnum (*Viburnum odoratissima* var. *awabuki*)	N, C, S

Orange or Yellow Fruit

Palm, many species	N, C, S
Pindo palm (*Butia capitata*)	N, C, S
Apricot (*Prunus armeniaca* 'Harcot')	N
African sumac (*Rhus lancea*)	N, C, S

Bronze, Tan, or Brown Fruit

Palm, many species	N, C, S
California horse chestnut (*Aesculus californica*)	S
Deodar cedar (*Cedrus deodara*)	N
Desert willow (*Chilopsis linearis*)	N, C, S
Floss silk tree (*Chorisia speciosa*)	C, S
Eucalyptus (*Eucalyptus* spp.)	S
Sausage tree (*Kigelia pinnata*)	S
Golden shower tree (*Koelreuteria elegans*)	N, C, S
Goldenrain tree (*Koelreuteria paniculata*)	N, C
Wild tamarind (*Lysiloma bahamensis*)	S
Pine (*Pinus* spp.)	N, C, S

Black Fruit

Paurotis palm (*Acoelorrhaphe wrightii*)	S
Variegated orchid tree (*Bauhinia variegata* 'Candida')	S
Black olive (*Bucida* spp.)	S
Prickly ash (*Zanthoxylum* spp.)	N, C, S

TREES WITH UNUSUALLY COLORFUL FOLIAGE

The colorful leaves of just one of these trees can give you more color than a whole flower garden. Some, such as the bronze undersides of Glen St. Mary magnolia, are fairly subtle; others, such as purple plum, are such strong accents that they must be used carefully. Ask about these trees at your nursery or read about them in garden books and magazines.

Red, Maroon, or Purplish Leaves

Japanese maple (*Acer palmatum* 'Bloodgood' and other cultivars)	N, C
Redbud (*Cercis canadensis* 'Forest Pansy')	N, C
Giant dracaena (*Cordyline australis* 'Atropurpurea')	S
Plum, purpleleaf, or myrobalan (*Prunus cerasifera* 'Newportii'+)	N, C

Variegated

Japanese maple (*Acer palmatum* 'Aureum')	N, C
Redbud (*Cercis canadensis* 'Silver Cloud')	N, C
Flowering dogwood (*Cornus florida* 'First Lady'+, 'Variegata')	N, C
Holly (*Ilex aquifolium* 'Argentea')	N
Sunny Foster holly (*Ilex × attenuata* 'Sunny Foster')	N, C, S
American sweet gum (*Liquidambar styraciflua* 'Variegata')	N, C, S
Screwpine (*Pandanus* spp.)	S
Veitch screwpine (*Pandanus veitchii*)	C, S
Cherry laurel (*Prunus caroliniana* 'Variegata')	N, C

Bluish Green to Silver

Acacia (*Acacia* spp.)	N, C, S
Mexican blue palm (*Brahea armata*)	C, S
Jelly, pindo palm (*Butia capitata*)	N, C, S
Blue Atlas cedar (*Cedrus atlantica* 'Glauca')	N, C
Deodar cedar (*Cedrus deodar*)	N, C
Blue palo verde (*Cercidium floridum*)	N, C, S
Atlantic white cedar (*Chamaecyparis thyoides*)	N, C, S
Silver palm (*Coccothrinax argentata*)	S
Silver buttonwood (*Conocarpus erectus* var. *sericeus*)	S
Texas wild olive (*Cordia boissieri*)	N, C, S
Silver dollar eucalyptus (*Eucalyptus cinerea*)	N, C, S
Lemon-scented eucalyptus (*Eucalyptus citriodora*)	S, shrub in C
Kaffir palm (*Jubaeopsis caffra*)	N, C, S
Australian tea tree (*Leptospermum laevigatum*)	C, S
Triangle palm (*Neodypsis decaryi*)	S
Screwpines (*Pandanus* spp.)	S
Big-cone pine (*Pinus coulteri*)	N, C, S
Durmast oak (*Quercus petrea*)	N, C
Silver trumpet tree, Tree of gold (*Tabebuia caraiba*)	C, S
Thatch palms (*Thrinax* spp.)	S

Black-Green Leaves

Monkey puzzle tree (*Araucaria araucana*)	N, C, S
Nellie Stevens holly (*Ilex cornuta* 'Nellie R. Stevens')	N, C
Florida yew (*Podocarpus macrophyllus*)	N, C, S

Broadleaf yew (*Podocarpus nagi*)   N, C

Chartreuse Leaves
Flowering dogwood (*Cornus florida* 'Rainbow')   N, C
Honey locust (*Gleditsia triacanthos* var. *iermis* 'Sunburst')   N, C
Cherry laurel (*Prunus laurocerasus* 'Castlewellan')   N, C

GIL WHITTON'S FAVORITE FLOWERING TREES FOR CENTRAL FLORIDA

Although he has vast stores of knowledge about many plants, this horticultural consultant and radio show host calls flowering trees his favorite. Talk about visual impact, the first sight of any of these in bloom almost knocks the socks off of a transplanted northerner who has seen trees blooming only for a brief week in early spring. These you can see from a mile away. Gil suggests leaving dogwood and redbud for north Florida. They do grow in much of the central area, but performance varies greatly from year to year. All of the following will grow in south Florida, and those marked with an asterisk will also grow in north Florida.

Hong Kong orchid (*Bauhinia blakeana*)—Deep magenta; blooms without foliage. Most *Bauhinias* come true from seed, but 'Hong Kong' must be grafted.
Cassia (*Cassia bicapsularis*)—Small tree; dependable for fall; bloom gets caterpillars.
Golden shower (*Cassia fistula*)—Slightly tender but will grow; huge clusters of yellow flowers in summer.
Floss silk tree (*Chorisia speciosa*)—Beautiful pink flowers in fall and no leaves; thorns on trunk and limbs. Very large upright tree; cold sensitive.
Citrus (*Citrus* spp.)—Great for flowers, fragrance, fruit.*
Jacaranda (*Jacaranda mimosifolia*)—Huge tree; spectacular lavender-blue flowers in late spring.
Crape myrtle (*Lagerstroemia* spp.)—Especially those that are mildew resistant.
Southern magnolia (*Magnolia grandiflora*)—Slow grower; huge tree. Messy seed cones and leaves drop continuously but are worth the extra clean-up.*
Jerusalem thorn (*Parkinsonia aculeata*)—Yellow flowers; lots of thorns; thin foliage; very salt tolerant; short lived.*
Copperpod (*Peltophorum dubium*)—Yellow but smaller than *P. pterocarpum*.
Yellow poinciana, copperpod (*Peltophorum pterocarpum*)—Yellow flowers in early summer.
Silver trumpet tree (*Tabebuia caraiba*)—Yellow; best grown from Sarasota south; rough bark.
Golden tabebuia (*Tabebuia chrysotricha*)—Largest flower in the group; blooms about the same time as the *impetiginosa*.
Pink trumpet tree (*Tabebuia heterophylla*)—Only evergreen; pink flowers; very frost tender. All other *Tabebuias* are deciduous and bloom without leaves.
Purple tabebuia (*Tabebuia impetiginosa*)—More pink than purple.
Tabebuia (*Tabebuia umbellata*)—Yellow; last to bloom in the spring (about Easter); most cold hardy of the group.

"Flowering trees are my thing, especially for the Tampa Bay area as well as central Florida. My favorite trees for the Tampa Bay area are those from the *Tabebuia* group." —Gil Whitton, horticultural consultant and radio and TV host.

TREES WITH INCONVENIENT LITTER

Weeping
willow

MB: All trees drop something. What and when they drop vary a bit in Florida. Deciduous trees can lose their leaves any time from August until March, depending on the kind and the season. The sycamores turn bronzy as early as August but hang on for quite a while. My mother was here for Thanksgiving one year and on a walk she said, "What's wrong with that tree?" "It's winter," I replied. "Oh, yes. I forgot," was her answer.

The pin oaks in our neighborhood usually turn a lovely red by Christmas and then drop very suddenly between then and March, depending on the cold spells. The laurel and live oaks actually drop most of their old leaves in March when the new ones push them off. Where dropped leaves and fruit fall on the garden, we call them mulch, and they enrich the soil.

Fruit dropping anywhere you don't want it is called a mess, however. The neighbors' driveway under our laurel oak did have a crunchy surface in alternate years when the acorn crop was heavy, but lately an enlarged population of squirrels has kept that under control.

The cones of the monkey puzzle tree could knock you out if they dropped on your head. They hide in the tops of the sticky evergreens and can weigh up to 12 pounds. Flowering trees are not listed here because most people don't mind their fallen petals unless they are slippery on walks or patios.

Big Leaves, Hard to Rake
Chinese parasol tree (*Firmiana simplex*)	N, C, S
Southern magnolia (*Magnolia grandiflora*)	N, C, S
Sycamore (*Platanus occidentalis*)	N, C

Narrow Leaves That Clog Gutters
Willow oak (*Quercus phellos*)	N, C

Drop Twigs or Twiggy Leaves
River birch (*Betula nigra*)	N, C
Hackberry, sugarberry (*Celtis laevigata*)	N, C, S
Weeping willow (*Salix babylonica*)	N, C, S

Messy Fruit
Sour orange (*Citrus aurantium*)	C, S
Ginkgo or maidenhair (female tree) (*Ginkgo biloba*)	N
Queen palm (*Syagrus romanzoffiana*)	C, S
Chinaberry (*Melia azedarach*)	N, C, S
Mulberry (*Morus* spp.)	N, C, S
Java plum (*Syzygium cumini*)	S

Messy Seeds, Cones, or Pods
Monkey puzzle tree (*Araucaria araucana*)	N, C, S
Hickory (*Carya* spp.)	N, C, S
Sweet gum (*Liquidambar styraciflua*)	N, C, S
Pine (*Pinus* spp.)	N, C, S

Sycamore (*Platanus occidentalis*)   N, C
Oak (*Quercus* spp.)   N, C, S
Bald cypress (*Taxodium distichum*)   N, C, S

STREET TREES FOR CITY CONDITIONS

City trees must withstand the pollution and fumes of city streets, the reflected heat, and limited open soil surface. Add to that constant traffic and soil compaction, and it's no wonder that the average life of a "downtown" tree is only seven years. Suburban trees do better, with an average life of thirty-one years. The following do well along streets (remember to watch for electric lines), in open medians, and along highways.

Although all these trees are tough, they *must* be watered and cared for in the first year or two. Ask your local urban forester (call the city or county parks department) or another experienced source how these or other species might fare on a specific site. Every tree has limitations. A sweet gum would be a nuisance where the gumballs would drop on sidewalks or create street litter but would be fine for a large neighborhood triangle or median. (The variety 'Rotundiloba' doesn't produce gumballs.)

Use this list as a springboard for suggestions and learn all you can from good references before making your final choice. Also check to see if your city or county forestry department has a list of trees that are not allowed in new street plantings.

Florida maple (*Acer barbatum*)   N, C
Red maple (*Acer rubrum*)   N, C, S
Hackberry, sugarberry (*Celtis laevigata*)   N, C
Fringe tree (*Chionanthus virginicus*)   N
Ash (*Fraxinus* spp.)   N, C
American holly (*Ilex opaca*)   N, C
Yaupon holly (*Ilex vomitoria*)   N, C, S
Crape myrtle (*Lagerstroemia indica*)   N, C, S
Sweet gum (*Liquidambar styraciflua*)   N, C
Southern magnolia (*Magnolia grandiflora*)   N, C, S
Black tupelo (*Nyssa sylvatica*)   N, C
Chinese pistache (*Pistacia chinensis*)   N, C, S
Sycamore (*Platanus occidentalis*)   N, C
Myrtle oak (*Quercus myrtifolia*)   N, C, S
Shumard red oak (*Quercus shumardii*)   N, C, S
Bald cypress (*Taxodium distichum*)   N, C, S
Japanese zelkova (*Zelkova serrata*)   N, C

"Trees planted in our urban public spaces often reflect the first impression of our cities and neighborhoods. The key is providing the proper maintenance—aeration, water, fertilization, and pruning—as part of a regular routine. Let's rethink the planting of trees in regard to our abilities to maintain them. By encouraging programs that involve the private and public sectors working together, we can protect this important community investment." —Kathy Beck, Tampa Parks superintendent.

TREES THAT RESEED MADLY OR ARE OTHERWISE INVASIVE

Have you weeded desperately to remove a hundred seedlings coming up in your yard from a tree next door or down the block? Or have you found seedling trees in your yard whose parent is so far away you can't even see it? The following list includes some trees that are nice enough in themselves but may bring too many relatives along to be welcome; they can take over an entire area and threaten the ecology. Some of these have better-behaved relatives in the same genus, such as the *Melaleuca decora* or Snow-in-Summer, and some such as the Schefflera are a threat only in south Florida. Frequent freezes keep them in check elsewhere.

As a rule, it is better not to plant the following. Nor is it necessary, when we have so many great trees from which to choose. The ones marked with asterisks are on the official state noxious weed list.

Paper
mulberry

Earleaf acacia (*Acacia auriculiformis*)*	N, C, S
Mimosa (*Albizia* spp.)	N, C
Orchid tree (*Bauhinia variegata*)*	N, C, S
Schefflera (*Brassaia actinophylla*)*	S
Paper mulberry (*Broussonetia papyrifera*)	N, C, S
Australian pine (*Casuarina* spp.)*	S
Camphor tree (*Cinnamomum camphora*)*	N, C, S
Carrotwood (*Cupaniopsis anacardiopsis*)*	S
Earpod tree (*Enterolobium* spp.)*	C, S
Murray red gum (*Eucalyptus camaldulensis*)*	S
Banyan tree (*Ficus altissima*)*	S
Weeping fig (*Ficus benjamina*)*	C, S
Indian rubber tree (*Ficus elastica*)*	S
Chinese parasol tree (*Firmiana simplex*)	N, C, S
Governor's plum (*Flacourtia indica*)*	S
Goldenrain tree (*Koelreuteria paniculata*)	N, C, S
Melaleuca (*Melaleuca quinquenervia*)*	C, S
Chinaberry (*Melia azedarach*)*	N, C, S
Sapodilla (*Minikara zapota*)*	S
Orange jessamine (*Murraya paniculata*)*	N, C, S
Canistel (*Pouteria camapechiana*)*	S
Chinese tallow tree (*Sapium sebiferum*)*	N, C, S
Brazilian pepper (*Schinus terebinthifolius*)	N, C, S
African tulip tree (*Spathodea campanulata*)*	S
Java plum (*Syzygium* spp.)*	S
Tropical almond (*Terminalia catappa*) *	S
Chinese elm (*Ulmus parvifolia*)	N, C

TREES THAT WILL OUTLIVE YOUR GREAT-GRANDCHILDREN

Would you like to do something good that will last a hundred years or more? If you plant one of these trees and do it right, it should live for generations to come. Some, such as the cypress, grow quickly at first but very slowly after the first thirty years. The oaks grow more slowly at first but faster in Florida than most people expect. Some oaks are short lived, especially compared to the ones listed here, so you might as well buy the best in this case. Live oaks have been known to live for 300 or 400 years in the wild.

Southern red cedar (*Juniperus silicicola*)   N, C, S
Longleaf pine (*Pinus palustris*)   N, C, S
Chestnut, chinquapin oak (*Quercus muehlenbergii*)   N
White oak (*Quercus alba*)   N, C
Overcup oak (*Quercus lyrata*)   N, C
Post oak (*Quercus stellata*)   N, C
Live oak (*Quercus virginiana*)   N, C, S
Cabbage palm (*Sabal palmetto*)   N, C, S
Pond cypress (*Taxodium ascendens*)   N, C, S
Bald cypress (*Taxodium distichum*)   N, C, S

"There are quite a few oaks that grow in Florida. Three are common in the urban environment of Tampa. The live oak is the best, hands down. It has the longevity and it has the genetic disposition to have strong structural limb attachments. The live oak is relatively pest free—just an all-round good species. Both the laurel and the water oak are relatively short lived, maxing out at sixty to seventy years. The live oak will live for hundreds of years." —Steve Graham, urban forester, Tampa.

SOME CHOICE TREES WITH FEW PEST PROBLEMS

We'd all prefer to plant trees that have no insect or disease problems, but, unfortunately, there are no such living things. Some trees have very few pests, however. Remember that even the best trees should not be planted under power lines or so close to the house that they take the shingles off. The invasive trees are also pest free—darn it—which is often why they tend to take over. We left them off this list.

Red maple (*Acer rubrum*)   N, C
Black olive (*Bucida* spp.)   S
Atlantic white cedar (*Cedrus*)   N, C
Fringe tree (*Chionanthus virginicus*)   N, C
Eucalyptus (*Eucalyptus* spp.)   C, S
Holly (*Ilex* spp.)   N, C, S
Magnolia (*Magnolia* spp.)   N, C, S
Dawn redwood (*Metasequoia glyptostroboides*)   N, C
Black tupelo (*Nyssa sylvatica*)   N, C
Chinese pistache (*Pistacia chinensis*)   N, C, S
Live oak (*Quercus virginiana*)   N, C, S
Mahogany (*Swietenia mahagoni*)   S
Bald cypress (*Taxodium distichum*)   N, C, S
Drake elm (*Ulmus parvifolia* 'Drake')   N, C
Rusty blackhaw (*Viburnum rufidulum*)   N, C
Japanese zelkova (*Zelkova serrata*)   N

"Sweet gums, which are pest free in the northern states, can get serious problems with lace bugs here. Sycamores get a lot of lace bugs, too. The drake elms are nearly pest free, and they are airy and give filtered sunlight. Live oaks and laurel oaks can get root rots and decays. They get a lot of insects, but these don't do much permanent damage. I've seen cases where caterpillars defoliate young oaks in spring, but they usually don't kill the tree. The oaks are strong and resilient, especially the live oak. My first choices for planting would depend on the yard, but bald cypress is good almost anywhere except in the middle of a parking lot." —Robert Irwin, Davey Tree, Tampa.

TREES WITH WEAK WOOD OR STRUCTURAL PROBLEMS

Use these trees with caution. It is amazing that so many Florida trees grow so quickly and yet are not weak wooded. On the whole, this list of weak or brittle trees is fairly short. Although there is no substitute for some trees on this list, such as the royal poinciana or the avocado, knowing their tendency toward weak or brittle limbs, you can place them where they won't do great harm if a limb or top does break off in a storm. Fast-growing trees will provide a canopy quickly, so look at them as temporary shade. Plant sturdier species nearby to eventually take their place.

Acacia (*Acacia* spp.)	N, C, S
Box elder (*Acer negundo*)	N
River maple, silver maple (*Acer saccharinum*)	N, C
Mimosa (*Albizia* spp.)	N, C
Orchid tree (*Bauhinia* spp.)	C, S
Bishopwood, toog tree (*Bischofia javanica*)	C, S
Bulnesia, vera (*Bulnesia arborea*)	S
Gumbo limbo (*Bursera simaruba*)	S
Catalpa (*Catalpa bignonioides*)	N
Buttercup tree, Brazilian rose (*Cochlospermum vitifolium*)	S
Indian rosewood (*Dalbergia sissoo*)	C, S
Royal poinciana (*Delonix regia*)	S
Eucalyptus (*Eucalyptus* spp.)	C, S
Silk oak (*Grevillea robusta*)	N, C, S
Mahoe, sea hibiscus (*Hibiscus tiliacaeus*)	C, S
Jerusalem thorn (*Parkinsonia aculeata*)	N, C, S
Yellow poinciana (*Peltophorum* spp.)	S
Avocado (*Persea americana*)	C, S
Bradford pear (*Pyrus calleryana* 'Bradford')	N, C
Weeping willow (*Salix babylonica*)	N, C
African tulip tree (*Spathodea campanulata*)	S

ROSENTHAL'S CUTTING-EDGE TREES FOR NORTH FLORIDA

LC: These trees should be planted more often; they are trees that Florida horticulturists consider to be on the cutting edge of horticultural fashion—I use the word *fashion* lightly, because some plants are the navy blue blazers of horticulture: classics. Below you will find a list of Stanton Rosenthal's suggestions and comments for the Tallahassee area and Leon County, which have two major soil types. The southern portion is sandy like much of the rest of the state. "The northern half is red hills country, and some of these trees do very well in this richer soil. There is also an area like that around Gainesville, where some of these northern hardwoods do well," he says. One of his favorites is the bigleaf magnolia. "The flowers are incredible. The tree is usually about 20–30 feet tall and fairly scrawny, but the flowers can be 17 inches across. There is nothing else that looks like it. I've run into it in the wild a couple times in a real rich site. They are pretty rare. I found one in a nursery for my yard. The leaves can be 20–30 inches long and 9 inches wide." Some of these trees will grow much farther south in the state as well.

Red buckeye (*Aesculus pavia*)   N, C
American hornbeam or musclewood (*Carpinus caroliniana*)   N, C
American holly (*Ilex opaca*)   N, C
Tulip poplar (*Liriodendron tulipifera*)   N, C, S
Ashe magnolia (*Magnolia ashei*)   N
Big-leaf magnolia (*Magnolia macrophylla*)   N, C
Southern crabapple (*Malus angustifolia*)   N, C
Black gum (*Nyssa sylvatica*)   N, C
Hop hornbeam (*Ostrya virginiana*)   N, C, S
Sourwood (*Oxydendrum arboreum*)   N, C
Spruce pine (*Pinus glabra*)   N
White oak (*Quercus alba*)   N, C
Bald cypress (*Taxodium distichum*)   N, C, S
Sparkleberry (*Vaccinium arboreum*)   N, C, S

 "Diversity is a good thing. Dutch Elm disease is something I observed in boyhood, and I don't want to see that happen again. We've got some real winners. Live oaks and dogwoods are very popular here and they deserve it, but there could be a problem if that's all anybody plants. Some of these gems require you to pick the right site. Do your research." — Stanton Rosenthal, extension agent, University of Florida/Leon County Cooperative Extension Service.

TREES FOR CONTAINERS

Obviously, no tree was meant to grow in a container. Nevertheless, some of the following do amazingly well in large pots and add greatly to areas that would otherwise have no trees at all. The secrets of success include occasionally pruning the tops and roots back if needed (almost like bonsai on a larger scale) or repotting to a larger container every year or two until it's too large to repot. Containers will usually keep a tree much smaller than it would grow in the ground and cut its natural lifespan at least in half. "The (tropical) figs all do well in containers, where their running roots are controlled," says Rob Irvin of Davey Tree in Tampa, "but I would never put one in the ground." Most of the palms, especially the smaller ones, do well in containers because palms have small root systems by nature. See the list "Palms for Containers" earlier in the chapter.

Japanese maple (*Acer palmatum*)   N, C
Redbud (*Cercis canadensis*)   N, C
Citrus (*Citrus* spp.)   N, C, S
Silver dollar eucalyptus (*Eucalyptus cinerea*)   N, C, S
Fig (*Ficus* spp.)   C, S
Weeping yaupon holly (*Ilex vomitoria* 'Pendula')   N, C, S
Crape myrtle (*Lagerstroemia indica*)   N, C, S
Pine (*Pinus* spp.)   N, C, S
Chinese elm (*Ulmus parvifolia* 'Drake')   N, C
Sparkleberry (*Vaccinium arboreum*)   N, C, S
Viburnum (*Viburnum* spp. and cultivars)   N, C, S

LARRY SCHOKMAN'S FAVORITE FLOWERING TREES FOR SOUTH FLORIDA

Larry Schokman, director of horticulture at the Kampong of the National Tropical Garden in Coconut Grove, is so excited about the wonderful spectrum of color and the possible uses of flowering trees in south Florida that he makes you want to move there and start planting right away. Also a past president of the City of Miami Beautification Committee (which has planted two thousand trees in the last six years) and of the Tropical Flowering Tree society, Larry says, "One of our goals is to make Miami the Flowering Tree Capital of the World. We are in both the temperate and tropical zones and have the best of both worlds. We have a Flowering Tree Park in South Miami, and every single day of the year there is something in bloom." Here are Larry's favorites; those marked with an asterisk will also grow in central Florida.

Red silk-cotton tree (*Bombax ceiba*)*
Red-orange flowers in winter, spectacular after leaves drop.

Bulnesia or vera (*Bulnesia arborea*)
Yellow-orange flower in spring, summer, and fall, very hard wood.

Ylang-ylang (*Cananga odorata*)
Showy, fragrant yellow flowers year-round, source of Chanel No. 5 perfume.

Golden shower (*Cassia fistula*)
Showy yellow flowers in summer.

Pink shower (*Cassia grande*)
Rosy pink flowers in spring.

Apple blossom shower (*Cassia javanica*)
Red-pink flowers, spring and summer.

Floss silk tree (*Chorisia speciosa*)*
White to pink to lavender flowers, many hybrids, exciting new 'Sugarloaf' has red autumn flowers.

Buttercup tree, Brazilian rose (*Cochlospermum vitifolium*)
Yellow single or double flowers in winter and spring.

Colville's glory (*Colvillea racemosa*)
Orange flowers in fall.

Royal poinciana (*Delonix regia*)
Red, orange, or yellow flowers.

Flamegold goldenrain tree (*Koelreuteria elegans*)*
Yellow flowers followed by coppery seed pods autumn and winter.

Queen's crape myrtle (*Lagerstroemia speciosa*)
Pink, lilac, or mauve flowers all summer; the tallest crape myrtle (up to 35 feet).

Champac (*Michelia champaca*)
Exquisite fragrance; double-narcissuslike yellow flowers. M. *alba* has white flowers year-round, mostly in April and May.

Shaving-brush tree (*Pseudobombax ellipticum*)
Red flowers in winter and spring; grafted trees have magenta, pink, and white flowers on one tree.

Sorrowless tree (*Saraca indica*)	Orange, yellow, and red fragrant flowers in winter.
Tree of gold (*Tabebuia caraiba*)*	Yellow flowers in spring; silver-green foliage.
Purple tabebuia (*Tabebuia impetiginosa*)*	Purple flowers in spring.
Long John (*Triplaris cumingiana*)	Tall columnar tree with stunning, iridescent magenta-red flowers in winter and spring; resists cold to 28 degrees F.

"All these trees are underutilized. We have planted trees in Flowering Tree Parks in abandoned parts of Miami, on abandoned road beds, without irrigation. Flowering trees are ideal xeriscape plants because they need a little stress factor to stimulate flowering. Our motto is 'Don't plant a $5 tree in a 50 cent hole.' We auger out the hole and fill it with organic matter and put mulch as deep as 2 feet but keep it 18 inches away from the trunk. Suddenly we have earthworms and extra bird life and all sorts of wonderful things."—Larry Schokman, director of horticulture, The Kampong of the National Tropical Garden, Coconut Grove.

JOE FREEMAN'S FAVORITE TREES

Joe Freeman spends a lot of time working with trees. He is the chief horticulturist at Florida's Cypress Gardens. Joe advises that, "Gardeners really need to consider a tree's characteristics before selecting and planting it in their landscape. Often a trade-off is made between fast growth and longevity, with someone eventually becoming the loser and inheriting a brittle, short-lived, messy tree. It's also important to look ahead to the mature size of a tree. Most people cringe when they see power-company-pruned trees, yet how many oaks and other large trees do you see planted too close to power lines? Far too many. A nice shade tree is important, but if the landscape doesn't have room for it, plant a grouping of small, more upright-growing trees such as crape myrtle to provide shade."

Heritage river birch (*Betula nigra* 'Heritage')	N
American hornbeam (*Carpinus caroliniana*)	N, C
Fringe tree (*Chionanthus virginicus*)	N
Loblolly bay (*Gordonia lasianthus*)	N, C, S
Crape myrtle (*Lagerstroemia indica* 'Natchez')	N, C, S
Southern magnolia (*Magnolia grandiflora*)	N, C, S
Sand pine (*Pinus clausa*)	N, C, S
Spruce pine (*Pinus glabra*)	N, C
Bluejack oak (*Quercus incana*)	N, C, S
Live oak (*Quercus virginiana*)	N, C, S
Trumpet tree (*Tabebuia* spp.)	C, S
Bald cypress (*Taxodium distichum*)	N, C, S
Winged elm (*Ulmus alata*)	N, C

"Exotic, tropical trees are very alluring, but I don't recommend that gardeners plant them outside of their hardiness zone. A cassia or royal poinciana is stunning in bloom, but if it suffers severe cold damage and dies partially or completely, it becomes a tremendous mess to prune back, cut down, or remove."—Joe Freeman, chief horticulturist, Cypress Gardens.

A SAMPLER OF TREES BY FLOWER COLOR AND SEASON

Every tree species has flowers, but most are fairly inconspicuous. The trees on this list are showy. In Washington, D.C. the cherry trees bloom briefly in the spring, and in Valley Forge Park the dogwoods are unbelievably glorious in May. But in Florida, there are trees that fill the sky with flowers in every season. This list will help you select flowering trees by the color of their blossom and their peak season. Aim to include at least one of these in each vista of your yard for each season and you'll have people driving by just to see them.

    The color categories here are very general. Also, the lavender list includes everything from the true purple glory of the jacaranda to the magenta of redbuds, and the yellow list has a few oranges as well. The red list needs the most concern, for some plants are orange red and some are lavender red. Trees listed more than once come in several colors. A + indicates that there are other cultivars in that color that we didn't have room to mention. For finer details we refer you to a good local source.

Aesculus californica

Please see other lists of flowering trees in this chapter for more possibilities.

Lavender and Purple Flowers

Orchid tree (*Bauhinia* spp.)	N, C, S	Fall, winter, spring
Redbud (*Cercis canadensis* 'Silver Cloud')	N, C	Spring
Oklahoma redbud (*Cercis reniformis* 'Oklahoma')	N, C	Spring
Jacaranda (*Jacaranda mimosifolia*)	C, S	Spring, summer
Crape myrtle (*Lagerstroemia* × 'Apalachee'+)	N, C, S	Summer
Japanese magnolia (*Magnolia soulangeana* hybrids)	N	Winter to spring
Texas mountain laurel (*Sophora secundiflora*)	N	Spring
Purple trumpet tree (*Tabebuia impetiginosa*)	C, S	Spring
Chaste tree (*Vitex negundo* 'Heterophylla')	N, C	Summer

Red Flowers

Red maple (*Acer rubrum*)	N, C, S	Winter, spring
Red buckeye (*Aesculus pavia*)	N, C	Spring
Red bauhinia (*Bauhinia punctata*)	C, S	Spring, summer, fall
Red silk-cotton tree (*Bombax ceiba*)	S	Winter
Bottlebrush (*Callistemon* spp.)	N, C, S	Spring, fall, winter
Coral tree (*Erythrina* spp.)	N, C, S	Spring, summer
Crape myrtle (*Lagerstroemia* × 'Tuscarora'+)	N, C, S	Summer

Yellow and Orange Flowers

Acacia (*Acacia* spp.)	N, C, S	Spring, summer, fall
Orchid tree (*Bauhinia* spp.)	N, C, S	Fall, winter, spring
Yellow bauhinia (*Bauhinia tomentosa*)	C, S	Spring, summer, fall
Bulnesia or vera (*Bulnesia arborea*)	S	Spring, summer, fall
Bridal-veil tree (*Caesalpinia* spp.)	C, S	Summer, fall
Golden shower (*Cassia* spp.)	C, S	Summer, fall
Medallion tree (*Cassia leptophylla*)	C, S	Summer
Mahoe, sea hibiscus (*Hibiscus tiliacaeus*)	C, S	Year-round
Goldenrain tree (*Koelreuteria* spp.)	N, C, S	Summer, fall
Fraser magnolia (*Magnolia fraseri*)	N	Spring

Yellow poinciana or copperpod (*Peltosporum* spp.)	S	Spring, summer
Fevertree (*Pinckneya pubens*)	N, C	Spring
Trumpet tree (*Tabebuia* spp.)	C, S	Spring
Rosewood (*Tipuana tipu*)	S	Spring, summer

White Flowers

Brazilian orchid tree (*Bauhinia forficata*)	C, S	Summer
Fringe tree (*Chionanthus virginicus*)	N, C	Spring
Floss silk tree (*Chorisia speciosa*)	C, S	Fall
Parsley hawthorn (*Crataegus Marshallii*)	N	Spring
Citrus (*Citrus* spp.)	N, C, S	Late winter
Dogwood (*Cornus* spp.)	N, C	Spring
Loblolly bay (*Gordonia lasianthus*)	N, C, S	Summer, fall
Carolina silverbell (*Halesia caroliniana*)	N, C	Spring
Japanese raisin tree (*Hovenia dulcis*)	N, C, S	Summer
Crape myrtle (*Lagerstroemia* × 'Natchez'+)	N, C, S	Summer
Star magnolia (*Magnolia stellata*)	N	Spring, summer, fall
Sweet bay magnolia (*Magnolia virginiana*)	N, C, S	Summer
Southern crabapple (*Malus angustifolia*)	N, C	Early spring
Sourwood (*Oxydendrum arboreum*)	N, C	Spring, summer
Chickasaw plum (*Prunus angustifolia*)	N, C	Spring
Purpleleaf, myrobalan plum (*P. cerasifera*)	N, C	Spring
Callery pear (*Pyrus calleryana* 'Aristocrat'+)	N, C	Winter, spring
Rusty blackhaw (*Viburnum rufidulum*)	N, C	Spring

Pink Flowers

California horse chestnut (*Aesculus californica*)	N	Spring
Butterfly flower (*Bauhinia monandra*)	S	Summer
Pink-and-white shower (*Cassia javanica*)	S	Spring, summer
Floss silk tree (*Chorisia speciosa*)	C, S	Fall
Dogwood (*Cornus florida* 'Welch's Jr. Miss')	N	Spring
Crape myrtle (*Lagerstroemia* × 'Biloxi'+)	N, C, S	Summer
Magnolia (*Magnolia* × 'Peter Smithers')	N	Winter, spring
Saucer magnolia (*Magnolia* × *soulangeana* 'Cupcake'+)	N	Winter, spring
Rhodoleia (*Rhodoleia championii*)	N, C, S	Spring
Trumpet tree (*Tabebuia* spp.)	C, S	Spring, summer
Fevertree (*Pinckneya pubens*)	N, C	Spring

SHRUBS

In any landscape, shrubs are among the most versatile of plants. They mature quickly, offer a huge variety of leaf color and texture, flower color, fragrance, and sometimes attractive or edible fruit as well. They can serve as hedges, screens, groundcovers, accents, or single specimen plants. Shrubs can give us that greatest kind of privacy, the ability to see out without being seen. They serve as the walls of our outdoor rooms—soft walls children can run through or hide in, barrier walls whose thorns will discourage intruders, blooming walls that bring birds and butterflies to our gardens. "There are more evergreen and flowering shrubs in Florida than in any other state. While trees are important to your landscape plan, they take years to achieve their full height, width, and beauty. Shrubs, on the other hand, develop quickly and give almost immediate results in completing the picture you are trying to create in your garden," says Stan DeFreitas, author of *The Complete Guide to Florida Gardening* and *The Stan Defreitas Garden Answer Book.*

Shrubs can be dainty enough to fit in the flower garden, low enough to serve as groundcover, or large enough to serve as small trees for shade or for framing a one-story house. Because of this great variation, it is important to select the right shrub for the right place. Otherwise, small and choice shrubs could disappear in the bushes and large ones could overgrow the windows and turn a pleasant yard into an impenetrable jungle. With proper selection, there is no need for extensive pruning. Laurel Schiller, wildlife biologist and co-owner of Florida Native Plants, Inc., in Sarasota, shares this opinion: "One of the biggest mistakes people make is planting their shrubs too close together. They want their plants to be drought tolerant, but they don't give the roots room to find the needed moisture."

LC: Although shrubs tend to be more permanent than smaller plants, their placement is not written in stone. We are in our fifteenth year of garden building at home and still have holes in the landscape and places we may have liked at one time but now just don't do. We move shrubs around the way some people move furniture and will continue doing so until we're dead or satisfied. Today we find ourselves increasingly mixing shrubs and perennials. I like what Georgia Tasker, garden editor of the *Miami Herald* and author of *Enchanted Ground* says: "A harmonious blend of different shrubs in a mixed border can work well, if you deal with half a dozen kinds and blend them skillfully, playing with leaf color and texture, shape and form. You may find that the round and scalloped leaves of elephant's ear (*Alocasia odora*) play nicely against the feathery, dark green leaves of a cat palm (*Chamaedorea cataractarum*). Or the palmately compound leaves of *Schefflera arboricola* will contrast well with the spike leaves of walking iris."

In Florida, many herbaceous perennials grow tall and broad enough to serve as shrubs, so check lists in the perennials chapter if you don't find your favorites here. In fact, some plants that are perennials in north Florida are shrubs in south Florida, so they are listed in both chapters. Be sure to check the edible landscaping chapter, also; there are some quite ornamental shrubs that bear delicious fruit. And if you learn of an improved variety or have something specific in mind that your local nursery doesn't have in stock, ask the staff to order it for you.

TO DO LIST FOR SHRUBS

MB: The first plant I bought when I moved to Florida was a gardenia because I love the blooms and I had killed so many trying to grow them as house plants in the Midwest. I planted it at the corner of the back porch, and it has done well there ever since. I'm glad now that it is in an inconspicuous place, for the gardenia is not pretty during bloom unless you are there to snip off every aged, brown blossom. One man in our church solves that problem by cutting every blossom every morning and passing them out to all the ladies he sees.

Research *before* you buy or plant. Check our list of reference books in the introduction and always consult with a local expert.

- Improve your soil with compost before planting.
- Mulch well and renew mulch as needed.
- Fertilize, at least twice a year, especially for the first 3 to 5 years as the plant matures.
- Water well until established, as needed thereafter.
- Allow enough space for the shrub to grow to its mature size. Don't plan on pruning, which ruins the natural form of a shrub.
- Group shrubs with like needs for sun, soil, and water.
- Put tender or iffy plants in sheltered spots and where frost damage won't be too serious.
- Include shrubs with fragrance, especially near doors and sitting areas.
- Include some bloom for all seasons.

"One of the most common problems of young landscapes is incorrect installation procedures. Be sure to set plants at the same depth at which they were growing in the container. This should be with only ⅛ to ¼ inch of soil on top of their roots. Cut any circling roots at the outside of the root ball. Then pack the soil gently around the root ball. You should not be able to shake the plant by its trunk after installation." — Frank Melton, horticulture Extension agent, Manatee County.

SHRUBS FOR SHOWY FOLIAGE IN THE SHADE

MB: I've been planting trees all my life and never managed to live in the same house long enough to enjoy much of the shade. Florida is the first place I've ever seen where some yards really do have more shade than I would want, since I am determined to grow a good deal of fruits and vegetables. But even for shady landscapes, there is a wide variety of choice shrubs.

We chose these plants because they have some characteristic that makes them interesting and showy. It may be flowers (camellia, oakleaf hydrangea), variegated or colorful foliage (aucuba, dragon tree, snowbush), or a particularly interesting form or texture (fatsia, bamboo, nandina). Plants with asterisks after their names will also do well in the sun.

Copperleaf, chenille plant (*Acalypha wilkesiana*, A. *hispida*)*	C, S
Japanese aucuba (*Aucuba japonica*)	N, C, S
Black bamboo (*Bambusa nigra*)*	N, C, S
Snowbush (*Breynia disticha* 'Rosea Picta')*	C, S
Camellia (*Camellia sasanqua*)*	N, C
Coco plum (*Chrysobalanus icaco*)*	S
Ti plant (*Cordyline terminalis*)*	C, S
King or queen sago (*Cycas revoluta*, C. *circinalis*)*	C, S
Spiny dioon (*Dioon spinulosum*)*	S
Dragon tree (*Dracaena marginata* 'Tricolor')*	N, C, S
Fatsia (*Fatsia japonica*)	N, C, S
Oakleaf hydrangea (*Hydrangea quercifolia*)*	N, C
Florida anise (*Illicium floridanum*)*	N, C, S
Ocala anise (*Illicium parviflorum*)*	N, C, S
Leatherleaf mahonia (*Mahonia bealei*)*	N, C
Grape holly (*Mahonia fortunei*)*	N, C
Nandina, heavenly bamboo (*Nandina domestica*)	N, C, S
Philodendrons (*Philodendron* spp.)*	N, C, S
Aralias (*Polyscias* spp.)	S
Lady palm (*Rhapis exelsa* 'Variegata')	C, S
Coontie (*Zamia* spp.)	N, C, S

*Cycas
revoluta*

SOME SHRUBS THAT BLOOM IN SHADE

Many shrubs will bloom in moderate shade in one part of Florida or another. This list contains some of the more showy and familiar. Those with an asterisk also fare well in the sun.

Red buckeye (*Aesculus pavia*)*	N, C
Marlberry (*Ardisia escallonioides*)	C, S
Azalea species and hybrids	N, C, S
Yesterday-today-and-tomorrow (*Brunfelsia australis*)	C, S
Red powderpuff (*Calliandra haematocephaia*)	N, C
Camellia (*Camellia japonica*, C. *sasanqua*)	N, C
Pagoda flower (*Clerodendrum paniculatum*)*	C, S
Golden dewdrop (*Duranta repens*)*	C, S
Thryallis (*Galphimia glauca*)*	C, S
Gardenia (*Gardenia jasminoides*)	N, C, S
Firebush (*Hamelia patens*)*	C, S

French hydrangea (*Hydrangea macrophylla*)*   N, C
Oakleaf hydrangea (*Hydrangea quercifolia*)   N, C, S
Jasminum (*Jasminum* spp.)*   N, C, S
Shrimp plant (*Justicia brandegeana*)*   N, C, S
Flamingo plant, jacobinia (*Justicia carnea*)   C, S
Sandhill laurel (*Kalmia hirsuta*)   N, C, S
Leatherleaf mahonia (*Mahonia bealei*)   N, C
Turk's cap (*Malvaviscus arboreus*)*   N, C, S
Nandina, heavenly bamboo (*Nandina domestica*)   N, C, S
Rhododendron   Mickey Mouse plant (*Ochna serrulata*)*   C, S
Tea olive (*Osmanthus fragrans*)   N, C
Golden shrimp plant (*Pachystachys lutea*)*   C, S
Florida flame azalea (*Rhododendron austrinum*)   N
Piedmont azalea (*Rhododendron canescens*)   N
Viburnums (*Viburnum* spp.)*   N, C, S

SHRUBS FOR DEEP SHADE

Deep shade, where the sun's rays never penetrate, is a difficult place to grow many plants, let alone a flower. So gardeners often rely on foliage for an interesting effect.

Shade is deepest on the north side of a building under trees or in the shade of a heavy stand of oaks. The shrubs on this list maintain their characteristic forms in heavy shade. Start with the largest size you can afford because growth in deep shade is generally slow. When planting under large shade trees, you must never forget to water for the first several seasons until roots are well established and have a fighting chance. Even then you may have to water in the hot, dry months of April and May, as tree roots are fierce competitors for water. Plants marked with an asterisk are especially useful for dry shade, usually found under big trees whose roots suck up water, leaving little for the less aggressive plants beneath their canopy.

Florida leucothoe (*Agarista populifolia*)*   N, C, S
Marlberry (*Ardisia escallonioides*)   C, S
Japanese acuba (*Acuba japonica*)*   N, C, S
Parlor palm, bamboo, parlor (*Chamaedorea erumpens*)   N, C, S
Ti plant (*Cordyline terminalis*)   C, S
Dioons (*Dioon* spp.)   N, C, S
Fatsia (*Fatsia japonica*)*   N, C, S
Leatherleaf mahonia (*Mahonia bealei*)*   N, C
Nandina, heavenly bamboo (*Nandina domestica*)*   N, C, S
Philodendrons (*Philodendron* spp., some)   C, S
Aralias (*Polyscias* spp.)   S
Lady palm (*Raphis* spp.)*   C, S
Needle palm (*Rhapidophyllum hystrix*)*   N, C, S
Variegated schefflera (*Schefflera arboricola*)   C, S

"Good plants for color in deep shade include Cordyline *'Red Sister' and* Philodendron *'Zanadu'." —Loren Rapport, Beachside Gardens, Satellite Beach.*

DROUGHT-TOLERANT SHRUBS

Although this list is extensive, many more shrubs do well with only occasional watering or with no watering at all once established. But every plant needs to be watered until it has established a good root system, usually within the first two years. Rain barrels are great for this because it is so easy to dip in a bucket and take some of that free water to the new plants in the area.

Glossy abelia (*Abelia* × *grandiflora*)	N, C
Allamandas (*Allamanda* spp.)	C, S
Pineland allamanda (*Angadenia berterii*)	S
Japanese aucuba (*Aucuba japonica*)	N, C, S
Red bauhinia (*Bauhinia punctata*)	C, S
Japanese barberry (*Berberis thunbergii*)	N, C
Bougainvilleas (*Bougainvillea* spp.)	C, S
Butterfly bush (*Buddleia davidii*)	N, C, S
Beautyberry (*Callicarpa americana*)	N, C, S
Croton (*Codiaeum variegatum* var. *pictum*)	C, S
King or queen sago (*Cycas revoluta, C. cercinalis*)	N, C, S
Dioon (*Dioon* spp.)	C, S
Dragon tree (*Dracaena* spp.)	C, S
Elaegnus (*Elaegnus pungens*)	N, C
Cardinal spear (*Erythrina herbacea*)	N, C, S
Fatsia (*Fatsia japonica*)	N, C, S
Feijoa (*Feijoa sellowiana*)	N, C, S
Kumquat (*Fortunella japonica*)	N, C, S
Burford holly (*Ilex cornuta* 'Burfordi')	N, C
Carissa holly (*Ilex cornuta* 'Carissa')	N, C, S
Galberry (*Ilex glabra*)	N, C
Yaupon holly (*Ilex vomitoria*)	N, C
Coral plant (*Jatropha multifida*)	C, S
Juniper (*Juniperus* spp.)	N, C, S
Lantanas (*Lantana* spp.)	N, C, S
Texas sage (*Leucophyllum texanum*)	N, C, S
Christmas berry (*Lycium carolinianum*)	N, C, S
Turk's cap (*Malvaviscus arboreus*)	N, C, S
Wax myrtle (*Myrica cerifera*)	N, C, S
Nandina, heavenly bamboo (*Nandina domestica*)	N, C, S
Oleander (*Nerium oleander*)	N, C, S
Pittosporum (*Pittosporum tobira*)	N, C, S
Aralia (*Polyscias* spp.)	C, S
Pomegranate (*Punica granatum*)	N, C, S
Firethorn (*Pyracantha* spp. and hybrids)	N, C, S
Indian hawthorn (*Raphiolepsis* spp. and hybrids)	N, C, S
Needle palm (*Rhapidophyllym hystrix*)	N, C, S
Sumac (*Rhus* spp.)	N, C
Firecracker plant (*Russelia equisetiformis*)	C, S
Dwarf palmetto (*Sabal minor*)	N, C, S
Beach naupaka, inkberry (*Scaevola plumieri*)	C, S
Reeve's spirea (*Spirea cantonensis*)	N, C

Bird-of-paradise (*Strelitzia* spp.)   C, S
Bay cedar (*Suriana maritima*)   S
Windmill palm (*Trachycarpus fortunei*)   N, C, S
Shiny blueberry (*Vaccinium myrsinites*)   N, C, S
Victorian rosemary (*Westringia rosmariniformis*)   C, S
Coontie (*Zamia* spp.)   N, C, S

"If you plant a variety of natives, your land will come alive with the lovely sights, floral fragrances, melodious bird and insect songs, and varied wildlife activity of our unique central Florida heritage. Used in suitable locations, native plants are easy and fun to grow and require exceptionally little maintenance. . . . Once your landscape is established, you can relax and enjoy it." — *The Right Plants for Dry Places* by Carl Strohmenger and other members of the Florida Native Plant Society.

EVERGREEN SHRUBS FOR A CLIPPED HEDGE

Shrubs with needle leaves or small broadleaves make the best clipped hedges because the cut margin of the leaf does not turn an unsightly, ragged brown. The whole hedge has a smoother, more uniform look with shrubs like those listed below. Some shrubs just don't tolerate frequent, close trimming and refuse to be confined. Keeping a hedge trimmed can be a labor-intensive project, so don't start it unless you can keep up with it. There is no doubt that a well-maintained hedge can add greatly to the richness of a garden scene. It can be a low outline or a tall background. Hedges add a sense of formality.

MB: James Bush-Brown, coauthor with his wife, Louise Carter Bush-Brown, of *America's Garden Book*, used to tell our landscaping classes at Temple University, "It didn't matter if it took three men four days three times a year to trim those hedges in the Italian villas and the English gardens. It gave people work." Our lifestyles have changed considerably, and I would much rather pick fruit than trim hedges. Nevertheless, many Florida homeowners don't mind doing the work or hiring the help for the walls of green.

Glossy abelia (*Abelia* × *grandiflora*)   N, C
Korean boxwood (*Buxus microphylla koreana*)   N, C, S
Powderpuff (*Calliandra* spp.)   C, S
Natal plum (*Carissa macrophylla*)   C, S
Coco plum (*Chrysobalanus icaco*)   S
Stoppers, redberry (*Eugenia* spp.)   C, S
Surinam cherry (*Eugenia uniflora*)   C, S
Wild olive (*Forestiera segregata*)   N, C, S
Dwarf yaupon holly (*Ilex vomitoria*)   N, C, S
Wax myrtle (*Myrica cerifera*)   N, C
Dwarf myrtle (*Myrtus communis*)   C, S
Ochrosia, kopsia (*Ochrosia parviflora*)   S
Tea olive (*Osmanthus fragrans*)   N, C
Florida yew (*Podocarpus macrophyllus*)   N, C, S
Aralia (*Polyscias* spp.)   C, S
Indian hawthorn (*Raphiolepis* spp.)   N, C, S
Beach naupaka (*Scaevola plumieri*)   C, S
Limeberry (*Triphasia trifolia*)   N, C, S
Victorian rosemary (*Westringia rosmariniformis*)   C, S

SHRUBS THAT TOLERATE WET FEET

MB: I gardened for my first five decades without taking water needs into consideration to any great degree. In the Midwest we left it to nature to take care of all watering beyond that for newly set plants. It was a revelation for me (and also good preparation for moving to Florida) the first time I visited California and realized that we can and sometimes must do the watering ourselves. When I wrote *Xeriscaping for Florida Homes*, I learned the fine details about how best to water so we can have both the plants now and the water for the future. Many a drought-tolerant plant will also tolerate wet feet, so you will find some of these plants on the list of drought-tolerant plants as well. Some are plants that naturally like a great deal of water, but many are just very forgiving.

Red buckeye (*Aesculus pavia*)	N, C
Copperleaf (*Acalypha wilkesiana*)	C, S
Elephant's ear (*Alocasia* spp.)	C, S
Marlberry (*Ardisia escallonioides*)	C, S
Salt bush (*Baccharis halimifolia*)	N, C, S
Sweetshrub (*Calycanthus florida*)	N, C
Myrtle-of-the-river (*Calyptranthes zuzygium*)	S
Buttonbush (*Cephalanthus occidentalis*)	N, C, S
Night-blooming jasmine (*Cestrum nocturnum*)	C, S
Sweetpepper bush (*Clethra alnifolia*)	N
Elaegnus (*Elaegnus pungens*)	N, C
Coral bean (*Erythrina herbacea*)	N, C, S
Firebush (*Hamelia patens*)	C, S
French hydrangea (*Hydrangea macrophylla*)	N, C
St. John's-wort (*Hypericum* spp.)	N, C, S
Chinese holly (*Ilex cornuta*)	N, C
Galberry (*Ilex glabra*)	N, C, S
Florida anise (*Illicium floridanum*)	N, C, S
Ocala anise (*Illicium parviflorum*)	N, C, S
Virginia sweetspire (*Itea virginica*)	N, C
Marsh elder (*Iva frutescens*)	N, C, S
Shrimp plant (*Justicia brandegeana*)	N, C, S
Florida leucothoe (*Leucothoe populifolia*)	N, C
Wax myrtle (*Myrica cerifera*)	N, C, S
Rapanea (*Myrsine gauanensis*)	S
Firespike (*Odontonema strictum*)	C, S
Tea olive (*Osmanthus fragrans*)	N, C
Philodendron (*Philodendron selloum*)	N, C, S
Needle palm (*Rhapidophyllum hystrix*)	N, C, S
Bird-of-paradise (*Strelitzia* spp.)	C, S
Blackhaw (*Viburnum ovovatum*)	N, C, S
Rusty blackhaw (*Viburnum rufidulum*)	N, C

Buttonbush

SHRUBS WITH FRAGRANT BLOSSOMS

Your landscape will be increasingly enjoyable if you make fragrance a definite element of your plan. Plant shrubs with fragrant flowers close to walks and sitting areas where you can enjoy them most or in contained gardens where the fragrance will be most intense.

LC: I find it very interesting the way people disagree on what smells good or sweet in a garden; a plant that smells good to one may not smell so to another. If the perfume of gardenia is too strong for you, omit it or put it far enough away to weaken before it reaches the porch. Refer to the lists of azaleas and the chapters on roses, annuals, perennials, and vines for added fragrance. Those marked with an asterisk in this list have flowers that are fragrant but not particularly showy. In some cases, such as with eleagnus, the tiny blossoms are nearly hidden beneath the leaves.

Sweet acacia (*Acacia farnesiana*)	C, S
Desert rose (*Adenium obesum*)	C, S
Marlberry (*Ardisia escallonioides*)*	C, S
Tarflower (*Befaria racemosa*)	N, C, S
Yesterday-today-and-tomorrow (*Brunfelsia australis*)	C, S
Butterfly bush (*Buddleia* hybrids)	N, C, S
Pink powderpuff (*Calliandra surinamensis*)	S
Sweetshrub (*Calycanthus florida*)*	N, C, S
Natal plum (*Carissa macrocarpa*)	C, S
Seven-year apple (*Casasia clusiifolia*)	S
Night-blooming jasmine (*Cestrum nocturnum*)	C, S
Cleyera (*Cleyera japonica*)*	N, C
Fragrant dracaena (*Dracaena fragrans*)*	C, S
Golden dewdrop (*Duranta repens*)	C, S
Elaegnus (*Elaegnus pungens*)	N, C
Surinam cherry (*Eugenia uniflora*)*	C, S
Gardenia (*Gardenia jasminoides*)	N, C, S
Joewood (*Jacquinia keyensis*)	S
Jasmine (*Jasminum* spp.)	N, C, S
Loropetalum (*Loropetalum chinense*)*	N, C, S
Banana shrub (*Michelia figo*)*	N, C
Dwarf myrtle (*Myrtus communis*)	C, S
Ochrosia, kopsia (*Ochrosia parviflora*)*	S
Tea olive (*Osmanthus fragrans*)	N, C
Holly olive (*Osmanthus heterophyllus*)	N
Mock orange (*Philadelphus coronarius*)	N
Pittosporum (*Pittosporum tobira*)	N, C, S
Native azalea (*Rhododendron austrinum*)	N
Piedmont azalea (*Rhododendron canescens*)	N
Snake plant (*Sansevieria* spp.)*	C, S
Cape jasmine (*Tabernaemontana divaricata*)	S
Limeberry (*Triphasia trifolia*)*	N, C, S
Sweet viburnum (*Viburnum odoratissimum*)	N, C, S
Angel trumpet, datura (*Brugmansia* × *candida*)	C, S

"Oleander fragrances are nearly as difficult to identify as those of plumerias. Many . . . have a jasmine-like fragrance, others a sweet-spice or musky scent. The scent most often described is that of vanilla, with certain cultivars imparting a magnolia or bitter almond aroma. Ted Turner, Sr. (owner of Gardenland Nursery in Corpus Christi, Texas) stated that he has found all of them to be most fragrant in the morning, becoming less so as the day proceeds." —Richard and Mary Helen Eggenberger, tropical plant specialists in Cleveland, Georgia, and authors of *The Handbook on Oleanders.*

Shrubs with Colorful Foliage Year-Round

One advantage of gardening in Florida is the wide variety of colorful foliage available in every season, not just spring and fall. It is possible to have great color in the landscape without any flowers at all. The following shrubs offer either bright or subtle foliage colors along with the easy maintenance and permanence of shrub plantings. Some are specific cultivars of a plant.

Red to Bronze, or with Red Markings

Copperleaf (*Acalypha wilkesiana*)	C, S
Barberry (*Berberis* cultivars)	N
Croton (*Codiaeum variegatum* var. *pictum*)	C, S
Fiery costus (*Costus igneous*)	C, S
Velvet spiral flag (*Costus pulverulentus*)	C, S
Ti plant (*Cordyline terminalis*)	C, S
Dracaena (*Dracaena marginata*)	C, S
Red spurge (*Euphorbia cotinifolia*)	C, S
False roselle (*Hibiscus acetosella*)	C, S
Redbird flower (*Pedilanthus tithymaloides* 'Variegatus')	C, S

Yellow to Golden

Croton (*Codiaeum variegatum* var. *pictum* cultivars)	C, S
Elaegnus (*Elaegnus pungens* 'Sunset')	N, C, S
Fernleaf aralia (*Polyscias filicifolia*)	C, S
Spirea (*Spirea* × *bumalda* 'Goldflame')	N, C

Gray, Silver, or Bluish

Century plant (*Agave* spp.)	C, S
Silver sea oxeye (*Borrichia arborescens*)	C, S
Elaegnus (*Elaegnus pungens*)	N, C, S
Silver leaf daisy (*Euryops pectinatus*)	C, S
Texas sage (*Leucophyllum frutescens*)	N, C, S
Sea lavender (*Mallotonia gnaphalodes*)	C, S
Screwpine, blue (*Pandanus baptistii*)	C, S
Victorian rosemary (*Westringia rosmariniformis*)	C, S

Variegated Purple

Snowbush (*Breynia disticha*)	C, S
Caricature plant (*Graptophyllum pictum*)	C, S
Cup-leafed aralia (*Polyscias scutellaria* 'Fabian')	C, S
Persian shield (*Strobilanthes dyeranus*)	C, S

Variegated Green, White, or Yellow

Abelia (*Abelia* × *grandiflora* 'Francis Mason')	N, C
Japanese aucuba (*Aucuba japonica*)	N, C
Japanese barberry (*Berberis thunbergii* 'Aurea Nana')	N
Crepe ginger (*Costus speciosus* 'Variegatus')	N, C, S
Jade plant (*Crassula argentea* 'Variegata')	C, S
Dracaena (*Dracaena warenecki, D. fragrans massengeana*)	C, S
Ribbon plant (*Dracaena sanderiana*)	C, S

Golden creeper (*Ernodea littoralis*)	C, S
Coral tree (*Erythrina variegata* var. *orientalis*)	C, S
Milk-striped euphorbia (*Euphorbia lactea*)	C, S
Fatsia (*Fatsia japonica* 'Variegata')	N, C, S
Gardenia (*Gardenia jasminoides* 'Radicans Variegata')	N, C, S
Chinese privet (*Ligustrum sinense* 'Variegatum')	N, C, S
Sander screwpine (*Pandanus sanderi*)	C, S
Mock orange (*Philadelphus coronarius* 'Aureus')	N
Pittosporum (*Pittosporum tobira* 'Variegata', 'Wheeler's Dwarf')	N, C, S
Spirea (*Spirea × bumalda* 'Variegata')	N
Cleyera (*Ternstroemia gymnanthera* 'Burnished Gold', 'Variegata')	C, S
Laurestinus (*Viburnum tinus* 'Variegatum')	N, C
Vitex (*Vitex trifolia* 'Variegata')	N, C, S
Weigela (*Weigela florida* 'Variegata Nana')	N

LOW SHRUBS THAT WON'T HIDE WINDOWS

Too many untrained landscapers put under windows shrubs that grow too large; these shrubs soon cover the window if not pruned several times a year. None of the experts we quote in this book would be caught dead doing that to a client. If you inherit such misplaced shrubs, take them out as soon as you can and replace them with well-behaved low shrubs. MB: To me the ideal shrub for under a window is one that grows just tall enough to see the top edge when sitting inside. An added bonus is one that blooms or attracts butterflies or birds. A plumbago under our family-room window does all that and needs pruning only every other year or so.

Some of the plant groups listed below, like the hollies and the junipers, have a good selection of low cultivars but also include many tall shrubs and trees, so read the fine print on their label, not just the first name. All of these are reliable evergreens that stay under 4 feet with little or no pruning and have few problems. They are also good for tight places like a side yard.

Gumpo azaleas (*Azalea* 'Gumpo')	N, C
Crimson pygmy barberry (*Berberis thunbergii atropurpurea*)	N, C
Japanese boxwood (*Buxus microphylla*)	N, C
Dwarf gardenia (*Gardenia jasminoides* 'Radicans')	N, C, S
French hydrangea (*Hydrangea macrophylla*)	N, C
Carissa holly (*Ilex cornuta* 'Carissa')	N, C, S
Rotunda holly (*Ilex cornuta* 'Rotunda')	N, C, S
Helleri holly (*Ilex crenata* 'Helleri')	N, C, S
Dwarf yaupon holly (*Ilex vomitoria* 'Nana', 'Schellings's Dwarf')	N, C
Showy jasmine (*Jasminum floridum*)	N, C, S
Shore juniper (*Juniperus conferta* 'Blue Pacific'+)	N, C, S
Creeping juniper (*Juniperus horizontalis* 'Blue Rug'+)	N, C, S
Flamingo plant or jacobinia (*Justicia carnea*)	C, S
Lantanas (*Lantana* spp.)	N, C, S
Coastal leucothoe (*Leucothoe axillaris*)	N
Dwarf wax myrtle (*Myrica cerifera* 'Dwarf')	N, C, S
Dwarf nandina (*Nandina domestica* 'Harbor Dwarf'+)	N, C, S
Plumbago (*Plumbago auriculata*)	C, S
Dwarf Indian hawthorn (*Raphiolepsis indica* 'Dwarf', 'Compacta')	N, C, S
Coontie (*Zamia* spp.)	N, C, S

SHRUBS WITH ORNAMENTAL FRUIT OR BERRIES

Gardeners north of the Florida-Georgia border associate ornamental fruit with late summer, fall, and winter, but many parts of Florida have shrubs with fruits almost year-round. These are interesting even in their green stage but grow more showy as they turn orange, red, blue, purple, or black. The Surinam cherry is one example of a shrub that often has green, orange, and red or black fruit ripening in the same cluster. Occasionally, you will also find yellow and white fruited selections of some plants. This fruit often attracts birds, which add another dimension of interest and color to the garden, as well as the best kind of pest patrol. Perhaps one of the most outstanding and easiest to grow is the native beautyberry. Its clusters of purple berries in late summer are spaced every inch or two along the stem and are magnificent enough for flower arrangers to spend a day scouring the roadsides for them.

LC: There will be some variation in how long the different berries last in your garden, based on the weather and the hunger of local birds. One winter, our nandina berries all disappeared in about two hours when a flock of starlings spotted our 12-foot-long screen and decided to have lunch.

Marlberry (*Ardisia escallonioides*)	C, S
Japanese aucuba (*Aucuba japonica* 'Rozeanne')	N, C
Japanese barberry (*Berberis thunbergii*)	N, C
Beautyberry (*Callicarpa americana*)	N, C, S
Pepper, ornamental (*Capsicum frutescens*)	C, S
Natal plum (*Carissa macrocarpa*)	C, S
Buttonbush (*Cephalanthus occidentalis*)	N, C
Cleyera (*Cleyera japonica*)	N, C
Quail berry (*Crossopetalum illicifolium*)	C, S
Golden dewdrop (*Duranta repens*)	N, C, S
Surinam cherry (*Eugenia uniflora*)	C, S
Kumquat (*Fortunella* spp.)	N, C, S
Burford holly (*Ilex cornuta* 'Burfordi')	N, C, S
Inkberry (*Ilex glabra*)	N, C, S
Yaupon holly (*Ilex vomitoria*)	N, C, S
Leatherleaf mahonia (*Mahonia fortunei*)	N, C
Nandina, heavenly bamboo (*Nandina domestica*)	N, C, S
Mickey Mouse plant (*Ochna serrulata*)	C, S
Firethorn (*Pyracantha* spp.)	N, C, S
Jerusalem cherry (*Solanum pseudocapsicum*)	C, S
Chindo viburnum (*Viburnum odoratissimum* var. *awabuki* 'Chindo')	N, C, S
Rusty blackhaw (*Viburnum rufidulum*)	N, C
Laurestinus (*Viburnum tinus* 'Variegatum')	N, C

SHRUBS TO TRAIN AS SMALL TREES

Some shrubs grow tall enough that they are about the height of small trees. If you remove their lower limbs to expose the "trunks," you can indeed turn them into trees. There is nothing so fascinating as the unusual; one azalea or hibiscus trained as a small tree will be a stand-out. These are great for the center of a bed of flowers. Large plants that will become small trees make good accents for the corner of a single-story house or to punctuate the end of a curving shrub border. They are also ideal under power lines because they will never grow tall enough to need pruning or cause trouble to the utility company.

There are two ways to train large shrubs into trees:

1. Start when the plant is very small and train it from the beginning by pruning to create one to three main trunks. This takes discipline, especially while the plant is very young. After the framework matures into a strong trunk, remove any growth that comes from below the point where the canopy branches appear.

2. Prune an existing shrub to encourage a main trunk by cutting back any side or additional branches part way. Leaving some will make both top growth and root growth more vigorous. As the plant develops, remove the basal and lower limbs one or two at a time. Sometimes you can reclaim an older shrub by pruning away the lower limbs to expose its multitrunk base.

Southern indica azalea (*Azalea indica*)	N, C
Camellia (*Camellia japonica, C. sasanqua*)	N, C
Burford holly (*Ilex cornuta* 'Burfordi')	N, C
Privet (*Ligustrum japonicum*)	N, C, S
Wax-leaf privet (*Ligustrum lucidum*)	N, C, S
Loropetalum (*Loropetalum chinense*)	N, C
Banana shrub (*Michelia figo*)	N, C
Wax myrtle (*Myrica cerifera*)	N, C
Rapanea (*Myrsine gulanensis*)	C, S
Sweet olive (*Osmanthus fragrans*)	N, C
Pittosporum (*Pittosporum tobira*)	N, C, S
Pomegranate (*Punica granatum*)	N, C, S
Native azaleas (*Rhododendron flammeum, R. canescens*)	N, C
Sumac (*Rhus* spp.)	N, C
Golden senna (*Senna polyphylla*)	C, S
Limeberry (*Triphasia trifolia*)	N, C, S
Sandwanka viburnum (*Viburnum suspensum*)	N, C, S

AZALEAS THAT REBLOOM IN FALL

If you've seen azaleas in bloom in the fall, you were not in the Twilight Zone. There are a few whose internal mechanisms respond to the short days of fall in Florida by producing a good show of flowers, starting in late summer and continuing all winter or until frost in north Florida. Although the show is not as tremendous as it is in spring, it is certainly enough to make you want these beauties for their surprise.

'Aaron White'
'Alaska White'
'Celestine'
'Duc de Rohan'
'Duchess of Cypress'
'Early Red'
'Fashion'

'Happy Days'
'Pink Ruffle'
'Red Ruffle'
'Vogel'
'Wakaebisu'
'White Duc'

"You can grow some azaleas out in the sun, but to me an azalea always looks better if it is planted in partial shade. Ours are field grown under many large oaks. Dense shade will reduce plant growth and flowering. You have to work a lot of organic amendments into the soil, especially farther south. Azaleas need plenty of water—thorough watering at least twice a week—because they have very shallow root systems."
—Jim Brogle, Vet's Wholesale Nursery, Seffner.

SOME AZALEAS BY HEIGHT

LC: One of the most common mistakes made when planting azaleas is not knowing how large they will eventually get. My friend Norman Johnson, a landscape architect from Louisiana, jokes about how they can grow to the size of Greyhound buses. Here we have categorized a few popular ones by height; there are dozens more, however, so do your homework before you buy.

The very low azaleas make good groundcovers as mass plantings, and they are especially great under dogwoods for a terrific spring show. Even the semidwarfs will stay neat under a window with little pruning.

Dwarf: 2 to 3 feet	Semidwarf: 3 to 6 feet	Large: 6 feet and up
'Celestine'	'Aron White'	'Formosa'
'Coral Bells'	'Dogwood'	'George Tabor'
'Happy Days'	'Duc de Rohan'	'G.G. Gerbing'
'Madonna'	'Duchess of Cypress'	'H.H. Hume'
'Pink and White'	'Early Red'	'Salmon Solomon'
'Red Ruffle'	'Evening Song'	'Southern Charm'
'Wakaebisu'	'Fashion'	'Sublanchalata'
'White Duc'	'Fedora'	
	'Glory of Sunny Hill'	
	'Little John'	
	'Pink Ruffle'	

"Azaleas are one of the easiest plants that I've ever propagated. If you keep them wet, you can get 80 percent rooted. Take 3-inch succulent cuttings (green stems) around the first of May. Strip off everything except for the top two or three leaves. Snip them at an angle just below the node. [A rooting hormone] may help a little, but it isn't necessary. It might give you 85 percent. I put them right in 6-inch pots of good potting medium and keep them damp. They will be rooted well by fall and can stay in the pots until the next spring and then be set out." —Floyd Joyner, groundskeeping supervisor, Ravine State Garden, Palatka.

SHRUBS FOR TIGHT PLACES

Shrubs that have a thin, vertical silhouette make good accents in any planting and give a feeling of more formality. They can, however, be easily misplaced. They draw attention, so they need to look good; some junipers are subject to spider mites and can soon become eyesores.

Use such accents carefully in the general landscape. They tend to blend in better in those tight, narrow places where shrubs would otherwise soon grow over the walk or need too much pruning—between a walk and a building, at the corner of the garage, or in between driveways. Choose shrubs that are narrow enough to fill—but not overfill—the space. There are many columnar cultivars of otherwise broader shrubs, such as the Teton firethorn, so look for these as you shop or browse through a catalog.

Marlberry (*Ardisia escallonioides*)	C, S
Japanese plum yew (*Cephalotaxus harringtonia* 'Fastigiata')	N, C
Parlor palm (*Chamaedorea* spp.)	S
Ti plant (*Cordyline terminalis*)	C, S

Dracaena or dragon tree (*Dracaena* spp.)   N, C, S*
Fatsia (*Fatsia japonica*)   N, C, S
Rose-of-Sharon (*Hibiscus syriacus*)   N, C
Juniper (*Juniperus chinensis* 'Blue Point' 'Torulosa'+)   N, C, S
Shrimp plant (*Justicia brandegeana*)   N, C, S
Flamingo plant or Jacobinia (*Justicia carnea*)   C, S
Leatherleaf mahonia (*Mahonia bealei*)   N, C
Nandina, heavenly bamboo (*Nandina domestica*)   N, C, S
Florida yew (*Podocarpus microphyllus*)   N, C, S
Teton firethorn (*Pyracantha coccinea* 'Teton')   N, C, S
Lady palm (*Rhapis excelsa*)   C, S
Bird-of-paradise (*Strelitzia* spp.)   C, S

JOHN W. SHIRAH'S FAVORITE CAMELLIAS FOR FLORIDA

Camellias grow as far south as Sebring and Avon Park, about 30 miles south of Highway 60. Local camellia society meetings throughout Florida help enthusiasts share knowledge and plants and stage some fantastic shows, including a very informational booth at the state fair in Tampa every February. Allena Halliday of Brandon grows two hundred different kinds of camellias under her orange trees and between plants of tomatoes, parsley, and amaryllis around the pool in her yard. Getting ready for shows takes hours of her loving care and time, but the thrill of winning over 178 ribbons in one year is well worth it. So are the lovely blooms she has to enjoy and to give away from November until June.

John W. Shirah, Jr., who also grows more than two hundred varieties of camellias, as his late father did before him, in his nursery in Lakeland, says, "Camellias perform best in partially shaded locations, which are enhanced by good water drainage and air movement. A location that meets the basic cultural requirements will enable plants to withstand adverse conditions." He says that camellias will grow in full sun but do better in partial shade. They like a pH of 5.0 to 5.5 but will grow in soil up to a pH of 6.5. Organic matter in the soil makes for better growth and also helps adjust the pH. Camellias need feeding before the spring flush of bloom, again in July, and in November. John offers the following lists of his favorite varieties. All of these are *Camellia japonica*.

North Florida
'Brassenia'
'Carter's Sunburst'
'Charlie Bettes'
'Cherrie's Jubilee'
'Happy Birthday'
'Julia France'
'Laura Walker'
'Mathotiana Rubra'
'Miss Charleston'
'Pink Perfection'
'Royal Velvet'
'Tomorrow's Dawn'

Central Florida
'Alba Plena'
'Bart Colbert Variegated'
'Betty Sheffield Silver'
'Betty Sheffield Supreme'
'Debutante'
'Dixie Knight Supreme'
'Faith'
'Happy Birthday'
'Johnnie S.'
'Kramer's Supreme'
'Mathotiana Rubra'
'Pink Perfection'
'Royal Velvet'
'Tomorrow Variegated'

HIBISCUS FOR FLORIDA

Hibiscus is a family of shrubs that grow all over Florida. Some are native; some are not. Some are perennial, but many are woody. Sea hibiscus can grow into a large tree. Though many hibiscus are reliably hardy only in the southern third of the peninsula, many of us in areas that are not frost free are satisfied when they come back from the roots after a freeze.

The false roselle and roselle are both edible, but the false can be an invasive weed.

False roselle (*Hibiscus acetosella*)	C, S
Confederate rose (*Hibiscus mutabilis*)	N, C, S
Chinese hibiscus (*Hibiscus rose-sinensis* cultivars)	C, S

 'Anderson Crepe'
 'Brilliant Red'
 'Carnation Red'
 'Celia'
 'Double'
 'Florida Sunset'
 'Fort Myers'
 'Hula Girl'
 'Joanne'
 'Kona Princess'
 'Lafrance'
 'Painted Lady'
 'President'
 'Ruth Wilcox'
 'Scarlet Red'
 'Seminole Pink'
 'Sherri'
 'White Wings'
 'Yellow Wings'

Hibiscus

Fringed hibiscus (*Hibiscus schizopetalus*)	C, S
Roselle (*Hibiscus sabdariffa*)	S
Rose-of-Sharon (*Hibiscus syriacus*)	N, C

"Hibiscus is the rose of the tropics. The hybrids especially are just like children—the more you do for them, the more they respond. I tell my customers to do something for them everyday. Water them. Feed them. Mulch them; they have shallow roots. Prune them to shape as needed. They bloom on new wood, so trimming is essential for continual bloom. Hibiscus grow easily, but they will just linger if you neglect them. Here in south Florida, the nights are too warm for much bloom in the summertime, but they begin blooming in October and continue until May."—Winn Soldani, owner and operator, Fancy Hibiscus, Pompano Beach.

SHRUBS FOR THE BEACH

LC: Like other plants that grow on the beach, shrubs that flourish there need to be the toughest and most resistant to wind, sun, and salt spray, especially along the Atlantic Coast. The Gulf Coast isn't as horribly windy, and the distinction between the beachfront and the leeward side of a house isn't as drastic. I grew up in Jacksonville and spent much time at the beach.

Below are some plants that I've seen used regularly, or that have been recommended by garden designers who work on the beach. Before you plant, look around and ask about what specifically works on the waterfront in your locale. Be aware that salt spray and wind damage can extend quite far inland during storms. Also, check other chapters in this book for trees, annuals, groundcovers, and perennials for the beach.

Plant	Zones
Century plant (*Agave americana*)	C, S
Marlberry (*Ardisia escallonioides*)	C, S
Salt bush (*Baccharis halimifolia*)	N, C, S
Jamaican caper (*Capparis* spp.)	S
Natal plum (*Carissa macrocarpa*)	C, S
Seven-year apple (*Casasia clusiifolia*)	S
Snowberry (*Chicococca alba*)	C, S
Coco plum (*Chrysobalanus icaco*)	S
Varnish leaf (*Dodanaea viscosa*)	N, C, S
Elaegnus (*Elaegnus* spp.)	N, C, S
Stoppers, redberry (*Eugenia* spp.)	C, S
Wild olive, Florida privet (*Forestiera segregata*)	N, C, S
Yaupon holly (*Ilex vomitoria* 'Stokes Dwarf', others)	N, C, S
Marsh or beach elder (*Iva* spp.)	N, C, S
Ixora (*Ixora coccinea*)	C, S
Joewood (*Jacquinia keyensis*)	S
Christmas berry (*Lycium carolinianum*)	N, C, S
Sea lavender (*Mallotonia gnaphalodes*)	C, S
Wax myrtle (*Myrica cerifera*)	N, C, S
Rapanea (*Myrsine gauanensis*)	S
Oleander (*Nerium oleander*)	N, C, S
Ochrosia, kopsia (*Ochrosia parviflora*)	S
Blackbead (*Pithecellobium guadelupense*)	C, S
Pittosporum (*Pittosporum tobira*)	N, C, S
White indigoberry (*Randia aculeata*)	C, S
Indian hawthorn (*Raphiolepsis indica*)	N, C, S
Maidenbush (*Savia bahamensis*)	S
Beach naupaka, inkberry (*Scaevola* spp.)	C, S
Saw palmetto (*Serenoa repens*)	N, C, S
Necklace pod (*Sophora tomentosa*)	C, S
Bay cedar (*Suriana maritima*)	S
Sandankwa viburnum (*Viburnum suspensum*)	N, C, S
Laurestinus (*Viburnum tinus*)	N, C
Spanish bayonet (*Yucca aloifolia*)	N, C, S

"There are several ways gardeners can partially overcome the problems caused by wind, salt, cold, and drought. Proper soil preparation is the place to start. Incorporate as much organic material into the soil as possible, including compost, peat, black dirt, and animal manures." —Mary Jane McSwain, author, *Florida Gardening by the Sea.*

CAMELLIAS FOR FIVE MONTHS OF BLOOM

If you choose the varieties carefully, you can have a camellia in bloom from November through March. The list below comes from Gene Ellis at Tallahassee Nurseries. Gene says that the show there begins with the earliest sasanqua in the fall, 'Sparkling Burgundy', and ends in late March with 'Mrs. Charles Cobb', a large-flowered japonica. It includes some old-fashioned standbys such as 'Debutante', 'Professor Sargent', and 'Pink Perfection', as well as some of the newer popular selections. 'Aunt Jetty' is a descendant of a plant in MacClay Gardens just out-side of Tallahassee.

Use camellias as framing trees for a one-story house, as a single specimen in a patio plant-ing, or as an effective privacy screen. Their dense, evergreen foliage is beautiful year-round. If space is at a premium, try camellias as espalier or in a pot. They train beautifully against a wall or solid fence and maintain an evergreen, glossy presence even when not in bloom.

To enjoy your camellias indoors, too, float the blooms in a shallow bowl or large goblet of water.

Month of Bloom	Variety	Color	Type
October/November	All sasanquas	white, pink, red, variegated	single and double
November	'Alba Plena'	white	formal double
	'Daikagura'	variegated	peony
	'Emmett Barnes'	white	semi-double
	'Debutante'	pink	peony
December	'Pink Perfection'	pink	formal double
	'Rubra'	rose red	formal double
	'White Empress'	white	semi-double
	'Professor Sargent'	red	peony
January	'Julia France'	shell pink	semi-double
	'Nucciorquote's Gem'	white	formal double
	'Jordan's Pride'	variegated	semi-double
	'Nuccior's Pearl'	white-pink	formal double
	'Carterr's Sunburst'	peppermint	peony
February/March	'Elegans Splendor'	pink-white	large anemone
	'Mrs. Charles Cobb'	red	loose peony
	'Tomorrow'	red or pink	semi-double
	'Dr. Clifford Parks'	red	peony

A FEW SHRUBS FOR GROUNDCOVERS

Many of the plants in the groundcover chapter are low, spreading shrubs with dense enough growth to cover the ground and create a solid mass. Woody groundcovers are not as good where there may be foot traffic, but they are excellent for interest, bloom, and barriers and for differ-ent textures and colors of foliage. Some of the plants in this list, like the junipers and jasmines, are from a genus with many cultivars, some of which make terrific groundcovers, though others are much too tall. Although some of these plants, such as dwarf abelia or dwarf yaupon, will get

4 feet tall in a large, open space, they can be excellent groundcovers. They cover a lot of ground, thus making a planting more economical. Check the groundcovers chapter as well as the perennial, fern, rose, and vine chapters for more good groundcover plants.

Dwarf abelia (*Abelia* × *grandiflora* 'Prostrata', 'Edward Groucher'+)	N, C
Japanese ardisia (*Ardisia japonica*)	N
Azalea hybrids (types shorter than 3 feet)	N, C
Crimson pygmy barberry (*Berberis thunbergii atropurpurea* 'Crimson Pygmy')	N
Shiny blueberry (*Vaccinium myrsinites*)	N, C, S
Pineland snowberry (*Chicococca pinetorum*)	S
False heather (*Cuphea hyssopifolia*)	C, S
Golden creeper (*Ernodea littoralis*)	S
Dwarf gardenia (*Gardenia jasminoides* 'Radicans')	N, C, S
Rotunda holly (*Ilex cornuta* 'Rotunda'+)	N, C
Japanese holly (*Ilex crenata* 'Stokes'+)	N, C
Dwarf yaupon holly (*Ilex vomitoria* 'Schelling's Dwarf'+)	N, C
Winter jasmine (*Jasminum nudiflorum*)	N
Parson's juniper (*Juniperus chinensis* 'Parsonii')	N, C, S
Shore juniper (*Juniperus conferta* cultivars)	N, C, S
Creeping juniper (*Juniperus horizontalis* 'Blue Rug'+)	N, C, S
Trailing lantana (*Lantana montevidensis*)	C, S
Singapore holly (*Malpighia coccigera*)	C, S
Twinflower (*Mitchella repens*)	N
Dwarf nandina (*Nandina domestica* 'Harbor Dwarf'+)	N, C
Formosan firethorn (*Pyracantha koidzumii*)	N, C, S
Dwarf Indian hawthorn (*Raphiolepsis indica* 'Enchantress'+)	N, C, S

SHRUBS THAT CAN BE INVASIVE

This list is not complete; there are even more. Most of the following plants can be used in certain sections and situations where either frost, summer heat, or a careful gardener can keep them in control. Edible figs are not invasive, and the other *Ficus* species can be well used in containers, where their rambling roots can't spread far. Many of the edible fruiting shrubs that could be a problem in south Florida are cut back often enough in the central counties to be no threat at all. Those with asterisks in the list below are considered noxious weeds in some parts of the state.

Spreading bamboo (*Bambusa* spp.)	N, C
Night-blooming cereus (*Cereus undatus*)*	C, S
Sickle bamboo (*Chimonobambusa falcata*)	N, C, S
Pagoda flower (*Clerodendrum paniculatum*)	C, S
Java glorybower (*Clerodendrum speciosissimum*)	C, S
Surinam cherry (*Eugenia uniflora*)*	C, S
Fig (*Ficus* spp.)*	C, S
Heliconias (*Heliconia* spp.)	S
False roselle (*Hibiscus acetosella*)	C, S
Sea hibiscus (*Hibiscus tiliaceus*)*	C
Lantana (*Lantana camara*)*	N, C, S
Japanese honeysuckle (*Lonicera japonica*)*	N, C, S

Christmas berry (*Lycium carolinianum*)*	N, C, S
Wax myrtle (*Myrica* spp.)	N, C, S
Black or golden bamboo (*Phyllostachys* spp.)	N, C
Pittosporum (*Pittosporum pentandrum*)*	N, C, S
Arrow bamboo (*Pseudosasa japonica*)	N, C, S
Guava (*Psidium guava*)*	C, S
Strawberry guava (*Psidium littorale*)*	C, S
Winged sumac (*Rhus copallina*)	N, C, S
Castor bean (*Ricinus communis*)*	N, C, S
Firecracker plant (*Russelia equisetiformis*)*	C, S
Java plum (*Syzygium cumini*)*	C, S
Rose apple (*Syzygium jambos*)*	C, S
Rice-paper plant (*Tetrapanax papyriferus*)	C, S

SAMPLER OF SHRUBS BY FLOWER COLOR

Use this list for a quick overview of some of the flowering shrubs in this chapter if you are interested in selecting a shrub for its flower color.

White Flowers

Glossy abelia (*Abelia* × *grandiflora*)	N, C
Marlberry (*Ardisia escallonioides*)	C, S
Azalea hybrids	N, C, S
Angel trumpet, datura (*Brugmansia* × *candida*)	C, S
Butterfly bush (*Buddleia* hybrids)	N, C
Camellia (*Camellia sasanqua, C. japonica*)	N, C
Natal plum (*Carissa macrocarpa*)	C, S
Buttonbush (*Cephalanthus occidentalis*)	N, C
Coco plum (*Chrysobalanus icaco*)	S
Golden dewdrop (*Duranta repens*)	N, C, S
Gardenia (*Gardenia jasminoides*)	N, C, S
Rose-of-Sharon (*Hibiscus syriacus* 'Diana')	N, C, S
Oakleaf hydrangea (*Hydrangea quercifolia*)	N, C
Joewood (*Jacquinia keyensis*)	S
Jasmine (*Jasminum* spp.)	N, C, S
Oleander (*Nerium oleander*)	N, C, S
Pentas (*Pentas lanceolata*)	N, C, S
Mock orange (*Philadelphus coronarius*)	N
Beach naupaka, inkberry (*Scaevola plumieri*)	C, S
Reeve's spirea (*Spirea cantonensis*)	N, C
Limeberry (*Triphasia trifolia*)	N, C, S
Viburnum (*Viburnum* spp.)	N, C, S

Blue Flowers

Yesterday-today-and-tomorrow (*Brunfelsia australis*)	C, S
Butterfly bush (*Buddleia* hybrids)	N, C
Blue-butterfly bush (*Clerodendron ungandense*)	C, S
Lignum-vitae (*Guaiacum* spp.)	S
French hydrangea (*Hydrangea macrophylla*)	N, C

Smooth hydrangea (*Hydrangea arborescens*)   N, C
Christmas berry (*Lycium carolinianum*)   N, C, S
Pentas (*Pentas lanceolata* 'Buderin Blue')   C, S
Plumbago (*Plumbago auriculata*)   C, S
White bird-of-paradise (*Strelitzia nicolai*)   C, S
Chaste tree (*Vitex agnus-castus*)   N, C, S

Lavender, Purple, or Pink Flowers
Azalea hybrids   N, C
Butterfly bush (*Buddleia* hybrids)   N, C
Locustberry (*Byrsonima lucida*)   S
Camellia (*Camellia sasanqua, C. japonica*)   N, C
Jamaican caper (*Capparis* spp.)   S
Golden dewdrop (*Duranta repens*)   N, C, S
Rose-of-Sharon (*Hibiscus syriacus*)   N, C
French hydrangea (*Hydrangea macrophylla*)   N, C
Flamingo plant,r jacobinia (*Justicia carnea*)   C, S
Texas sage (*Leucophyllum frutescens*)   N, C, S
Barbados cherry (*Malpighia glabra*)   C, S
Oleander (*Nerium oleander*)   N, C, S
Pentas (*Pentas lanceolata*)   C, S
Blackbead (*Pithecellobium guadelupense*)   C
Indian hawthorn (*Raphiolepsis* spp.)   N, C, S
Princess-flower (*Tibouchina* spp.)   C, S

Red Flowers
Chenille plant (*Acalypha hispida*)   C, S
Red buckeye (*Aesculus pavia*)   N, C
Azalea hybrids   N, C, S
Dwarf poinciana (*Caesalpinia pulcherrima*)   C, S
Powderpuff (*Calliandra haematocephala*)   C, S
Camellia (*Camellia sasanqua, C. japonica*)   N, C
Coral bean (*Erythrina herbacea*)   N, C, S
Poinsettia (*Euphorbia pulcherrima*)   C, S
Firebush (*Hamelia patens*)   C, S
Hibiscus (*Hibiscus* spp.)   C, S
Ixora (*Ixora coccinea*)   C, S
Peregrina, coral-, or gout-plant (*Jatropha* spp.)   C, S
Turk's cap (*Malvaviscus arboreus*)   N, C, S
Oleander (*Nerium oleander*)   N, C, S
Pentas (*Pentas lanceolata*)   C, S
Firecracker plant (*Russelia equisetiformis*)   C, S

Orange or Yellow Flowers
Sweet acacia (*Acacia farnesiana*)   C, S
Candlebush (*Cassia alata*)   C, S
Cassia shrub (*Cassia* spp.)   C, S
Snowberry (*Chicococca alba*)   C, S
Dwarf poinciana (*Delonix regia*)   S

Orange or Yellow Flowers (*continued*)

Thryallis (*Galphimia glauca*)	C, S
African bush daisy (*Gamolepsis chrysanthemoides*)	N, C, S
Hibiscus (*Hibiscus* spp.)	C, S
Ixora hybrids	C, S
Lantanas (*Lantana* spp.)	C, S
Mahonias (*Mahonia* spp.)	N, C
Golden shrimp plant (*Pachystachys lutea*)	C, S
Florida flame azalea (*Rhododendron austrinum*)	N, C
Necklace pod (*Sophora tomentosa*)	C, S
Bird-of-paradise (*Strelitzia reginae*)	C, S
Beach buttercup (*Turnera ulmifolia*)	S

VINES

Vines are like the stitching in a patchwork quilt. They can give you in a short time the screening, privacy, shade, flowers, and fragrance that it would take trees and shrubs many months to achieve. These often unappreciated, underutilized landscape plants can bind the elements of a garden and add a feeling of opulence and romance. The possible choices of vines multiply the farther south one lives in Florida. There are fifty times as many vines in tropical countries as in the cooler regions of the world, according to Edwin Menninger in *Flowering Vines of the World*.

MB: We built an arbor over our front door and bay window that has made all the difference in the world in our home, both indoors and out. It is presently covered with moonflowers, Muscadine grapes, and double allamanda, which looks like roses but has no thorns. It is practically an outdoor room, the foyer we wouldn't otherwise have. My daughter Teresa sits on the swing in the shade to wait for her school bus, and her cat, Powder, basks among the plants on the bench opposite. This vine-covered arbor adds tremendously to the feeling of privacy inside. It cools the living room all summer, yet because the vines are deciduous or frost tender, they let in plenty of sun in the winter.

There can be disadvantages to vines if you plant the wrong one in the wrong place or if you are afraid to prune, but these can be overcome by choosing wisely from the following lists. Let vines decorate your arbor, deck rail, fence, lamppost, or latticework or add some of these elements to your garden. Vines can hide or disguise the entrance to the shed or garage, soften a big blank wall, or frame the scenes you enjoy most from your windows or patio. Check magazines and books and the gardens you admire most for additional ideas.

TO DO LIST FOR GROWING VINES

With perennial and woody vines it is increasingly important to know what a plant will and will not do before you bring it home. Growing annual vines can be a hands-on learning experience. You can mix and match them with more permanent vines on the same arbor or support;

or try one annual one year, another the next. To keep evergreens from getting out of hand and taking over your whole yard, follow the steps listed here.

- Decide what you want each vine to provide: shade, fragrance, flowers, fruit, foliage, or texture. Will it be year-round or seasonal?
- Choose a vine adapted to the site. Is the site sunny or shady? What is the soil pH? Is the spot particularly hot, dry, or wet? Does the vine need to tolerate ocean spray?
- Get the full particulars on any vine you are considering. If possible, find it growing somewhere and ask the person who tends it what kind of pruning or support is needed. Ask if it sends out runners or spreads a million seedlings (like the black-eyed Susan does).
- Find out whether the vine withstands frost. With vines, frost is not always bad; it can help with control. Some, like the passionflowers, can get out of hand even between frosts.
- Once you've made a selection, plant it properly in enriched soil. Water well until established. Mulch to keep weeds down and moisture in, and then stand back. Vines grow quickly, and you'll have flowers, fruit, or shade before you know it.
- Take your pruning shears every time you go for a garden walk to snip vines back into place before they get out of hand. Their almost instant growth is one of the things that makes them so useful. But we can hardly expect them to stop when they get to the edge of the porch. Frequent snipping is not much trouble, a habit easily developed that makes living with vines easy and pleasant.
- Learn to recognize seedlings of the vines in your yard and transplant or remove the ones you don't want while they are small—another little job that prevents a large mess.

DECIDUOUS VINES

True deciduous vines are less common in Florida than in the rest of the country. These are the ones to put on arbors over windows and around porches, where you want all the sun you can get in the winter but leafy shade in the summer's heat. Bear in mind that this means falling leaves. MB: I have to sweep the walk under our front door arbor every day in the fall, but I consider that a small price for winter sunlight. The framework of bare branches has its own appeal. Most people never notice the swelling buds and interesting seedpods, but gardeners consider them promises for the future and find them fascinating. Quite a few vines may lose their leaves in a freeze and then leaf out again, but those often have to be cut back to the ground, so they are not included on this list.

Five-leaf akebia (*Akebia quinata*)	N
Pepper vine (*Ampelopsis arborea*)	N, C, S
Cross vine (*Bignonia capreolata*)	N, C, S
Trumpet vine (*Campsis radicans*)	N, C, S
Orange trumpet vine (*Campsis* × *tagliabuana* 'Madame Galen')	N
Marine ivy (*Cissus incisa*)	N, C, S
Poet's jasmine (*Jasminum officinale*)	N, C, S
Virginia creeper (*Parthenocissus quinquefolia*)	N, C, S
Grape (*Vitis* spp.)	N, C, S
American wisteria (*Wisteria frutescens*)	N, C
Japanese wisteria, Chinese wisteria (*Wisteria floribunda, W. sinensis*)	N, C

VINES FOR SUN OR PARTIAL SHADE

So many of the plants that need full sun elsewhere in the country are happy for a bit of shade in Florida's warm weather. Partial shade can mean sunlight for four to six hours a day or mottled sunlight peeping through a tree canopy or under tall limbs. The west side of a building or a tree that gets the long, hot afternoon sun is the hardest on plants that prefer shade, but all of the vines in this list can take it. Many of those listed for central or south Florida will grow as annuals in north Florida.

Passion-
flower

Pepper vine (*Ampelopsis arborea*)	N, C, S
Pipe vine (*Aristolochia* spp.)	C, S
Herald's trumpet (*Beaumontia grandiflora*)	S
Cross vine (*Bignonia capreolata*)	N, C, S
Trumpet vine (*Campsis radicans*)	N, C, S
Marine ivy (*Cissus incisa*)	N, C, S
Armand clematis (*Clematis armandii*)	N
Bleeding heart vine (*Clerodendrum thomsoniae*)	C, S
Devil's potato (*Echites umbellata*)	S
Wintercreeper (*Euonymous fortunei*)	N, C
Creeping fig (*Ficus pumila*)	N, C, S
Carolina yellow jessamine (*Gelsemium sempervirens*)	N, C
Gloriosa lily (*Gloriosa rothschildiana*)	N, C, S
Night-blooming cereus (*Hylocereus undatus*)	C, S
Jacquemontia (*Jacquemontia* spp.)	C, S
Trumpet honeysuckle (*Lonicera sempervirens*)	N, C, S
Passionflower (*Passiflora* spp.)	N, C, S
Queen's wreath (*Petrea volubilis*)	C, S
Flame vine (*Pyrostegia ignea*)	C, S
Rangoon creeper (*Quisqualis indica*)	C, S
Hunter's robe (*Scindapsus aureus*)	S
Smilax (*Smilax* spp.)	N, C, S
Chalice vine (*Solandra guttata*)	C, S
Madagascar jasmine (*Stephanotis floribunda*)	C, S
Brazilian golden vine, golden creeper (*Stigmaphyllon ciliatum*)	C, S
Black-eyed Susan vine (*Thunbergia alata*)	C, S
Bengal clock vine (*Thunbergia grandiflora*)	C, S
Confederate jasmine (*Trachelospermum jasminoides*)	N, C, S
Wild allamanda (*Urechites lutea*)	C, S

"Most vines will get as big as you let them, and most people overplant. Give them strong support and plenty of room. Passionflowers are one of my favorite vines for butterflies, and I've had one cover a 60-foot length of fence 8 feet tall from a single root. The red passionflower is not at all invasive for us here, because it does not seed in a cultivated landscape; it just spreads. Figure to give most vines a good 20 feet to run." —Chris Maler, Alexander's Landscaping and Plant Farm, Davie.

VINES FOR DEEP SHADE

The hardest spots to plant are those with deep shade, where the sunlight never settles, such as the shaded north side of a home or where trees form too dense a canopy. I couldn't even imagine too much shade for the first fifty years of my life, while I was planting trees in the Midwest that took decades to cast a shadow. But it can happen quickly in Florida. When it does, you might want to consider removing some of the least choice trees or having lower limbs removed for a higher canopy. This not only lets in more light but also allows for more air circulation. Get a professional to prune once trees get too large for you. MB: We had ours done recently, and it was worth every penny, almost like getting a whole new yard. In the meantime, vines are of one of Mother Nature's prime choices for deep shade, as a walk in the woods will prove. Here are some that will flourish there.

Sicklethorn vine (*Asparagus falcatus*)	C, S
Grape ivy (*Cissus rhombifolia*)	S
Climbing hydrangea (*Decumaria barbara*)	N
Creeping fig (*Ficus pumila*)	N, C, S
Algerian ivy (*Hedera canariensis*)	N, C, S
English ivy (*Hedera helix*)	N, C
Monstera (*Monstera deliciosa*)	S
Philodendrons (*Philodendron* spp.)	C, S
Confederate jasmine (*Trachelospermum jasminoides*)	N, C, S
Greater periwinkle (*Vinca major*)	N, C

VINES FOR THE BEACH

Vines for the beach need to be happy in full sun and driving wind—in other words, the toughest of plants. It helps if their roots bind the sand into place, as do the roots of the beach bean, to help prevent erosion. Otherwise, that wonderful waterside property can wash right out to sea. Even careful planting cannot always prevent this, but it can sometimes help. Some plants are not fully tolerant of salt, either in spray or in the soil, and are usually found behind the dunes; they are still considered valuable because they help prevent erosion—those are marked in this list with an asterisk.

Pepper vine (*Ampelopsis arborea*)	N, C, S
Bougainvillea (*Bougainvillea spectabilis*)	C, S
Trumpet vine (*Campsis radicans*)*	N, C, S
Beach bean (*Canavalia maritima*)	S
Snowberry (*Chicococca* spp.)	C, S
Marine ivy (*Cissus incisa*)	N, C, S
Madagascar rubber vine (*Cryptostegia madagascariensis*)	S
Rubber vine (*Cryptostegia* spp.)	C, S
Garlic vine (*Cydista aequinoctialis*)*	S
Devil's potato (*Echites umbellata*)*	S
Wintercreeper (*Euonymous fortunei*)	N, C
Carolina yellow jessamine (*Gelsemium sempervirens*)	N, C, S
Algerian ivy (*Hedera canariensis*)	N, C, S
Morning glory (*Ipomoea* spp.)	N, C, S
Railroad vine (*Ipomoea pes-caprae*)	S
Jacquemontia (*Jacquemontia* spp.)*	C, S
Coral honeysuckle (*Lonicera sempervirens*)	N, C, S

Lonicera sempervirens

Virginia creeper (*Parthenocissus quinquefolia*)   N, C, S
Barbados gooseberry, lemon vine (*Pereskia aculeata*)   S
Lady bank's rose (*Rosa banksia*)*   N, C
Confederate jasmine (*Trachelospermum jasminoides*)*   N, C, S
Wild allamanda (*Urechites lutea*)   C, S

 "Most sources say coral honeysuckle is not salt tolerant, but I've found otherwise. Three of my vines have thrived after sitting in a saltwater flood for hours." — Beth Dolan, garden editor and writer, *Tampa Tribune.*

VINES THAT DEMAND FULL SUN

The amount of light a vine needs is one of the main points to consider when matching it to a location in your garden. Vines will seek what they need and often stretch a long distance to find it. The vines in this list can take, indeed thrive on, the full blaze of Florida's sun, whether it is in the dry heat of late spring or the damp and humid heat of full summer. Those listed for only central and south Florida will grow as annuals or perennials in north Florida.

Yellow allamanda (*Allamanda cathartica*)   C, S
Purple allamanda (*Allamanda violacea*)   C, S
Woolly morning glory (*Argyreia nervosa*)   S
Calico flower (*Aristolochia elegans*)   C, S
Bougainvillea (*Bougainvillea spectabilis*)   C, S
Beach bean (*Canavalia maritima*)   S
Snowberry (*Chicococca* spp.)   C, S
Purple painted trumpet (*Clytostoma callistegioides*)   N, C, S
Showy combretum (*Combretum grandiflorum*)   S
Woolly congea (*Congea tomentosa*)   C, S
Rubber vine (*Cryptostegia* spp.)   C, S
Madagascar rubber vine (*Cryptostegia madagascariensis*)   C, S
Garlic vine (*Cydista aequinoctialis*)   C, S
Jewel vine (*Derris scandens*)   S
Morning glory (*Ipomoea* spp.)   N, C, S
Railroad vine (*Ipomoea pes-caprae*)   S
Mandevillas (*Mandevilla* spp.)   C, S
Tropical wisteria (*Millettia reticulata*)   C, S
Bower plant (*Pandorea jasminoides*)   S
Barbados gooseberry, lemon vine (*Pereskia aculeata*)   S
Snow creeper (*Porana paniculata*)   S
Mexican flame vine (*Senecio confusus*)   C, S
Cape honeysuckle (*Tecomaria capensis*)   C, S
Sweet clock vine (*Thunbergia fragrans*)   C, S

 "If you can choose only one vine for your garden, the tropical wisteria (*Millettia reticulata*) may be the one. The wine and purple sweetpea-like flowers are real show-stoppers, blooming in surges spring through fall. Glossy, evergreen leaves about 3 inches long decorate strongly architectural curves of tough dark-brown stems. It is not aggressive and has no pests of consequence." — *Leu Gardens Quarterly*, Orlando.

VINES WITH FRAGRANT FLOWERS

Does anything accentuate the charm of living in a warm climate more than the romantic picture of the vine-covered porch or arbor? Take the same scene and add the sweet fragrance of jasmine or moonflowers. Use the vines on this list near your indoor and outdoor living areas and entranceways, and they will double your enjoyment every time the breeze wafts their fragrance your way. They will make you feel that Florida is the best-smelling part of God's green earth.

Vanilla planifolia

Showy and Fragrant

Yellow allamanda (*Allamanda cathartica*)	C, S
Sicklethorn vine (*Asparagus falcatus*)	N, C, S
Herald's trumpet (*Beaumontia grandiflora*)	S
Armand clematis (*Clematis armandii*)	N, C
Garlic vine (*Cydista aequinoctialis*)	C, S
Jewel vine (*Derris scandens*)	S
Wax plant (*Hoya purpurea-fusca* 'Silver pink')	C, S
Night-blooming cereus (*Hylocereus undatus*)	C, S
Moonflower (*Ipomoea alba*)	C, S,
Jasmine (*Jasminum* spp.)	N, C, S
Chilean mandevilla (*Mandevilla lava*)	C, S
Snow creeper (*Porana paniculata*)	S
Rangoon creeper (*Quisqualis indica*)	C, S
White Lady bank's rose (*Rosa banksia alba plena*)	N, C
Chalice vine (*Solandra guttata*)	C, S
Madagascar jasmine (*Stephanotis floribunda*)	C, S

Fragrant but Inconspicuous Flowers

Five-leaf akebia (*Akebia quinata*)	N
Madeira vine (*Anredera cordifolia*)	C, S
Dalbergia (*Dalbergia brownea*)	S
Vanilla orchid (*Vanilla planifolia*)	C, S

Foul-smelling

Pipe vine (*Aristolochia* spp.)	N, C, S

EVERGREEN WOODY VINES

Many woody vines are evergreen in Florida. These are the ones you want to use for screening and privacy, to hide downspouts, dog kennels, and service areas, or for permanent groundcovers. A few of the frost-tender ones may shed leaves if they get a freeze, so be aware of this in marginal zones of hardiness. Many will leaf out again or, at worst, come back from the roots if the freeze has been more severe or long lasting. Every decade or so a long, hard freeze could wipe them out. Because of this, we have listed here only the regions where the following vines are reliably evergreen (other lists may indicate a wider region where they will grow even though they might occasionally die down from frost).

Smilax

Some very common vines, such as pothos, Japanese honeysuckle, and coral vine, are omitted because they appear on Florida's list of noxious weeds.

Allamandas (*Allamanda* spp.)	S
Woolly morning glory (*Argyreia nervosa*)	S
Pipe vine (*Aristolochia* spp.)	S
Sicklethorn vine (*Asparagus falcatus*)	C, S
Herald's trumpet (*Beaumontia grandiflora*)	S
Bougainvillea (*Bouganvillea spectabilis*)	S
Snowberry (*Chicococca* spp.)	S
Grape ivy (*Cissus rhombifolia*)	S
Armand clematis (*Clematis armandii*)	N
Bleeding heart vine (*Clerodendrum thomsoniae*)	S
Purple painted trumpet (*Clytostoma callistegioides*)	N, C, S
Showy combretum (*Combretum grandiflorum*)	S
Woolly congea (*Congea tomentosa*)	S
Wintercreeper (*Euonymus fortunei*)	N, C
Carolina yellow jessamine (*Gelsemium sempervirens*)	N, C
Algerian ivy (*Hedera canariensis*)	N, C, S
English ivy (*Hedera helix*)	N, C
Wax plant (*Hoya* spp.)	S
Jasmine (*Jasminum* spp.)	S
Coral honeysuckle (*Lonicera sempervirens*)	N, C, S
Tropical wisteria (*Millettia reticulata*)	S
Bower plant (*Pandorea jasminoides*)	S
Barbados gooseberry, lemon vine (*Pereskia aculeata*)	S
Flame vine (*Pyrostegia venusta*)	S
Cherokee rose (*Rosa laevigata*)	N, C, S
Mexican flame vine (*Senecio confusus*)	S
Southern smilax (*Smilax smallii*)	N, C
Potato vine (*Solanum jasminoides*)	N, C, S
Brazilian golden vine, golden creeper (*Stigmaphyllon ciliatum*)	S
Cape honeysuckle (*Tecomaria capensis*)	S
Clock vine (*Thunbergia* spp.)	S
Asian jasmine (*Trachelospermum asiaticum*)	N, C, S
Confederate jasmine (*Trachelospermum jasminoides*)	N, C, S

"Vines will not hurt a tree as long as you do regular maintenance. I have never seen or heard of any vine choking a tree. They have enough give and aren't like putting wire on the tree that the tree would have to grow over. Most vines don't squeeze tight enough to do harm. My main worry with vines on a tree is that some aggressive vines such as air potato or grapes may grow to the point where their leaves block out the sunlight to the leaves of the tree. If they are let go, they will cause the leaves to become dysfunctional, and then the branches will begin to die. From my point of view, the vines make it difficult to diagnose tree problems. They may cover wood rot or decay, fungus under the bark, or insects hiding or moisture held against the tree. As long as you cut them completely back every couple of years or thin them out, they're okay." —Robert Irwin, certified arborist, Davey Tree, Tampa.

Drought-Tolerant Vines

It is estimated by the experts of the Florida Water Management Districts that up to 50 percent of Florida's treated water is used for landscaping—not for agriculture but for home and commercial ornamental use. More and more people, however, are following the xeriscape concept of planning their yard with water needs in mind, with plants grouped according to need. All of the plants in this list will thrive, once established, with only occasional watering at most, perhaps every few weeks in the hot, dry spring and only during unusually dry times otherwise.

If you want the nicest plantings for the least work, select from this list those marked with an asterisk, for they are very drought tolerant and, once they are settled in and have developed good root systems, can thrive on natural rainfall.

Yellow allamanda (*Allamanda cathartica*)	C, S
Purple allamanda (*Allamanda cviolacea*)	C, S
Woolly morning glory (*Argyreia nervosa*)	S
Calico flower (*Aristolochia elegans*)	C, S
Pelican flower (*Aristolochia grandiflora*)	C, S
Sicklethorn vine (*Asparagus falcatus*)*	N, C, S
Herald's trumpet (*Beaumontia grandiflora*)	S
Bougainvillea (*Bougainvillea spectabilis*)*	C, S
Trumpet vine (*Campsis radicans*)*	N, C, S
Beach bean (*Canavalia maritima*)	S
Snowberry (*Chicococca* spp.)	C, S
Marine ivy (*Cissus incisa*)*	N, C, S
Purple painted trumpet (*Clytostoma callistegioides*)	N, C, S
Showy combretum (*Combretum grandiflorum*)	S
Woolly congea (*Congea tomentosa*)	S
Madagascar rubber vine (*Cryptostegia madagascariensis*)*	C, S
Rubber vine (*Cryptostegia* spp.)	C, S
Garlic vine (*Cydista aequinoctialis*)*	C, S
Climbing hydrangea (*Decumaria barbara*)	N
Devil's potato (*Echites umbellata*)	S
Creeping fig (*Ficus pumila*)*	N, C, S
Carolina yellow jessamine (*Gelsemium sempervirens*)	N, C
Algerian ivy (*Hedera canariensis*)	N, C, S
Night-blooming cereus (*Hylocereus undatus*)*	C, S
Morning glory (*Ipomoea* spp.)	C, S
Railroad vine (*Ipomoea pes-caprae*)	S
Jacquemontia (*Jacquemontia* spp.)	C, S
Coral honeysuckle (*Lonicera sempervirens*)	N, C, S
Mandevillas (*Mandevilla* spp.)*	C, S
Monstera (*Monstera deliciosa*)	S
Virginia creeper (*Parthenocissus quinquefolia*)*	N, C, S
Passionflower (*Passiflora* spp.)	N, C, S
Barbados gooseberry, lemon vine (*Pereskia aculeata*)	S
Queen's wreath (*Petrea volubilis*)	C, S
Philodendrons (*Philodendron* spp.)	C, S
Flame vine (*Pyrostegia venusta*)*	C, S
Rangoon creeper (*Quisqualis indica*)*	C, S
Southern smilax (*Smilax smallii*)	N, C, S

| Madagascar jasmine (*Stephanotis floribunda*) | C, S |
| Bengal clock vine (*Thunbergia grandiflora*) | C, S |

THE PLANT SHOPPE'S VINE LIST

The Plant Shoppe in Gainesville, just off I-75 at exit 76, has a great variety of all kinds of landscaping plants, including new and improved varieties. Ellen Shapiro gave us this list of the vines they grow there, just about on the border between north Florida and central Florida. Many, like the mandevilla that blooms for them for one season, will bloom longer the farther south one lives. The vines with an asterisk are native to Florida.

Coral vine (*Antigonon leptopus*)	N, C, S	Pink
Dutchman's pipe (*Aristolochia elegans*)	N, C	Red, purple
Cross vine (*Bignonia capreolata*)	N, C, S	Yellow w/orange
Orange trumpet vine (*Campsis × tagliabuana* 'Madame Galen')	N, C, S	Orange
Bleeding heart vine (*Clerodendrum thomsoniae*)	C, S	Red and white
Purple painted trumpet vine (*Clytostoma callistegioides*)	N, C, S	Purple
Dipladenia (*Dipladenia sanderi*)	C, S	Pink
Hyacinth bean (*Dolichos lablab*)	C, S	Lavender or white
Carolina yellow jessamine (*Gelsemium sempervirens*)*	N, C, S	Yellow
Black sweet potato vine (*Ipomoea batatas* 'Blackie')	N, C, S	Pink/lavender
Chartreuse sweet potato vine (*Ipomoea batatas* 'Margarita')	N, C, S	Pink/lavender
Indian jasmine (*Jasminum sambac*)	C, S	White
Purple-leaf Japanese honeysuckle (*Lonicera japonica* 'Purpurea')	N, C, S	White to yellow
White honeysuckle (*Lonicera japonica*)	N, C, S	White
Coral honeysuckle (*Lonicera sempervirens*)*	N, C, S	Coral
Cat's claw (*MacFadyena unguis-cati*)*	N, C, S	Yellow
Mandevilla (*Mandevilla splendens*)	C, S	Bright pink
Tropical wisteria (*Milletia reticulata*)	C, S	Mauve
Blue passionflower (*Passiflora caerulea*)	N, C, S	Blue
Red passionflower (*Passiflora coccineum*)	N, C, S	Red
Pink trumpet vine (*Podranea ricasoliant*)	N, C, S	Pink
Potato vine (*Solanum jasminoides* 'Variegata')	N, C, S	Blue/lavender
Confederate jasmine (*Trachelospermum jasminoides* 'Variegata')	N, C, S	White
Wisteria, Chinese wisteria (*Wisteria sinensis*)	N, C	Blue or white
American wisteria, dwarf wisteria (*Wisteria frutescens*)	N, C	Blue

"One of my favorite vines is the purple painted trumpet. It is reliably evergreen for us here, with glossy, pale green leaves and flowers much like the allamanda. It doesn't die back and doesn't have a time when it looks bad like the Carolina jasmine does. There are some new varieties of the sweet potato vine, *Ipomoeas*, like 'Blackie' with its burgundy foliage and 'Margarita' with lime-colored foliage. Lime and burgundy seem to be the latest fashion and setting a new trend in the plant world. The annual hyacinth bean, *Dolichos lablab*, is also very striking, with the purple in the leaves, the flowers, and the seedpods." —Ellen Shapiro, owner, The Plant Shoppe, Gainesville.

VINES TOLERANT OF ALKALINE SOIL

It is always a good idea to have the soil tested when you have a new yard and every few years thereafter. Most of us in Florida are blessed with a soil that is mildly acid, not extreme enough to be a problem. But fill soils, often found next to canals and waterfronts, are usually very alkaline. So are the marl soils of south Florida and areas near the beach. You can amend the soil with sulfur to make it less alkaline, but it will revert to form. It is much easier to choose plants that thrive in what you have. The plants that follow have been tried and tested and found best for alkaline soils. The ones marked with an asterisk are annuals easily started from a packet of seed. Those listed for central and south Florida will grow as annuals in north Florida.

Pepper vine (*Ampelopsis arborea*)	N, C, S
Madeira vine (*Anredera* species)	C, S
Dutchman's pipe (*Aristolochia durior*)	C, S
Pelican flower (*Aristolochia grandiflora*)	C, S
Cross vine (*Bignonia capreolata*)	N, C, S
Trumpet vine (*Campsis radicans*)	N, C, S
Hyacinth bean (*Dolichos lablab*)*	N, C, S
Creeping fig (*Ficus pumila*)	N, C, S
Moonflower (*Ipomoea alba*)	C, S
Cypress vine (*Ipomoea quamoclit*)*	C, S
Morning glory (*Ipomoea* spp.)*	N, C, S
Cardinal climber (*Ipomoea × multifida*)*	N, C, S
Mandevilla (*Mandevilla × amabilis*)	C, S
Virginia creeper (*Parthenocissus quinquefolia*)	N, C, S
Passionflower (*Passiflora* spp.)	C, S
Rangoon creeper (*Quisqualis indica*)	C, S
Mexican flame vine (*Senecio confusus*)	C, S
Marriage vine (*Solanum* spp.)	S

Hyacinth bean

LONG-BLOOMING VINES

Some of the vines in this chapter are seasonal, as are most flowers in most places. And some of them are quite phenomenal in the profusion of their blossoms, the brightness of their colors, and especially the length of their bloom time in Florida. Length of bloom time tends to increase the farther south one lives in the state. Mandevillas bloom only in the summer and fall and perhaps a part of the spring in the Tampa area but all year in Miami. We are often awestruck by months of flame vine blooming in blankets of orange. Then a freeze sets them back, and we don't see any for two years. We have seen bougainvillea blooming to the top of a two-story building in Pompano Beach and Vero Beach. If you live in north Florida, you might want to try some of the following plants in containers or in the ground from spring until frost.

Bougainvillea (*Bougainvillea spectabilis*)	C, S
Beach bean (*Canavalia maritima*)	S
Bleeding heart vine (*Clerodendrum thomsoniae*)	C, S
Rubber vine (*Cryptostegia* spp.)	C, S
Devil's potato (*Echites umbellata*)	S
Gloriosa lily (*Gloriosa rothschildiana*)	N, C, S
Jacquemontia (*Jacquemontia* spp.)	C, S
Gold coast jasmine (*Jasminum dichotomum*)	C, S
Azores jasmine (*Jasminum fluminense*)	C, S

Downy jasmine (*Jasminum multiflorum*)	C, S
Poet's jasmine (*Jasminum officinale*)	N, C, S
Wax jasmine (*Jasminum volubile*)	C, S
Tropical wisteria (*Millettia reticulata*)	C, S
Passionflower (*Passiflora* spp.)	C, S
Mexican flame vine (*Senecio confusus*)	C, S
Brazilian golden vine, golden creeper (*Stigmaphyllon ciliatum*)	C, S
Cape honeysuckle (*Tecomaria capensis*)	C, S
Black-eyed Susan vine (*Thunbergia alata*)	S
Wild allamanda (*Urechites lutea*)	C, S

"Passionflowers are excellent host plants for butterflies, and everyone loves the beautiful blooms. Some will produce fruit as well. The Clerodendrums are another favorite. The 'Bleeding Heart' has white and red flowers, and another, 'Delectum', has even more purple and red, and these bloom all year here in south Florida." — Linda Hunter, owner, Canterbury Farm and Nursery, Miami.

VINES WITH ATTRACTIVE FRUIT

Showy fruit adds interest to any plant and extends the seasons of display. Some of this fruit, such as passionfruit and grapes, is both edible and delicious to humans. Most of it, even some that is poison to us, is edible and useful to wildlife and helps to draw birds to our gardens for song and great natural help with insect problems.

If you're looking for atypical vines, we suggest that you contact Woodlanders Nursery, a mail-order nursery in Aiken, South Carolina, that specializes in native and noteworthy exotic plants and often carries outstanding selections of our "common" natives. Woodlanders' impressive plant list is enough to keep any gardener or landscaper designer excited year after year. And you won't find more knowledgeable or dedicated plant folk.

Blue or Purple Fruit

Pepper vine (*Ampelopsis arborea*)	N, C, S
Wintercreeper (*Euonymous fortunei*)	N, C
Virginia creeper (*Parthenocissus quinquefolia*)	N, C, S
Smilax (*Smilax laurifolia, S. glauca*)	N, C, S

Red Fruit

Cherokee rose (*Rosa laevigata*)	N, C, S
Smilax (*Smilax walteri, S. pumila, S. smallii*)	N, C, S

Interesting Seedpods

Woolly morning glory (*Argyreia nervosa*)	S
Pipe vine (*Aristolochia* spp.)	N, C
Garlic vine (*Cydista aequinoctialis*)	C, S
Hop vine (*Humulus* spp.)	N, C,
Wood rose (*Merremia dissecta*)	N, C, S
Monstera (*Monstera deliciosa*)	C, S
Brazilian golden vine, golden creeper (*Stigmaphyllon ciliatum*)	C, S
Vanilla orchid (*Vanilla planifolia*)	C, S

VINES FOR MAILBOXES AND LAMP POSTS

These vines are so well behaved that basic pruning can make them a shrub, a vine, or a vining shrub. They are ideal on short structures such as a mailbox, lamp post, or fence post because they don't grow too long, are not too heavy, and are easily kept in bounds.

Allamandas (*Allamanda* spp.)	C, S
Sicklethorn vine (*Asparagus falcatus*)	N, C, S
Snowberry (*Chicococca* spp.)	C, S
Bleeding heart vine (*Clerodendrum thomsoniae*)	C, S
Wintercreeper (*Euonymus fortunei*)	N, C
Carolina yellow jessamine (*Gelsemium sempervirens*)	N, C
Chilean mandevilla (*Mandevilla lava*)	C, S
Mandevilla (*Mandevilla sanderi*)	C, S
Dipladenia (*Mandevilla splendens*)	C, S
Chalice vine (*Solandra guttata*)	C, S
Madagascar jasmine (*Stephanotis floribunda*)	C, S
Cape honeysuckle (*Tecomaria capensis*)	C, S
Confederate jasmine (*Trachelospermum jasminoides* 'Mandaianum')	N, C, S

CLINGING VINES

These vines will climb a solid wood fence or the side of your house. They have various kinds of adhesive pads, roots, or hooks that sprout from their stems, so they seem to glue themselves to their support. Pulling one off is like ripping packing tape from a box, only it takes more strength. LC: Our climbing fig always leaves a trail where we pull it off a painted brick wall, but the pads soon disintegrate. MB: We find the pads do not stain our painted stucco walls but do leave marks on the aluminum under the eaves and on the side of the above-ground pool. The Virginia creeper, however, clings loosely enough to the screen to be harmless there. It does leave little bits of pads, but that is small payment for the summer shade. It has not torn the screen in the ten years or more that it's been climbing there. Clingers are especially good for covering low walls.

Madeira vine (*Anredera species*)	C, S
Cross vine (*Bignonia capreolata*)	N, C, S
Trumpet vine (*Campsis radicans*)	N, C, S
Bleeding heart vine (*Clerodendrum thomsoniae*)	S
Blue butterfly pea (*Clitoria ternata*)	C, S
Showy combretum (*Combretum grandiflorum*)	S
Wintercreeper (*Euonymous fortunei*)	N, C
Creeping fig (*Ficus pumila*)	C, S
Algerian ivy (*Hedera canariensis*)	N, C, S
English ivy (*Hedera helix*)	N, C
Virginia creeper (*Parthenocissus quinquefolia*)	N, C, S
Rangoon creeper (*Quisqualis indica*)	C, S
Hunter's robe (*Scindapsus aureus*)	S
Sweet potato vine (*Solanum* spp.)	N, C, S
Vanilla orchid (*Vanilla planifolia*)	C, S

A Sampler of Vines by Flower Color and Season

It is always important to know what color the flowers will be so that they will harmonize with other colors nearby—of other flowers that bloom at the same time, of buildings, and even of patio furnishings. Vines can produce dozens to hundreds of flowers, so there is no chance to cover a mistake by cutting the blooms for bouquets as one can do with annuals or even perennials. Also, by the time a vine blooms, it is rather settled in its spot and hard to transplant. So check first. Those marked with asterisks are fragrant. All the vines marked for central or south Florida will grow as annuals or perennials in north Florida.

White Flowers

Madeira vine (*Anredera* spp.)	Summer, fall
Bleeding heart (*Clerodendrum thomsoniae*)	Summer
Woolly congea (*Congea tomentosa*)	Winter, spring
Rubber vine (*Cryptostegia* spp.)	Year-round
Devil's potato (*Echites umbellata*)	Year-round
Wax plant (*Hoya purpurea-fusca* 'Silver pink')*	Spring, summer, fall
Night-blooming cereus (*Hylocereus undatus*)*	Summer
Morning glory (*Ipomoea* spp.)*	Year-round
Jacquemontia (*Jacquemontia* spp.)	Spring, summer
Poet's jasmine (*Jasminum officinale*)*	Spring, summer, fall
Bower plant (*Pandorea jasminoides*)	Summer
Madagascar jasmine (*Stephanotis floribunda*)	Summer
Sweet clock vine (*Thunbergia fragrans*)	Summer, fall
Bengal clock vine (*Thunbergia grandiflora*)	Summer, fall
Confederate jasmine (*Trachelospermum jasminoides*)	Spring, summer

Blue Flowers

Blue butterfly pea (*Clitoria ternata*)	Spring, summer
Morning glory (*Ipomoea* spp.)	Year-round
Jacquemontia (*Jacquemontia* spp.)	Spring, summer

Orange Flowers

Trumpet vine (*Campsis radicans*)	Summer
Flame vine (*Pyrostegia venusta*)	Winter, spring
Mexican flame vine (*Senecio confusus*)	Summer, fall
Cape honeysuckle (*Tecomaria capensis*)	Summer, fall
Black-eyed Susan vine (*Thunbergia alata*)	Spring, summer, fall

Yellow Flowers

Yellow allamanda (*Allamanda* spp.)*	Summer
Cross vine (*Bignonia capreolata*)	Spring
Yellow trumpet vine (*Campsis radicans* 'Flava')	Summer
Carolina yellow jessamine (*Gelsemium sempervirens*)*	Winter, spring
Yellow jasmine (*Jasminum humile*)	Spring, summer
Japanese honeysuckle (*Lonicera japonica*)*	Summer
Coral honeysuckle (*Lonicera sempervirens* 'Sulphurea')	Spring
Barbados gooseberry, lemon vine (*Pereskia aculeata*)	Spring, summer
Chalice vine (*Solandra guttata*)	Summer, fall
Brazilian golden vine, golden creeper (*Stigmaphyllon ciliatum*)	Spring, summer, fall

Yellow Flowers (continued)

Cape honeysuckle (*Tecomaria capensis*)	Summer
Black-eyed Susan vine (*Thunbergia alata*)	Year-round
Wild allamanda (*Urechites lutea*)	Winter, spring

Lavender and Purple Flowers

Beach bean (*Canavalia maritima*)	Year-round
Purple painted trumpet (*Clytostoma callistegioides*)	Spring, summer
Woolly congea (*Congea tomentosa*)	Winter, spring
Morning glory (*Ipomoea* spp.)	Year-round
Railroad vine (*Ipomoea pes-caprae*)	Summer, fall
Tropical wisteria (*Millettia reticulata*)	Spring, summer, fall
Queen's wreath (*Petrea volubilis*)	Summer
Bengal clock vine (*Thunbergia grandiflora*)	Summer, fall
Wisteria (*Wisteria floribunda, W. frutescens, W. sinensis*)*	Spring

Pink Flowers

Coral vine (*Antigonon leptopus*)	Summer, fall
Garlic vine (*Cydista aequinoctialis*)*	Spring
Morning glory (*Ipomoea* spp.)*	Spring
Bower plant (*Pandorea jasminoides*)	Spring, summer, fall
Pink trumpet vine (*Podranea ricasoliana*)	Summer

Red Flowers

Cross vine (*Bignonia capreolata*)	Spring
Showy combretum (*Combretum grandiflorum*)	Summer
Morning glory (*Ipomoea* spp.)	Spring, summer
Coral honeysuckle (*Lonicera sempervirens* 'Magnifica')*	Spring, summer
Rangoon creeper (*Quisqualis indica*)	Summer
Tecomanthe (*Tecomanthe venusta*)	Spring, summer
Cape honeysuckle (*Tecomanthe capensis*)	Summer, fall

FERNS

Florida is a land of ferns—more ferns grow here than in any other continental state. In north Florida the species are much like those of the northern United States, but in central and south Florida the ferns are more tropical.

Used in the landscape, ferns quiet the senses with their soothing feathery fronds. The ones with soft, airy foliage and soft colors impart a feeling of distance. They clothe bare, shaded areas with lush, green textures as a groundcover or in small clumps. In nature, they blanket old branches, boulders, and banks and grow up the trunks of trees. They evoke a sense of grace, comfort, and permanency.

Ferns grow as herbaceous perennials and are essentially hardy foliage plants. Most of them need shade and a fairly moist and acid soil, and they are most at home under trees or in a woodland setting. LC: I've seen talented designers combine ferns with coleus, aspidistra, wildflowers, and other foliages and textures for an impact that would rival that of the most renowned English flower borders. This technique seems most perfected with the contrasting textures of gingers and other bold perennials that also thrive in the ferns' lush climate.

In the lists that follow you will find ferns to suit almost every situation from sun to shade and dry soil to wet. But beware: Although they are generally easy to grow, ferns are not easy to know—at first they all seem to look alike. Fern societies have members who are experts at both growing and identifying and who are happy to share information with anyone who is interested. Your library reference section should have books like David L. Jones' *Encyclopedia of Ferns* and Barbara Joe Horshizaki's *Fern Growers' Manual*. These will give you photos and details of hundreds of ferns and fernlike plants.

Special thanks to Donna Legare and Jody Walthall of Native Nurseries in Tallahassee for their help with the ferns of north Florida.

TO DO LIST FOR FERNS

The first requisite for fern growing is some shade, so if you don't have any, you'll need to plant some trees and shrubs first. It won't take long in Florida for them to cast the needed shadows, especially if you place them carefully on the north side of a building. In the meantime, you could grow ferns in containers indoors or, better yet, on a covered porch, where they will have the benefit of outdoor humidity.

- Study shade and sun patterns in your yard and select a spot that has only partial sun, at the most. Many ferns are great for the darkest corners of the landscape.
- Start with fern plants. Divisions, or pups, will do, and gardeners who have the common ferns will be glad to share.
- Enrich the soil with humus and peat.
- Keep the soil around most ferns constantly moist. Once their leaves wilt, they seldom recover completely.
- Fertilize as needed, more often in the spring and summer when growth is more active and rains leach the soil.
- Remove any ferns that spread too much. A few species can come close to being weeds.
- Observe the many kinds of ferns in catalogs, books, and public and private gardens and try new ones. Find out if there is a fern society near you and join it if there is.

SOME FERNS THAT GROW WILD

The diverse climatic conditions, soil types, and geological features of the state offer a variety of habitats for ferns. Chances are you will find some in your garden whether you plant them or not. Take advantage of their presence, but watch out for the climbing ferns—they can be quite invasive.

Royal fern

Venus hair fern (*Adiantum capillus-veneris*)	N, C, S
Blackstem spleenwort (*Asplenium resiliens*)	N, C
Lady fern (*Athyrium filix-femina*)	N, C, S
Aquatic mosquito fern (*Axolla caroliniana*)	N, C, S
Vegetable fern (*Diplazium esculentum*)	C, S
Climbing fern (*Lygodium japonicum, L. palmatum*)	N, C, S
Boston fern (*Nephrolepis exaltata*)	N, C, S
Cinnamon fern (*Osmunda cinnamomea*)	N, C, S
Royal fern (*Osmunda regalis*)	N, C, S
Resurrection fern (*Polypodium polypodioides*)	N, C, S
Bracken fern (*Pteridium aquilinum*)	N, C, S
Netted chain fern (*Woodwardia areolata*)	N, C, S

POPULAR FERNS FOR LANDSCAPING

These are the ferns that are most used in landscaping for Florida gardens. They vary from groundcover to tree size and from the most delicate of foliage to the undivided fronds of the bird's-nest fern and the interesting shapes of the stag's-horn and elk's-horn ferns. The area of Pierson in Volusia County in north central Florida boasts the largest fern industry in the world, where ferns grow by the acre in tree-shaded fields and under opaque plastic screening. Trucks full of ferns are regularly sent to florists who could not do without the fronds.

Leather fern (*Acrostichum daneifolium*)	N, C, S
Maidenhair fern (*Adiantum* spp.)	N, C, S
Bird's-nest fern (*Asplenium nidus; A. serratum*)	C, S
Dwarf tree fern (*Blechnum gibbum*)	N, C, S
Swamp fern (*Blechnum serrulatum* or spp.)	N, C, S

Holly fern (*Cyrtomium falcatum*)	N, C, S
Rabbit's-foot fern (*Davallia fejeensis*)	C, S
Autumn fern (*Dryopteris erythrosora*)	N, C, S
Southern shield fern (*Dryopteris ludoviciana*)	N, C, S
Erect sword fern (*Nephrolepis cordifolia*)	N, C, S
Boston fern (*Nephrolepis exaltata*)	C, S
Basket fern (*Nephrolepis pectinata*)	C, S
Sword fern (*Nephrolepis biserrata*)	C, S
Royal fern (*Osmunda regalis*)	N, C, S
Polypody fern (*Polypodium spp.*)	N, C, S
Elk's-horn fern (*Polypodium grandiceps*)	C, S
Wart fern (*Polypodium scolopendria*)	C, S
Whisk fern (*Psilotum nudum*)	N, C, S
Leatherleaf fern (*Rumohra adiantiformis*)	N, C, S
Australian tree fern (*Sphaeropteris cooperi*)	C, S
Marsh fern (*Thelypteris palustris*)	N, C, S

"People should use ferns more often because, once you get them established, they make a wonderful groundcover. They are nearly maintenance free. They make a nice background for other plantings and do well in a shady area. They are tough plants that anybody can grow, and even the ones that spread abundantly are easy to control." —Nancy Lichtenstein, ground supervisor, Historic Spanish Point (which includes a fern garden), Sarasota.

TALL FERNS

When fern growers in other states refer to tall ferns, they may mean any that grow 30 inches high or more. In Florida a tall fern may be anywhere from 4 feet to 20 feet. The Australian tree fern grows only about 6 to 8 feet in the Tampa area but up to 20 feet where it is never reduced by frost in south Florida. All of these make fine soft backdrops and accent plants that set off the lower-growing plants of contrasting texture or color.

		Height (in feet)
Leather fern (*Acrostichum daneifolium*)	N, C, S	6–8
Silver tree fern (*Alsophila tricolor*)	C, S	15–20
Dwarf tree fern (*Blechnum gibbum*)	N, C, S	4–5
Mexican tree fern (*Cibotium schiedei*)	C, S	10–15
American tree fern (*Ctenitis sloanei*)	S	3½–7½
Bramble fern (*Hypolepis repens*)	C, S	3–10
Sword fern (*Nephrolepis biserrata*)	C, S	3–4
Cinnamon fern (*Osmunda cinnamomea*)	N, C, S	3–4
Royal fern (*Osmunda regalis*)	N, C, S	4–5
Bracken fern (*Pteridium aquilinum*)	N, C, S	3–4
Australian tree fern (*Sphaeropteris cooperi*)	C, S	18–20
Black tree fern (*Sphaeropteris medullaris*)	C, S	7½–17
Mariana maiden fern (*Thelypteris torresiana*)	N, C, S	3–6

FERNS THAT TAKE THE MOST LIGHT

LC: Most of us grow ferns under a canopy of trees, but some ferns can move into more sunny situations, though never full sun in Florida. At home we have a bed of southern shield fern that used to get hit by the hot afternoon sun before a young tree grew enough to shade it. It has been there ten years and has done well under both situations. In another bed, a corner proved too hot for impatiens, but the Japanese painted fern I put there four years ago is doing fine. The thing to remember about stretching the limits for a fern is that those grown in more sun need good soil and enough water to minimize their stress on hot summer days. Check with other gardeners or fern enthusiasts in your area for the limits on how much sun these ferns will take. The ones with an asterisk will generally take the most sun if they have constant moisture.

Lady fern (*Athyrium filix-femina*)	N, C, S
Dwarf tree fern (*Blechnum gibbum*)	N, C, S
Florida marsh fern (*Blechnum occidentale*)*	C, S
Holly fern (*Cyrtomium falcatum*)	N, C, S
Rabbit's-foot fern (*Davallia fejeensis*)	C, S
Hay-scented fern (*Dennstaedtia punctilobula*)*	N, C, S
Autumn fern (*Dryopteris erythrosora*)	N, C, S
Shield fern (*Dryopteris noveboracensis*)*	N, C, S
Japanese climbing fern (*Lygodium japonicum*)	N, C, S
Boston fern (*Nephrolepis exaltata*)	C, S
Sensitive fern (*Onoclea sensibilis*)*	N, C, S
Cinnamon fern (*Osmunda cinnamomea*)*	N, C, S
Royal fern (*Osmunda regalis*)*	N, C, S
Tassel fern (*Polystichum polyblepharum*)	N, C, S
Bracken fern (*Pteridium aquilinum*)	N, C, S
Leatherleaf fern (*Rumohra adiantiformis*)	N, C, S
Australian tree fern (*Sphaeropteris cooperi*)	C, S
Southern shield fern (*Thelypteris kinthii, T. normalis*)	N, C, S
Chain fern (*Woodwardia areolata*)	N, C, S

Lady fern

FERNS FOR DRY GROUND

MB: You don't have to live on a bog or have automatic irrigation to enjoy ferns in your Florida garden. True, none are terribly drought tolerant, but still some will survive in spots that don't always stay moist, especially if the location is partly shaded. A stand of Boston fern sprung up on its own in my yard and thrives where I never water. More choice ferns, such as my bird's-nest fern, do very well with only occasional watering once they are well established. The more organic matter in the soil, the less stress ferns will suffer.

Bear's-paw fern (*Aglaomorpha coronara*)	C, S
Blackstem spleenwort (*Asplenium resiliens*)	N, C
Bird's-nest fern (*Asplenium serratum*)	C, S
Florida marsh fern (*Blechnum occidentale*)	C, S
Hairy lip fern (*Cheilanthes lanosa*)	N, C, S
Holly fern (*Cyrtomium falcatum*)	N, C, S
Rabbit's-foot fern (*Davallia fejeensis*)	C, S
Hay-scented fern (*Dennstaedtia punctilobula*)	N, C, S
Boston fern (*Nephrolepis exaltata*)	C, S

Elk's-horn fern (*Polypodium grandiceps*)	C, S
Wart fern (*Polypodium scolopendria*)	C, S
Tassel fern (*Polystichum polyblepharum*)	N, C, S
Whisk fern (*Psilotum nudum*)	N, C, S
Bracken fern (*Pteridium aquilinum*)	N, C, S
Cretan brake fern (*Pteris cretica*)	N, C, S
Chinese brake fern (*Pteris vittata*)	N, C, S
Leatherleaf fern (*Rumohra adiantiformis*)	C, S
Giant chain fern (*Woodwardia fimbriata*)	N, C, S

 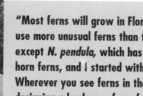

"Most ferns will grow in Florida. The possibilities are limitless. People should try to use more unusual ferns than the Boston. I stay away from all the *Nephrolepis* except *N. pendula*, which has fronds about 4 feet long. Most men prefer the stag's-horn ferns, and I started with them, but now I've moved on to many others. Wherever you see ferns in the landscape, you also see water and rocks. I am designing a landscape for a friend that will be at least 85 percent ferns." —Cliff Brown, member of the Tampa Bay Fern Club and park supervisor of Eureka Springs Botanical Gardens, Tampa, where there are interesting fern displays both outdoors and in the greenhouse.

FERNS FOR HANGING BASKETS OR MOUNTING

Many of the Florida ferns are epiphytes and will thrive in hanging baskets or mounted on a board or a tree. The stag's-horns and various members of the *Platycerium* genus are especially showy from the time you plant them until they are too huge to move. The latter is a problem where frost can kill them, but nevertheless there are some hanging from trees in every neighborhood in the central Florida area. These have two kinds of fronds, the fertile, forward fronds and the flat, round, shield fronds that cover the roots.

Maidenhair fern (*Adiantum* spp.)	N, C, S
Rabbit's-foot fern (*Davallia fejeensis*)	C, S
Basket fern (*Drynaria rigidula* 'Whitei')	C, S
Ant fern (*Lecanopteris carnosa*)	C, S
Boston fern (*Nephrolepis exaltata*)	C, S
Stag's-horn fern (*Platycerium* spp.)	C, S
Polypodium disimile	N, C, S
Elk's-horn fern (*Polypodium grandiceps*)	C, S
Tongue fern (*Pyrrosia lingua*)	C, S
Felt fern (*Pyrrosia longifolia*)	C, S

"The ant fern, *Lecanopteris carnosa,* is a neat plant but notoriously difficult. *Pyrrosia* should not be overlooked, as many of these species make beautiful baskets. For outdoor growing, the best stag's-horn ferns are, of course, species and cultivars of the bifurcatum complex, which includes *Platycerium bifurcatum*, subspecies *veitchii*, ssp. *willinckii*, and variety *hillii*. Virtually all of the large stag's-horn ferns seen in baskets or established on trees are from this group. *Platycerium superbum*, usually sold as *P. grande*, which makes immense shield fronds and impressive pendant fertile fronds, is the most cold hardy of the *Platycerium*, but it is sensitive to overwatering." —Charles Alford, owner, Charles Alford Plants, Vero Beach.

FERNS THAT GO DORMANT

So many plants are evergreen in Florida that we have to make a conscious effort to accommodate the ones that go dormant and remember that they aren't dead, just gone for a while. They will be back in the spring. And spring can almost overlap fall in many parts of Florida, so the time of dormancy can vary. The resurrection fern goes dormant whenever it is dry and turns green again even as you sprinkle it with the hose or the rain comes down.

Lady fern (*Athyrium filix-femina*)	N, C, S
Glade fern (*Athyrium pycnocarpon*)	N, C, S
Rabbit's-foot fern (*Davallia fejeensis*)	C, S
Hay-scented fern (*Dennstaedtia punctilobula*)	N, C, S
Climbing fern (*Lygodium palmatum, L. japonicum*)	N, C, S
Sensitive fern (*Onoclea sensibilis*)	N, C, S
Cinnamon fern (*Osmunda cinnamomea*)	N, C, S
Royal fern (*Osmunda regalis*)	N, C, S
Resurrection fern (*Polypodium polypodioides*)	N, C, S
Marsh fern (*Thelypteris thelypterioides*)	N, C, S

FERNS THAT LIKE WATER

Unless listed otherwise, figure that most ferns like partial shade and a constantly moist soil rich in decaying organic matter. That is why so many of them grow in woodlands. In the home garden this translates to areas that stay moist but not soggy. Put plants from the "Moist Site" list below in those areas. If you have a spot that is constantly soggy, because of irrigation, poor drainage, or the drip of an air conditioner, or a shaded area on the bank of a lake, pond, or slow-moving stream where the water level will never fall below the root extension, select from the "Wet Site" list. The mosquito fern is actually an aquatic plant that forms a solid but easily separated mat on the water surface.

Moist Site

Maidenhair fern (*Adiantum* spp.)	N, C, S
Venus hair fern (*Adiantum capillus-veneris*)	N, C
Bird's-nest fern (*Asplenium nidus*)	C, S
Lady fern (*Athyrium filix-femina*)	N, C, S
Dwarf tree fern (*Blechnum gibbum*)	N, C, S
Walking fern (*Camptosorus rhizophyllus*)	C, S
Holly fern (*Cyrtomium falcatum*)	N, C, S
Autumn fern (*Dryopteris erythrosora*)	N, C, S
Goldie's fern (*Dryopteris goldiana*)	N, C, S
Climbing fern (*Lygodium palmatum*)	N, C, S
Sword fern (*Nephrolepis biserrata*)	C, S
Erect sword fern (*Nephrolepis cordifolia*)	C, S
Cinnamon fern (*Osmunda cinnamomea*)	N, C, S
Royal fern (*Osmunda regalis*)	N, C, S
Polypody fern (*Polypodium* spp.)	N, C, S
Sword fern (*Polystichum munitum*)	N, C, S
Leatherleaf fern (*Rumohra adiantiformis*)	C, S
Spikemoss (*Selaginella* spp.)	N, C, S
Australian tree fern (*Sphaeropteris cooperi*)	C, S
Chain fern (*Woodwardia areolata*)	N, C, S
Virginia chain fern (*Woodwardia virginica*)	N, C, S

Wet Site

Leather fern (*Acrostichum daneifolium*)	N, C, S
Lady fern (*Athyrium filix-femina*)	N, C, S
Mosquito fern (*Axolla caroliniana*)	N, C, S
Florida marsh fern (*Blechnum occidentale*)	C, S
Swamp fern (*Blechnum serrulatum* or spp.)	N, C, S
Walking fern (*Camptosorus rhizophyllus*)	N, C, S
Climbing fern (*Lygodium palmatum*)	N, C, S
Sensitive fern (*Onoclea sensibilis*)	N, C, S
Cinnamon fern (*Osmunda cinnamomea*)	N, C, S
Royal fern (*Osmunda regalis*)	N, C, S
Serpent fern (*Phlebodium aureum*)	N, C, S
Ostrich fern (*Pteris umbrosa*)	N, C, S
Marsh fern (*Thelypteris palustris*)	N, C, S
Netted chain fern (*Woodwardia areolata*)	N, C, S
Virginia chain fern (*Woodwardia virginica*)	N, C, S

Sensitive
fern

FERNS FOR GROUNDCOVER

Some ferns send out underground stems that spring up around the original plant in an expanding mass of foliage. So what isn't good for a confined space (unless you want to keep digging up the runaway fronds), you can use elsewhere for a groundcover. If you want only a single plant, beware of the following. But if you want an easy groundcover that will spread fairly quickly to provide easy maintenance for a bed, then embrace the following. These are great ferns to share with friends because there are always new plants to dig up and give away.

Leather fern (*Acrostichum danaeafolium*)	N, C, S
Maidenhair fern (*Adiantum* spp.)	N, C, S
Lady fern (*Athyrium filix-femina*)	N, C, S
Glade fern (*Athyrium pycnocarpon*)	N, C, S
Florida marsh fern (*Blechnum occidentale*)	C, S
Swamp fern (*Blechnum serrulatum*)	N, C, S
Holly fern (*Cyrtomium falcatum*)	N, C, S
Rabbit's-foot fern (*Davallia fejeensis*)	C, S
Cup fern (*Dennstaedtia* spp.)	C, S
Florida shield fern (*Dryopteris ludoviciana*)	N, C, S
Giant sword fern (*Nephrolepis biserrata*)	C, S
Tuberous sword fern (*Nephrolepis cordifolia*)	C, S
Boston fern (*Nephrolepis exaltata*)	C, S
Sensitive fern (*Onoclea sensibilis*)	N, C
Royal fern (*Osmunda regalis*)	N, C, S
Wart fern (*Polypodium scolopendria*)	C, S
Polypody fern (*Polypodium* spp.)	N, C, S
Whisk fern (*Psilotum nudum*)	N, C, S
Japanese felt fern (*Pyrrosia lingua* and cultivars)	C, S
Leatherleaf fern (*Rumohra adiantiformis*)	C, S
Spikemoss (*Selaginella* spp.)	N, C, S
Marsh fern (*Thelypteris palustris*)	N, C, S
Broad beech fern (*Thelypteris hexagonoptera*)	N, C, S
Virginia chain fern (*Woodwardia virginica*)	N, C, S

FERNLIKE PLANTS

Plants that bloom and bear seeds are not ferns, but some with finely cut and delicate foliage are sometimes called by the name "fern" because of their appearance. A great portion of the fern industry of Florida consists of two asparagus ferns that actually belong to the lily family, as well as the leatherleaf, which is a true fern. The *Asparagus sprengeri* fern is almost a weed, but several exotic types of it like the Ming are quite unusual and lovely. Spikemoss is a fern ally. These reproduce by spores but have small leaves with unbranched veins.

Plumosa fern (*Asparagus plumosus*)	N, C, S
Asparagus fern (*Asparagus springerii*)	N, C, S
Spikemoss (*Selaginella* spp.)	N, C, S

"The *Selaginellas* are an overlooked fern ally, prehistoric plants that are an integral part of the fern world. These forerunners of all ferns are absolutely fascinating for baskets and groundcovers. The fronds come in a blue green, in a rainbow of reddish browns, and in other subtle color combinations." — Murline Lydon, Lydon Horticultural Enterprises, Dover. Murline collects, grows, and sells rare and unusual plants to botanical gardens and collectors.

FERNS WITH COLORFUL FOLIAGE

Everyone knows that ferns come in many shades of green. But these ferns have subtle colors that contrast beautifully with the deeper greens of mondo grass or other ferns. The Japanese painted fern combines silver, green, and burgundy in what is one of the most striking ferns around. Autumn fern rises from the ground each spring with a beautiful reddish cast that turns green as the leaves mature. If you really like ferns and have a good place for them, we suggest you take a walk through a fern garden to better acquaint yourself with this large and diverse group. Or go to the reference section in the library and look through *Tropica* or *Exotica*. When you do, you'll probably think we should have included fiddleheads and some with colorful fertile fronds on this list. Add them as you find them.

Rosy maidenhair (*Adiantum hispiculum*)	C, S	Red new growth
Silver dollar fern (*Adiantum peruvianum*)	N, C, S	Reddish silver growth
Variegated maidenhair (*Adiantum raddianum* 'Variegatum')	C, S	Variegated white
Variegated shield fern (*Arachniodes aristata variegata*)	N, C, S	White and yellow
Japanese painted fern (*Athyrium nipponicum* 'Pictum')	N, C, S	Silver and purple
Mosquito fern (*Axolla caroliniana*)	N, C, S	Green or dark red
Florida marsh fern (*Blechnum occidentale*)	C, S	Red new growth
Japanese shield, autumn, or wood fern (*Dryopteris erythrosora*)	C, S	Red new growth
Polypody fern		
(*Polypodium aureum* cv. 'Glaucum')	C, S	Blue green
(*P. aureum* 'Mandianum')	C, S	Blue green
(*P. aureum* 'Mexican tasseled')	C, S	Blue green

(*P. aureum* 'Variegatum')	C, S	Variegated yellow
Brake fern (*Pteris* spp.)	C, S	Variegated white
Victoria fern (*Pteris ensiformis victoriae*)	C, S	Variegated white
(*P. quadriaurita*)	C, S	Variegated red
Japanese felt fern (*Pyrrosia lingua* and cultivars)	C, S	Variegated yellow
Spikemoss (*Selaginella* spp. and cultivars)	N, C, S	Blue, red, gold

FERNS THAT DON'T NEED ACID SOIL

Most ferns do best in acid soil, but the following will adapt to a wider variety of soils. Choose from this list if you know your soil is alkaline, or for use in fill soil along a canal or water-front.

Leather fern (*Acrostichum daneifolium*)	N, C, S
Autumn fern (*Dryopteris erythrosora*)	C, S
Boston fern (*Nephrolepis exaltata*)	C, S
Sword fern (*Nephrolepis biserrata*)	C, S
Erect sword fern (*Nephrolepis cordifolia*)	C, S
Elk's-horn fern (*Polypodium grandiceps*)	C, S
Wart fern (*Polypodium scolopendria*)	C, S
Polypody fern (*Polypodium* spp.)	N, C, S
Whisk fern (*Psilotum nudum*)	N, C, S
Leatherleaf fern (*Rumohra adiantiformis*)	C, S
Australian tree fern (*Sphaeropteris cooperi*)	C, S
Marsh fern (*Thelypteris palustris*)	N, C, S

GROUNDCOVERS

For decades Americans have used grass as the groundcover of choice for any spot not covered by something else. We like grass for its simplicity and function, but in Florida grass takes more time, energy, water, work, and worry than many handsome groundcovers you could plant.

MB: When we first moved to Florida, I noticed that all my neighbors were working hard to manicure their lawns, while I was working to make mine smaller. I tilled up huge sections of lawn for other plantings. For a long time I was aiming for islands of other plants in a sea of grass; then I changed to a few islands of grass among the other plantings. We are in the process of learning to use turf as a design element instead of a cover-all.

LC: I have gone from a small lawn to no lawn. The space that was once grass is now a water garden and terrace. We will add a few square feet of grass because it is low and green and open, but it is selected on its merits, like other plants, and not as a cover-all. Grass, after all, is a groundcover. Unless you have reason for turf, such as children who play outdoors, or a place for croquet, grass doesn't need to dominate your landscape.

Groundcover plants are the ideal alternative to too much grass. They take a bit of weeding and water until they become established, but then many are almost maintenance free. Moreover, they add a whole new dimension of elegance to a landscape with their varied textures, colors, and flowers. You can even plant some that are fragrant.

In this chapter we have gathered, not just plants of the same botanical category, as we've done in other chapters, but plants of every sort: vines, perennials, low shrubs, and ornamental grasses that have a spreading growth habit and cover the ground densely. Many of the plants here are also listed elsewhere in this book.

There are so many plants that make good groundcovers in various parts of Florida that we couldn't begin to list them all. Those listed here are some of the most noteworthy. Also check lists in the chapters on shrubs and ferns. Write in new ones as you discover them.

TO DO LIST FOR GROUNDCOVERS

You can start your groundcover planting by killing the existing grass or weeds with a non-selective herbicide such as Roundup. Or you can just spread several thicknesses of newspaper over the grass, wet it thoroughly, and cover it with an attractive mulch such as pine needles, leaves, eucalyptus, or pine bark. (We discourage the use of cypress mulch because most of it is not a by-product of tree farming or the timber industries but comes from native trees being cut to use as mulch.) You can leave the mulch in place until the grass beneath rots away. It actually looks better than a patchy lawn. Pull back the mulch to plant through or on top of the newspaper, and before long, *voila!* you have an instant groundcover. MB: Since my tiller stopped running years ago, I have used the newspaper-mulch method with great success. Keep the groundcover plants and surrounding mulch well watered, and the roots will penetrate the newspaper soon enough. Also fertilize regularly, and your plants will spread and grow together more quickly than you ever expected. Below are some additional tips for planting groundcovers.

- Study the patterns of sunlight in your yard. Plant groundcovers that will thrive in sun, shade, or both—whatever you have.
- Decide how much watering you are willing to do. If you don't want to water much, select only groundcovers tolerant of drought once they are established.
- Water, fertilize, weed, and mulch until groundcover is well established.
- Plant in masses. The colors and textures of groundcovers will be more dramatic if you use them in large masses that cover many square feet. You may want to use more than one groundcover for a contrast in the colors and textures of various beds.

"Everyone knows that groundcovers look great and are easier to maintain than grass. But one thing I've learned about gardening in the subtropics is that keeping the soil cool is very important. Ever walk barefoot across a Florida beach on a sunny summer's day? Groundcovers absorb heat and provide much-needed shade to our garden soils, helping them keep cool, hold moisture, and be healthier in general." —Kathy Nelson, editor, *Florida Gardening* magazine.

GROUNDCOVERS FOR FULL SUN

The Florida sun can be intense, so we must choose carefully the plants we expose to its full power. The plants in this list can take full sun, although you may want to check locally to see how they hold up in times of drought in your local soil type. Most plants can take a lot more sun without looking parched if the soil can hold a bit of water during extended drought—especially if the sun is hot, as may be the case in late spring or fall.

We have subdivided this list into woody plants, grasses, and herbaceous plants, but check the shrubs chapter for more woody, low-growing shrubs useful as groundcovers. All of the herbaceous plants are listed only for the regions where they tend to be evergreen, even through the winter. Wedelia is a groundcover that is very popular, but it is becoming invasive in central and south Florida, so we have omitted it from this list.

Those that are marked with an asterisk are also at home in some shade, making them good choices for groundcover beds large enough to span both sun and shade in your landscape; a few will even tolerate deep shade, so don't be confused when you see them appear in lists for shade and deep shade.

Woody Shrubs or Vines

Pineland snowberry (*Chicococca pinetorum*)	S
False heather (*Cuphea hyssopifolia*)*	C, S
Golden creeper (*Ernodea littoralis*)*	S
Creeping fig (*Ficus pumila*)*	N, C, S
Carolina yellow jessamine (*Gelsemium sempervirens*)*	N, C
Railroad vine (*Ipomoea pes-caprae*)	S
Jasmine (*Jasminum* spp.)*	N, C, S
Dwarf lantana (*Lantana ovatifolia* var. *reclinata*)	C, S
Gopher apple (*Lincania michauxii*)	N, C, S
Asian jasmine (*Trachelospermum asiaticum*) *	N, C, S
Big-leaf periwinkle (*Vinca major*)*	N

Grasses or Grasslike Plants

Lilyturf (*Liriope muscari, L. spicata*)*	N, C
Maiden grass (*Miscanthus* spp.)	N
Fountain grass (*Pennisetum* spp.)	N, C, S
Ribbon grass (*Phalaris arundinacea picta*)	N, C
Blue-eyed grass (*Sisyrinchium angustifolium*)*	N, C, S
Sea oats (*Uniola paniculata*)	N, C, S

Herbaceous Plants

Lily-of-the-Nile (*Agapanthus africanus*)*	C, S
Bugleweed (*Ajuga reptans*)*	N, C
Aloe (*Aloe* spp.)*	C, S
Asparagus fern (*Asparagus springerii*)*	C, S
Beach bean (*Canavallia maritima*)	C, S
Beach sunflower (*Helianthus debilis*)	N, C, S
Daylily (*Hemerocallis* hybrids)*	N, C, S
Blood leaf (*Iresine lindenii*)*	C, S
Beach elder (*Iva umbricata*)	N, C, S
Kalanchoes (*Kalanchoe* spp.)*	C, S

Blue-eyed grass

Trailing lantana (*Lantana montevidensis*)*	C, S
Twinflower (*Mitchella repens*)*	N
Artillery plant (*Pilea microphllya*)*	C, S
Oyster plant (*Rhoeo spathacea*)*	C, S
Purple heart (*Setcreasea pallida*)*	N, C, S
Society garlic (*Tulbaghia violacea*)*	N, C, S

"If you choose a plant that forms a thick cover, weeding will not be much of a problem. If you select bromeliads, crinum lilies, or another type of plant that allows light to penetrate to the soil, weeding will have to be done. Groundcovers may take several months to become established, during which time the soil should be kept moist. Planting, as with trees and shrubs, is best done at the beginning of the rainy season but may be done any time." —Georgia Tasker, garden editor, *Miami Herald*, author of *Enchanted Ground* and coauthor with Tom MacCubbin of *Florida Gardener's Guide*.

GROUNDCOVERS FOR WET SOIL

If you have a spot that is often soggy, the following groundcovers can tolerate wet feet, at least for a while. You'll also find some of these on lists of drought-tolerant plants, making them good choices for use in a landscape that has both wet and dry spots (as many low, sandy Florida soils do).

How to we define wet spots? Ordinarily, these are areas to which the yard drains and where water may stand. They may be areas where water collects after a rain, where the water table is high, or where the subsoil is clay hardpan and drainage is poor. One way you can determine whether you have poor drainage is to dig a hole about 2 feet deep and fill it with water. If it takes more than a day to drain, you have poor drainage. If it is hot and sunny when you do this, cover the hole with cardboard to avoid too much loss from evaporation.

Plants marked with an asterisk in the following list can spread quickly and be difficult to limit, so plant them only in locations where they will be limited by a structure or your shovel.

Grassy-leafed sweet flag (*Acorus gramineus*)	N, C, S
Lily-of-the-Nile (*Agapanthus africanus*)	N, C, S
Swamp fern (*Blechnum serrulatum*)	N, C, S
Japanese sedge (*Carex morrowii*)	N
Green and gold (*Chrysogonum virginianum*)	N
Swamp lily (*Crinum americanum*)	N, C, S
African iris (*Dietes vegeta*)	N, C, S
Horsetail (*Equisetum hyemale*)*	N, C, S
Oakleaf fig (*Ficus montana*)	C, S
Carolina jessamine (*Gelsemium sempervirens*)	N, C
Algerian ivy (*Hedera canariensis*)	N, C, S
English ivy (*Hedera helix*)	N, C
Liriope (*Liriope muscari*)	N, C, S
Mondo grass (*Ophiopogon japonicus*)	N, C, S
Artillery plant (*Pilea microphylla*)	C, S
Swedish ivy (*Plectranthus madagascariensis*)	N, C, S
Asian jasmine (*Trachelospermum asiaticum*)	N, C, S
Big-leaf periwinkle (*Vinca major*)*	N

GROUNDCOVERS FOR PARTIAL SHADE

Many plants that like full sun in other parts of the country (and even those that will tolerate it here) appreciate some shade in Florida, especially during summer. Because we do not have lawn grasses that tolerate shade, at least not well enough to make a dense cover, beds of groundcover are often a terrific alternative to a thin, weedy lawn. These groundcovers grow in the dappled shade of pines, or under the partial shade of hardwoods whose lower limbs are high overhead.

Grassy-leaved sweet flag (*Acorus gramineus*)	N, C, S
Cast-iron plant (*Aspidistra elatior*)	N, C, S
Gumpo azalea (*Azalea* 'Gumpo')	N, C
Spider plant (*Chlorophytum comosum*)	C, S
Grape ivy (*Cissus rhombifolia*)	S
Dwarf dracaena (*Dracaena sanderana, D. surculosa, D. thaliodes*)	C, S
Algerian ivy (*Hedera canariensis*)	N, C, S
English ivy (*Hedera helix*)	N, C
Dwarf yaupon holly (*Ilex vomitoria*)	N, C, S
Blood leaf (*Iresine lindenii*)	C, S
Shore juniper (*Juniperus conferta*)	N, C, S
Prayer plant (*Maranta* spp.)	C, S
Mondo grass (*Ophiopogon japonicus*)	N, C, S
Peperomia (*Peperomia* spp.)	S
Swedish ivy (*Plectranthus madagascariensis*)	N, C, S
Snake plant (*Sansevieria* spp.)	C, S
Strawberry geranium (*Saxifraga stolonifera*)	N
Dwarf peace lily (*Spathyphyllum* spp.)	C, S
Nephthytis (*Syngonium podophyllum*)	C, S
Wandering Jew (*Zebrina pendula*)	C, S

Azalea

"People ask what kind of turf grass will grow under large oaks, and the answer is none. They try to grow grass anyway, and the St. Augustine lasts a year and then goes into decline. I tell them they are wasting their money. Instead, cut a natural outline around the area where the grass is doing poorly. Then put in clumps of groundcovers. Giant liriope is my favorite because it lives on neglect. I like to add a section of caladiums for summer color and perhaps a lady palm for added interest. I also like ivies. They may climb a tree, but you can always clip them off before they get into the branches. I like various shades of green, but if you want bloom, impatiens are also a great groundcover. They just take more maintenance. Be sure that most of the planting grows taller than the grass, or it will look like it just needs weeding and mowing." — Mike Ryan, garden sales and TV garden clinics, Home Depot, Brandon.

GROUNDCOVERS THAT CAN BE INVASIVE

The very qualities that make a good groundcover can sometimes make for too much of a good thing. A plant that spreads rampantly can become a pest—sometimes to the point of invading the entire state! In 1997 the governor proclaimed October as the Invasive, Nonnative Plant Eradication Awareness Month. Would you believe St. Augustine grass is on the noxious list? Yes, it can get out of control, spreading from yards into places where it competes unfettered with our native plants. Of course, there is plenty of room for disagreement among gardeners, ecologists, and plant people on how to define noxious.

We have marked with an asterisk groundcovers that are more or less agreed upon to easily spread beyond your control even if you are vigilant—birds and wind have a part in this. However, we are not the final word. Find out as much as you can about any of these plants from a local source, and then use your common sense. The Extension Service will have the latest list of plants considered noxious by the state, and in some cases of plants that you may be prohibited, by law, from planting.

However, some on this list, such as sea oats and lantana, can be just the right solution for a particular area, their spreading habit quickly covering what was once a barren spot of your yard. Just read and research carefully.

Bamboo (*Arundinaria* spp.)	N, C, S
Asparagus fern (*Asparagus springerii*)*	N, C, S
Ganges primrose (*Asystasia gangetica*)*	C, S
Sea oxeye daisy (*Borrichia frutescens*)	N, C
Madagascar periwinkle (*Catharanthus roseus*)*	C, S
Pineland snowberry (*Chicococca pinetorum*)	S
Leatherleaf (*Colubrina asiatica*)*	C, S
Pothos (*Epipremnum aureum*)*	C, S
Horsetail (*Equisetum hyemale*)	N, C
Creeping fig (*Ficus pumila*)	C, S
Morning glory (*Ipomoea* spp.)	N, C, S
Blood leaf (*Iresine lindenii*)	C, S
Kalanchoes (*Kalanchoe* spp.)	C, S
Lantana (*Lantana camara*)*	N, C, S
Matchweed (*Lippia nodiflora*)	N, C, S
Japanese honeysuckle (*Lonicera japonica*)*	N, C, S
Muhly grass (*Muhlenbergia capillaris*)	N, C, S
Oyster plant (*Rhoeo spathacea*)*	C, S
Monkey plant (*Ruellia makoyana*)	N, C, S
Sea purslane (*Sesuvium portulacastrum*)	N, C, S
Purple heart (*Setcreasea pallida*)	N, C, S
Sea oats (*Uniola paniculata*)	N, C, S
Wedelia (*Wedelia trilobata*)*	C, S
Wandering Jew (*Zebrina pendula*)*	C, S
Rain lily (*Zephyranthes* spp. and hybrids)	N, C, S

GROUNDCOVERS WITH COLORFUL FOLIAGE

Foliage color is even more important than flower color. Most foliage colors are fairly subtle and blend with other plants well. They give excellent accent and interest to a landscape and add an air of elegance while they cut down on the work of mowing and trimming. You will find others to add to this list, for many of the groundcover plants have variegated varieties. Also check the lists in the annual, perennial, and fern chapters.

Variegated

Bugleweed (*Ajuga reptans* 'Burgundy Glow')	N, C, S
Joseph's coat (*Amaranthus tricolor*)	C, S
Variegated cast-iron plant (*Aspidistra elatior*)	N, C, S
Japanese sedge (*Carex morrowii* 'Goldband')	N
Spider plant (*Chlorophytum comosum*)	C, S
Pothos (*Epipremnum aureum*)	C, S
Variegated ivy (*Hedera* spp.)	N, C, S
Variegated lilyturf (*Liriope* spp.)	N, C, S
Swedish ivy (*Plectranthus madagascariensis*)	N, C, S
Dwarf sansevieria (*Sansevieria* spp.)	C, S
Nephthytis (*Syngonium podophyllum*)	C, S

Purple or Red

Bugleweed (*Ajuga reptans*)	N, C, S
Blood leaf (*Iresine* spp.)	C, S
Purple heart (*Setcreasea pallida*)	N, C, S
Wandering Jew (*Zebrina pendula*)	C, S

Silver

Silver vase (*Aechmea* spp.)	S

Blue

Juniper (*Juniperus horizontalis*)	N, C, S

GROUNDCOVERS THAT NEED ONLY OCCASIONAL WATERING

The ideal groundcover for the Florida yard is one that, once established, needs water only occasionally—every several weeks if there is no rain, perhaps every two weeks in hot, dry April and May. Better yet are those that need no watering at all, once established. Add to this list as plants thrive for you with little or no added water and group them accordingly, even if it means moving plants around a bit. Or at least be aware of what you can skip over when you are out with the hose.

Those marked with an asterisk can thrive on natural Florida rainfall.

Yellow allamanda (*Allamanda cathartica*)	C, S
Aloe (*Aloe* spp.)*	N, C, S
Asparagus fern (*Asparagus springerii*)*	N, C, S
Star begonia (*Begonia heracleifolia*)	S
Sea oxeye daisy (*Borrichia frutescens*)*	N, C, S
Beach bean (*Canavallia maritima*)*	C, S

Dwarf natal plum (*Carissa macrocarpa*)	C, S
Pineland snowberry (*Chicococca pinetorum*)*	S
African iris (*Dietes vegeta*)	C, S
Blanket flower (*Gaillardia pulchella*)	C, S
Algerian ivy (*Hedera canariensis*)	N, C, S
English ivy (*Hedera helix*)	N, C
Beach sunflower (*Helianthus debilis*)*	N, C, S
Daylily (*Hemerocallis* spp.)*	N, C, S
Jasmine (*Jasminum* spp.)	N, C, S
Shore juniper (*Juniperus conferta*)*	N, C, S
Kalanchoes (*Kalanchoe* spp.)*	C, S
Dwarf lantana (*Lantana* spp.) *	C, S
Gopher apple (*Licania michauxii*)*	N, C, S
Liriope (*Liriope muscari*) *	N, C, S
Mondo grass (*Ophiopogon japonicus*)	N, C, S
Artillery plant (*Pilea microphylla*)	C, S
Oyster plant (*Rhoeo spathacea*)*	C, S
Sea purslane (*Sesuvium portulacastrum*)*	N, C, S
Asian jasmine (*Trachelospermum asiaticum*)	N, C, S
Society garlic (*Tulbaghia violacea*)	N, C, S
Sea oats (*Uniola paniculata*)*	N, C, S
Wild allamanda (*Urechites lutea*)*	S
Wedelia (*Wedelia trilobata*)	N, C, S
Coontie (*Zamia floridana*)	N, C, S

NATIVE GROUNDCOVERS AND GRASSES

Native plants, used under the same conditions in which they grow wild, are some of the toughest, most dependable of all groundcovers. Combine the vertical foliage and plumy spires of grasses with more sprawling vines and perennials for contrast. Natives can be mixed with other hardy plants that behave as well and have the same light and water needs. You don't have to be a purist. If you get your yard to 60 percent natives, you'll notice a happy improvement in thriving plants with less work and water.

As yet, most of us are not so familiar with the natives, and they are not always easy to find because they are going by the thousands to mitigation projects and roadside plantings.

Beach bean (*Canavalia maritima*)	C, S
Inland sea oats (*Chasmanthium latifolium*)	C, S
Golden creeper (*Ernodea littoralis*)	S
Gopher apple (*Licania michauxii*)	N, C, S
Matchweed (*Lippia nodiflora*)	N, C, S
Beach peanut (*Okenia hypogaea*)	S
Blue-eyed grass (*Sisrynchium augustifolium*)	N, C, S
Smooth cordgrass (*Spartina alterniflora*)	N, C, S
Sand cordgrass (*Spartina gakeri*)	N, C, S
Saltmeadow cordgrass (*Spartina patens*)	N, C, S
Dwarf fakahatchee grass (*Tripsacum floridana*)	N, C, S
Wild allamanda (*Urechites lutea*)	S
Coontie (*Zamia floridana*)	N, C, S

GROUNDCOVERS FOR DEEP SHADE

Areas where trees form dense canopies present a challenge because of the deep shade and the competition from tree roots. Remember that tree roots can suck up all the moisture and nutrients, so you'll have to water and feed more in such situations. Or you can use a 2- to 3-inch layer of mulch alone for a groundcover. Simply replenish it every few months as it decomposes. If you want plants as well, the following will thrive where less adaptable ones would grow very slowly if at all.

Cast-iron plant (*Aspidistra elatior*)	N, C, S
Swamp fern (*Blechnum serrulatum*)	N, C, S
Spider plant (*Chlorophytum comosum*)	C, S
Grape ivy (*Cissus rhombifolia*)	S
Kaffir lily (*Clivia miniata*)	S
Holly fern (*Cyrtomium falcatum*)	N, C, S
Dwarf dracaena (*Dracaena* spp.)	C, S
Algerian ivy (*Hedera canariensis*)	N, C, S
English ivy (*Hedera helix*)	N, C
Liriope (*Liriope muscari*)	N, C, S
Prayer plant (*Maranta* spp.)	C, S
Sword fern (*Nephrolepis biserrata*)	C, S
Mondo grass (*Ophiopogon japonicus*)	N, C, S
Peperomia (*Peperomia* spp.)	S
Philodendrons (*Philodendron* spp.)	C, S
Artillery plant (*Pilea microphylla*)	C, S
Dwarf oyster plant (*Rhoeo discolor*)	C, S
Leatherleaf fern (*Rumohra adiantiformis*)	N, C, S
Snake plant (*Sansevieria* spp.)	C, S
Dwarf peace lily (*Spathyphyllum* spp.)	C, S
Nephthytis (*Syngonium podophyllum*)	C, S
Asian jasmine (*Trachelospermum asiaticum*)	N, C, S
Wandering Jew (*Zebrina pendula*)	C, S

 "Liriope is my favorite groundcover to use in the shade. It is low maintenance and grows vigorously. I like to contrast the evergreen giant with the variegated giant liriope and use the dwarf mondo grass, also. It gives you a nice color feature and height variation. The peace lily does especially well in a shady area by a front door for accent." — Lesli Larmon Wiley, Lesli Larmon Landscape Design, St. Petersburg.

GROUNDCOVERS FOR CRACKS AND CREVICES

"I need something to grow between stepping stones to crowd out the weeds," said one gardener. She preferred herbs, and thyme is the standard in northern states. It is possible here but difficult in the summer. We have to be careful in Florida because so many plants that can do this job, like dichondra and Aztec sweet shrub, would also soon cover the stepping stones or the patio.

Use the taller ones, such as dwarf fountain grass and artillery plant, only in pockets where you aren't going to walk; they will grow over a foot tall.

Bugleweed (*Ajuga reptans*) — N, C, S
Gotu kola (*Centella asiatica*) — N, C, S
Pinks (*Dianthus* spp.) — N, C
Sweet woodruff (*Galium odoratum*) — N
Candytuft (*Iberis sempervirens*) — N
Lysimachia (*Lysimachia congestiflora* 'Eco Dark Satin') — N, C
Dwarf Creeping Jenny (*Lysimchia japonica* 'Minutissima') — N, C, S
Corsican mint (*Mentha requienii*) — N, C, S
Dwarf mondo grass (*Ophiopogon japonicus* 'Nana') — N, C, S
Black mondo grass (*Ophiopogon planiscapus* 'Arabicus') — N, C, S
Creeping oregano (*Origanum* spp.) — N, C, S
Dwarf fountain grass (*Pennisetum alopecuroides* 'Little Bunny') — N, C, S
Thrift (*Phlox sublata*) — N, C
Artillery plant (*Pilea microphylla*) — C, S
Pennyroyal (*Piloblephis rigida*) — C, S
Portulaca, purslane, or moss rose (*Portulaca* spp.) — N, C, S
Baby's tear (*Solierolia solierolii*) — S
Creeping thyme (*Thymus* spp.) — N, C, S
Moss verbena (*Verbena tenuisecta*) — N, C, S
Creeping veronica (*Veronica repens*) — N
Australian violet (*Viola hedera*) — N, C, S

"Ajuga makes an excellent groundcover for sun or shade. In full sun its leaves are velvet blue, red, and green in color. It also blooms with a blue to purple flower spike. It likes well-drained soil and has a slight salt tolerance. Great for under trees, on banks, and in open areas, it can also be used for edging. If kept cut, it is tolerant of light foot traffic." —Arthur Yambor, owner, Shelton's Nursery, Brandon.

GROUNDCOVERS FOR THE BEACH

The beach is a challenging situation for which God has provided amazingly well—many plants will stand up to the sun, wind, and salt spray. Mary Alice Harley, who has a rather famous garden in St. Petersburg, has a wide strip of beach at the edge of her lovely xeriscaped yard and lets anything grow there that will. The result is a sweep of grasses and wildflowers that she never waters, feeds, or mows.

Asparagus fern (*Asparagus springerii*) — N, C, S
Sea oxeye daisy (*Borrichia frutescens*) — N, C
Beach bean (*Canavallia maritima*) — C, S
Dwarf natal plum (*Carissa macrocarpa*) — C, S
Madagascar periwinkle (*Catharanthus roseus*) — C, S
Golden creeper (*Ernodea littoralis*) — S
Blue daze (*Evolvulus glomeratus*) — C, S
Creeping fig (*Ficus pumila*) — C, S
Blanket flower (*Gaillardia pulchella*) — N, C, S
Carolina yellow jessamine (*Gelsemium sempervirens*) — N, C
Algerian ivy (*Hedera canariensis*) — N, C, S

Groundcovers for the Beach (*continued*)

Beach sunflower (*Helianthus debilis*)	N, C, S
Spider lily (*Hymenocallis latifolia*)	C, S
Yaupon holly (*Ilex vomitoria*)	N, C, S
Railroad vine (*Ipomoea pes-caprae*)	S
Beach elder (*Iva imbricata*)	N, C, S
Star jasmine (*Jasminum multiflorum*)	N, C, S
Shore juniper (*Juniperus conferta*)	N, C, S
Trailing lantana (*Lantana montevidensis*)	C, S
Gopher apple (*Licania michauxii*)	N, C, S
Liriope (*Liriope muscari*)	N, C
Virginia creeper (*Parthenocissus quinquefolia*)	N, C, S
Snake plant (*Sansevieria* spp.)	C, S
Sea purslane (*Sesuvium portulacastrum*)	N, C, S
Purple heart (*Setcreasea pallida*)	N, C, S
Cordgrass (*Spartina patens*)	N, C, S
Sea oats (*Uniola paniculata*)	N, C, S
Wedelia (*Wedelia trilobata*)	N, C, S
Adam's needle (*Yucca* spp.)	N, C, S
Coontie (*Zamia floridana*)	N, C, S

"Research your plants before you incorporate them into your landscape. But don't be afraid to take chances with accent plants. The worst thing that will happen is that you'll have to pull up some dead ones. But then you'll get to try something new." — Beth Dolan, garden editor and writer, *Tampa Tribune*.

A SAMPLER OF GROUNDCOVERS BY FLOWER COLOR AND SEASON

Although flower color may not be the purpose of your groundcover planting, it is definitely something you will want to know and coordinate with your other plantings. The possibilities of added color, not to mention texture and fragrance, make a plain green lawn seem dull by comparison. Asterisks denote fragrance.

White Flowers

Lily-of-the-Nile (*Agapanthus africanus albus*)	Summer
Gumpo azalea (*Azalea* 'Gumpo')	Spring
Dwarf natal plum (*Carissa macrocarpa*)	Winter, spring
Madagascar periwinkle (*Catharanthus roseus*)*	Year-round
Swamp lily (*Crinum americanum*)*	Winter, spring, summer
African iris (*Dietes vegeta*)*	Year-round
Dwarf gardenia (*Gardenia jasminoides*)*	Winter, spring
Spider lily (*Hymenocallis latifolia*)*	Summer
Morning glory (*Ipomoea* spp.)	Year-round
Jasmine (*Jasminum* spp.)*	Year-round
Lilyturf (*Liriope muscari* 'Monroe White')	Summer
Snake plant (*Sansevieria* spp.)*	Summer
Dwarf peace lily (*Spathyphyllum* spp.)	Summer

Asian jasmine (*Trachelospermum Asiaticum*)   Spring, summer
Rain lily (*Zephyranthes* spp. and hybrids)   Winter, spring, summer

Red Flowers
Blanket flower (*Gaillardia pulchella*)   Year-round
Daylily (*Hemerocallis* spp.)   Winter, spring, summer
Kalanchoes (*Kalanchoe* spp.)   Winter, spring
Portulaca, purslane, or moss rose (*Portulaca* spp.)   Summer

Blue Flowers
Silver vase (*Aechmea* spp.)   Winter, spring
Lily-of-the-Nile (*Agapanthus africanus*)   Summer
Bugleweed (*Ajuga reptans*)   Spring
Conradina (*Conradina grandiflora*)   Year-round
Blue daze (*Evolvulus glomeratus*)   Year-round
Twinflower, partridge berry (*Mitchella repens*)   Year-round
Big-leaf periwinkle (*Vinca major*)   Spring

Yellow or Orange Flowers
Aloe (*Aloe* spp.)   Year-round
Sea oxeye daisy (*Borrichia frutescens*)   Spring, summer
Kafir lily (*Clivia miniata*)   Spring
Carolina yellow jessamine (*Gelsemium sempervirens*)   Winter, spring
Beach sunflower (*Helianthus debilis*)   Year-round
Daylily (*Hemerocallis* spp.)   Winter, spring, summer
Kalanchoes (*Kalanchoe* spp.)   Winter, spring
Dwarf lantana (*Lantana montevidensis*)   Year-round
Portulaca, purslane, or moss rose (*Portulaca* spp.)   Summer

Purple, Pink, and Lavender Flowers

Carrion flower

Gumpo azalea (*Azalea* 'Gumpo')   Spring
Beach bean (*Canavallia maritima*)   Year-round
Madagascar periwinkle   Year-round
    (*Catharanthus roseus*)
False heather (*Cuphea hyssopifolia*)   Year-round
Golden creeper (*Ernodea littoralis*)   Year-round
Daylily (*Hemerocallis* spp.)   Winter, spring, summer
Railroad vine (*Ipomoea pes-caprae*)   Year-round
Kalanchoes (*Kalanchoe* spp.)   Winter, spring
Trailing lantana (*Lantana montevidensis*)   Year-round
Liriope (*Liriope muscari*)   Summer
Portulaca, purslane, or moss rose (*Portulaca* spp.)   Summer
Purple heart (*Setcreasea pallida*)   Year-round
Carrion flower (*Stapelia nobilis*)   Summer
Society garlic (*Tulbaghia violacea*)   Spring, summer

ROSES

MB: Most people think that growing roses requires great care and dedication. True, many roses do require frequent spraying and tending for that ultimate perfection we see in catalog pages. But, I have grown roses without doting care in two states and have found that I can grow many as well in Florida as I did in Iowa. When I start to cut off the deadheads, I am pleased by how many blooms my bushes have produced, even if they are not exhibition quality.

Roses vary greatly in size and growth habit. As you investigate any rose on these lists, be sure to inquire about its size and form. We include everything from tiny miniatures to midsize shrub roses, such as the Fairy, to big roses such as the sprawling Lady Banks, which is large enough to drape a two-story house.

Specific rose species or cultivars may vary in their performance in different parts of the state, depending on soil, climate, and other conditions. Even viruses can influence success; a rose that does well in one garden may fail in another because of virus strains found in the unfortunate garden. For this reason, check with rose gardens and gardeners in your area to see what is locally proven. One place to start is the network of gardeners that comprise the American Rose Society (ARS). The ARS has consulting rosarians throughout the United States willing to make recommendations and answer your questions. You can contact the ARS (you may want to become a member just to receive their helpful magazine) at Box 30,000, Shreveport, LA 71130-0030. Or visit their web site: http://www.ars.org. For information and for camaraderie with folks who like old roses, try the Heritage Rose Society. The chapter for central Florida (in Lakeland) meets monthly and has a good newsletter. Contact Carol Hoffman, 1423 Glendale Street, Lakeland, FL 33803.

The lists on these pages reflect the opinions we have gathered from a number of rosarians throughout the state. We include roses that have, in an experienced rose gardener's opinion, proven their value in Florida gardens.

The roses in this chapter include both modern roses and old roses. The last few years have brought a renaissance of antique roses. And no wonder. The old roses have many advantages. Generally, they are easier to grow.

You may see a few roses listed here that are difficult to find. Because of the surging interest in old roses, we believe that many hard-to-find roses may be more available soon and so should remain on these lists. More and more mail-order businesses have their catalogs on-line, so you may want to check the web for sources.

LC: I want to thank Camille Hunter (master gardener, Jacksonville), Kelly Tesiero (designer, Landscapes by Design, and owner of The Elegant Garden, Jacksonville), and Bill Tevepaugh (Deep South District director of the American Rose Society, Jacksonville) for their review of this chapter. Mr. Tevepaugh didn't agree with all the roses on our original lists, and we made some changes based on his very helpful and deep knowledge. However, this is where our job as writers gets so difficult. So again, we urge you to always consult with local sources, because if there is one thing we can be sure of, it's that opinion is going to vary!

TO DO LIST FOR GROWING ROSES

Doing your homework is crucial to successful rose growing. Before you buy anything, study carefully the varieties available and match them to your place and purpose. Know what is needed for their growth and make a plan to provide it. Special thanks to Camille Hunter of Jacksonville for sharing her experiences as a master gardener to help us put together the following tips.

- Select a location that gets at least 6 hours of sunlight a day, has soil that drains well, and has water available. The site needs good air circulation, although not constant exposure to steady winds (such as on the coast). Stagnant air leaves plants vulnerable to disease.
- Have the soil tested for pH and nutrient content. Forms and instructions are available at your County Extension Office.
- Spring, fall, and winter are the best times for planting container-grown plants. Avoid summer planting unless you are willing to water plants religiously. Winter is the best time to plant bare-root roses.
- Arrange plants. Five-foot spacing works well for hybrid teas. Larger plants will need more room. Antique roses vary tremendously in size and form. Check with your source to determine their spacing.
- You may find recommendations that tell you to dig planting holes twice as wide and deep as the container. However, current University of Florida guidelines are to dig the hole no deeper than the root ball. If holes are deeper, the plants tend to settle to a point where they are too deep.
- Thoroughly mix soil amendments throughout the planting area. The width of the amended area should be a minimum of three times the width of the planting hole. Amend the entire bed. Good amendments include compost or a purchased planting mix. (You will find that local rose societies have their own recommendations for planting and amending the soil, so check with a nearby source.)
- Water a container-grown rose thoroughly before removing it from the pot. If the rose is bare-root, soak the roots for at least two hours before planting.
- Remove the rose from the container with root ball intact. A sharp hit on the rim should loosen the ball. Turn the plant upside down and slide it from the pot. Do not yank it.
- Put the plant in the hole and turn it so the best side faces you. The top of the soil on the root ball should be even with the ground. Fill half the space around the plant. Add water to the top and let it drain. Then fill the hole with soil and water again.
- Watch for roses that are planted incorrectly at the nursery when they are moved up to larger pots. To be sure the planting depth is correct, run your fingers down the stem and into the soil. The first lateral roots should be just at the soil surface. If they are buried, raise the plant in the hole so that the first roots are just below the surface.

- Mulch well with bark, compost, or pine straw. We do not recommend cypress mulch unless it is from a source where the trees are not being taken from our cypress swamps.
- Water new plants regularly at first. Drip irrigation is the best way to water, but whatever method you use, water slowly, thoroughly, and deeply. An inch of water per application is standard. Water less in winter.
- Spray insecticides and fungicides as needed. Modern hybrids such as hybrid teas need spraying weekly or even more often (depending on rain).
- Feed plants as needed. Hybrid teas for cutting will need more fertilizer than old-fashioned roses, which may only need a single application of controlled-release fertilizer in spring. The more you feed, the more the plant will need watching for aphids, mites, and other pests.
- Do yearly pruning in February. When pruning, be sure to strip off any leaves left on the plant and dispose of them. Also clean up any leaf litter on the ground. By so doing, you are removing any leaf disease that might be present and giving the plant a fresh start.
- Walk around the garden every morning, pick flowers, and remove dead flower heads (unless you want the hips).

ROSE TYPES

The lists that follow identify roses as belonging to a certain group or class. All roses generally fall into one of two categories: modern roses (varieties developed after 1867) and Old Garden Roses (varieties introduced before 1867). However, gardeners often loosely use the term "antique rose" to refer to any old rose. To make things more confusing, new hybrids whose parents are Old Garden Roses can also be called OGR, even though they are new!

Classes of Modern Roses
Modern roses include hybrid tea, floribunda, grandiflora, and polyantha roses.

Hybrid tea roses originated in 1867 when a tea rose was crossed with a hybrid perpetual to create 'La France'. It and such subsequent crosses become known as Hybrid Teas. Hybrid Teas produce one exquisite rose per stem and are popular for cutting. This is the rose you typically see exhibited in soda pop bottles at rose shows.

Floribundas were introduced in 1930. They are relatively compact bushes with clusters of small blooms. Many are respectable as landscape roses.

Grandifloras were so called beginning in 1954 as a way to describe new hybrids that were crosses between hybrid teas and floribundas. They have one or two blooms per stem, straight, long stems, and continuous bloom. 'Queen Elizabeth' is a popular grandiflora.

Polyanthas have large clusters of small roses and give a great deal of color in the garden.

Classes of Antique or Old Garden Roses
The American Rose Society identifies any variety belonging to a rose class known before 1867 as an Old Garden Rose. However, except in the lists, we will refer to all old roses as antique roses. Varieties listed as "found" have been collected from old gardens and are awaiting final classification. All of these roses have stood the test of time and are generally more carefree than the modern ones. They don't take nearly as much water or need fertilizer as often, and they can be grown without sprays. They will get some black spot, but they usually outlive it. "Not all antique roses are suitable for Florida," says Valerie Oppenheim, owner of Valrose Nursery (wholesale) in Gainesville. "To be sure of getting the best varieties for an area, a beginner should select roses by their class. The Chinas, teas, noisettes, polyanthas, and hybrid musks are examples of classes that are repeat bloomers and will grow well in Florida."

Most of the antiques are landscape roses. They generally make much fuller plants than modern roses. However, they vary greatly in habit from shrubby to climbing, so, as we said earlier, you need to learn more about each rose variety listed here before buying it. The blossoms of some antique roses will hold in a vase, but most shatter easily.

There is some debate about whether it is best to buy grafted antique roses. It is not essential as it is for the modern roses. Grafted antique roses grow more quickly. Leaves and blooms are bigger. But heavy top growth above a high graft may break the graft if it is not staked. As you will learn from the lists, some rosarians prefer old roses grafted on Fortuniana rootstock (the rootstock best for Florida conditions).

Martha Davies, owner of Martha Davies Antique Roses in Bartow, shares similar sentiments: "I've been growing and selling old roses since the 1930s. There are limited varieties that have been here long enough to prove their resistance to nematodes. Years ago people just planned to replace them every two or three years. Now we grow them on virus-free Fortuniana rootstock."

The advantages of growing antique roses on their own rootstocks include the fact that if a bush freezes to the ground, it will come back true to variety, not from a rootstock. You can root most antique roses easily in early spring (February or March) by stripping ½ inch of bark off one end of a cane and laying the cane down so that the stripped part is in contact with the soil, weighting the cane down with a brick to maintain that contact and burying the section with soil. By fall the stem should be rooted and you can sever the new rooted plant from the mother plant.

You will find the following major classes of Old Garden Roses in our lists.

Bourbons have large flowers, a rich scent, and some repeat bloom. They are leggy and thus are often trained horizontally in a technique known as pegging. Unfortunately, most are prone to disease in Florida.

Chinas match the floral display of azaleas in spring and will rebloom until frost. They are generally disease resistant.

Hybrid musks are useful landscape roses that tolerate more shade, have good disease resistance, and are very fragrant. They bloom best in spring, and some have a strong fall repeat. They have large bushes with long canes that can be trained on a fence.

Hybrid perpetuals are the forerunners of Hybrid Teas. Some repeat-bloom in the fall. Unfortunately, many are prone to disease in Florida, but some gardeners would rather spray than not enjoy their beautiful flowers and rich scent.

Kordesii hybrids were introduced by a German breeder in the 1930s. They are among the most dependable of roses. They include both shrub and climbing types and are descendants of an old species, *Rosa kordesii*.

Noisettes are hybrids of Chinas and Musk Roses. They produce loose, mounding bushes that can be trained to a pillar or fence; they have fragrant blooms mostly in spring and fall.

Old European roses are once-bloomers. They do better in colder climes; as a rule these don't do well in Florida, unless they are grafted on Fortuniana rootstock.

Polyanthas are a cross of Chinas with rambling Japanese Multiflora roses. They grow compact, bushy, and 2 to 5 feet tall, with small flowers in large clusters. They offer excellent repeat bloom from spring to frost. Some are fragrant; some are not.

Rugosa roses are coastal roses of cooler climates and generally do not do well in the South, but a few exceptions are listed here. The foliage is coarsely veined and tolerant of salt spray.

Species roses are simply that, just a simple species, and are listed as such.

Teas (not Hybrid Teas) are very similar to Chinas but more classic, and most have beautiful repeating blooms, with the greatest show in spring and fall. Flowers are small to large, single to doubles on large, healthy, upright bushes, good for cutting.

Misc. OGR stands for the category of "miscellaneous Old Garden Rose." The majority are once-bloomers.

 "The antique roses are ideal for Florida, the only way to go. I've been growing and selling roses, starting with my mother in the 1930s. Now we grow them on virus-free *Fortuniana* rootstock. There are only four or five varieties that have been here long enough to prove their resistance to nematodes. We started with the old early teas, and people just planned to replace them every two or three years. In the early 1930s my mother was selling grafted roses for a dollar each and plants on their own rootstock for 35 cents." — Martha Davies, owner, Martha Davies Antique Roses, Bartow.

GENERAL COMPARISONS BETWEEN HYBRID TEAS AND ANTIQUE ROSES

Hybrid Tea Roses	Antique Roses
Need weekly spraying throughout the growing season	Need little, if any, spraying
Are heavy feeders; need weekly liquid feed or controlled-release granular fertilizer on schedule	Need little fertilizing
Generally have a poor growth habit; have long stems for cutting but do not make a pretty bush	Many grow into lush shrubs or pillars; many make excellent landscape roses
Prefer good soil with excellent drainage	A little more tolerant of less-than-ideal soil
Have long stems and classic blossoms for cutting and showing	Blooms of the different species and cultivars vary greatly in shape, size, and longevity; some shatter quickly; stems short on most cultivars
Bloom continuously, or almost so, throughout spring, summer, and fall	Some bloom several times a year, with the spring flush being the greatest; others bloom only once (in the spring)
Have a short lifespan, often three to five years; usually longer if grafted on *Fortuniana* rootstock	Some plants live a hundred years
Cultivars are grafted onto a rootstock; the longest-lived are on *Fortuniana* rootstock, which is not always easy to find	Grow on their own roots
Not easily started from cuttings	Easily started from cuttings

ROSES FOR FRAGRANCE

Roses vary greatly in fragrance, but fragrance remains one of the driving reasons for growing and giving them. Roses have been used for perfumes and cosmetics since 1200 B.C. The following is just the tip of a lovely iceberg of fruit, spicy, citrus, licorice, myrrh, and musk scents. Because appreciation of fragrance is personal, make a point of sniffing before you buy when possible.

'Abraham Darby'	Shrub	1990
'Alec's Red'	Hybrid Tea	1970
'Alister Stella Gray'	Noisette	1894
'Angel Face'	Floribunda	1969
'Blue Moon'	Hybrid Tea	1964
'Blush Noisette'	Shrub	1817
'Buff Beauty'	Shrub	1922
'Cecile Brunner'	Climbing Polyantha	1881
'Celine Forestier'	Noisette	1858
'Champney's Pink Cluster'	Noisette	1811
'Clotilde Soupert'	Polyantha	1890
'De Rescht'	Damask	1940s
'Double Delight'	Hybrid Tea	1977
'Duchesse de Brabant'	Tea	1857
'Erfurt'	Hybrid Musk	1939
'Fortuniana'	Misc. OGR	1850
'Fragrant Cloud'	Hybrid Tea	1963
'Lamarque'	Noisette	1830
'Louis Philippe'	China	1834
'Maggie'	Found Bourbon	Unknown
'Marechal Neil'	Noisette	1864
'Marie Pavie'	Polyantha	1888
'Mr. Lincoln'	Hybrid Tea	1964
'Mrs. B.R. Cant'	Tea	1901
'Paul Neyron'	Hybrid Perpetual	1869
'Peace'	Hybrid Tea	1945
'Penelope'	Hybrid Musk	1924
'Reine des Violettes'	Hybrid Perpetual	1860
'Royal Highness'	Hybrid Tea	1962
'Secret'	Hybrid Tea	1993
'Sombreuil'	Climbing Tea	1850
'Sun Flare'	Floribunda	1981
'Souvenir de la Malmaison'	Bourbon	1843
'Stanwell Perpetual'	Scotch	1838
Swamp rose (*Rosa Palustris scandens*)	Species	Pre-1824

"I always tell people that our roses will never have the look you see in the garden magazines all the time. Rose bushes can only bloom so much over the entire ten to twelve months of our growing season. Florida roses are not going to be full of blossoms and gorgeous all the time. You must be realistic. Customers call and say, 'Why hasn't this rose bloomed for a month? Well, yes, it did bloom for six weeks before that.' And it will again and again all year." —Trish Montesano, owner, Sweet Annie's Antique Roses, Riverview.

BEST MODERN ROSES FOR FLORIDA GARDENS

The following are names that appear again and again on the lists of favorites of many rosarians around the state. One thing you will be sure to notice is that many of these are 20 years old or older. We think that is indicative of the time it takes for the plants to earn a spot as tried-and-true. However, be aware that all of these are likely to need some spraying to control disease. They appear on this list simply because most folks think they are worth the effort, or they survive problems better than others in their class.

'Alec's Red'	Hybrid Tea	1970
'Angel Face'	Floribunda	1969
'Anisley Dickson'	Floribunda	1983
'Anne Harkness'	Floribunda	1980
'Aquarius'	Grandiflora	1971
'Blue Moon'	Hybrid Tea	1964
'Bonica '82'	Shrub	1981
'Brigadoon'	Hybrid Tea	1992
'Century Two'	Hybrid Tea	1971
'Chicago Peace'	Hybrid Tea	1962
'Christian Dior'	Hybrid Tea	1958
'Chrysler Imperial'	Hybrid Tea	1952
'Color Magic'	Hybrid Tea	1978
'Confidence'	Hybrid Tea	1951
'Dainty Bess'	Hybrid Tea	1925
'Dearest'	Floribunda	1960
'Don Juan'	Climber	1958
'Double Delight'	Hybrid Tea	1977
'Elegant Beauty'	Hybrid Tea	1982
'Elina'	Hybrid Tea	1985
'Europeana'	Floribunda	1968
'First Prize'	Hybrid Tea	1970
'Fragrant Cloud'	Hybrid Tea	1963
'Garden Party'	Hybrid Tea	1959
'Gene Boerner'	Floribunda	1969
'Granada'	Hybrid Tea	1963
'Hannah Gordon'	Floribunda	1983
'Iceberg'	Floribunda	1958
'Ivory Fashion'	Floribunda	1958
'Just Joey'	Hybrid Tea	1973
'Keepsake'	Hybrid Tea	1980
'King's Ransom'	Hybrid Tea	1961
'Kordes' Perfecta'	Hybrid Tea	1957
'Korresia (Sunsprite)'	Floribunda	1974
'Lady X'	Hybrid Tea	1966
'Medallion'	Hybrid Tea	1973
'Miss All-American Beauty'	Hybrid Tea	1965
'Mister Lincoln'	Hybrid Tea	1964
'Pascali'	Hybrid Tea	1963
'Peace'	Hybrid Tea	1945

'Pink Favorite'	Hybrid Tea	1956
'Polar Star (Polarstern)'	Hybrid Tea	1992
'Queen Elizabeth'	Grandiflora	1955
'Red Gold'	Floribunda	1971
'Regenberg'	Floribunda	1979
'Royal Highness'	Hybrid Tea	1962
'Sea Foam'	Shrub	1964
'Sexy Rexy'	Floribunda	1984
'Sonia'	Grandiflora	1973
'Swarthmore'	Hybrid Tea	1963
'Tiffany'	Hybrid Tea	1954
'Tropicana'	Hybrid Tea	1964
'White Masterpiece'	Hybrid Tea	1969

"Exhibitors favor modern roses for their more perfect look and their wider color range. The modern roses will bloom more during the summer. What you want to do with them and how much you are willing to maintain are the deciding factors. Buds hold longer in the vase, up to almost ten days for some like St. Patrick." —Patti Barfield, who plans, plants, and takes care of rose gardens as owner of Personal Touch Roses, Dover.

ROSES WITH FEW OR NO THORNS

MB: Actually, no rose has thorns—just epidermal prickles. But these prickles are perfectly capable of drawing blood from a gardener or flower arranger, and one under the fingernail once led to blood poisoning for my husband. They are not to be taken lightly. It has always seemed a significant lesson in life that the loveliest of flowers should bear such peril. It is no wonder that roses with smooth canes are cherished. The 'Lady Banks' rose is truly thornless and the others on this list enough so to offer relief to wounded rose lovers. Jim and Diane Giles of Giles Rose Nursery say, "'Reine des Violettes' doesn't do well in the heat. 'Mrs. Dudley Cross' is a great rose, and 'Tausendschen' is easy to grow."

'Climbing Pinkie'	Polyantha	1952
'Marie Pavie'	Polyantha	1888
'Mrs. Dudley Cross'	Tea	1907
'Old Blush'	China	1752
'Paul Neyron'	Hybrid Perpetual	1869
'Playgirl'	Floribunda	1986
Prairie rose (*Rosa setigera serena*)	Species	1924
'Reine des Violettes'	Hybrid Perpetual	1860
Swamp rose (*Rosa palustris scandens*)	Species	Pre-1824
'Tausendschen'	Hybrid Multiflora	1906
'White Lady Banks' (*Rosa banksia*)	Species	1807
'Yellow Lady Banks' (*Rosa banksia* 'Lutea')	Species	1824

ROSES FOR SHADE

Most roses need at least four to six hours of direct sun, but there are a few varieties that will bloom with less. None will grow in total shade, but the following are most likely to tolerate bright shade or dappled shade. They manage to bloom and stay relatively disease free even in adverse conditions. But it never hurts to add a little encouragement when you plant them. Roses in shade will benefit from extra bonemeal to encourage blooming and applications of seaweed, which contains branching and rooting hormones and minerals. Any of the Chinas and Hybrid Musks are good candidates for this list.

'Ballerina'	Hybrid Musk	1937
'Carefree Beauty'	Floribunda	1977
'Carefree Wonder'	Meidiland	1990
'Cecile Brunner'	Climbing Polyantha	1894
Chestnut rose (*R. roxburghii*)	Species	Pre-1814
'Christian Dior'	Hybrid Tea	1958
'Cornelia'	Hybrid Musk	1925
'Garden Party'	Hybrid Tea	1959
'Green Ice'	Miniature	1971
'Kathleen'	Hybrid Musk	1922
'Marie Pavie'	Polyantha	1888
'Mrs. B.R. Cant'	Tea	1901
'Old Blush'	China	1752
'Penelope'	Hybrid Musk	1924
'Perle d'Or'	Polyantha	1884
'Pinata'	Climber	1978
'Playgirl'	Floribunda	1986
'The Fairy'	Miniature	1965
'Vanity'	Hybrid Musk	1920

ROSES THAT BLOOM IN MAD ABUNDANCE ONCE A YEAR

Although many people want roses that bloom repeatedly during the growing season (repeat-bloomers), there is a place in the landscape for roses that bloom only once a year, especially when the show is overwhelming. 'Lady Banks' and 'Seven Sisters' are tried-and-true examples that would not still be around if folks didn't think their yearly show was worth the wait. When their show is over, you can rely on other selections or use creative gardening techniques such as Bruce Cavey's of Gainesville's Plant Shoppe. Bruce uses the stems of his 'Lady Banks' as a support for nonaggressive annual vines for summer and fall color. He also mixes repeat-bloomers with the once-bloomers for the best of both worlds, with the following serving as a backdrop to other plants when they are past their fantastic peak.

'American Pillar'	Rambler	1908
Cherokee rose (*Rosa laevigata*)	Species	1759
'Dr. W. Van Fleet'	Large-flowered Climber	1910
'Fortune's Double Yellow'	Misc. OGR	1845
'Fortuniana'	Misc. OGR	1850

'Seven Sisters'	Hybrid Multiflora	1817
Swamp rose (*Rosa palustris scandens*)	Species	Pre-1824
'Tausendschen'	Hybrid Multiflora	1906
'Veilchenblau'	Hybrid Multiflora	1909
'White Lady Banks' (*Rosa banksia*)	Species	1807
'Yellow Lady Banks' (*Rosa banksia* 'Lutea')	Species	1824

MINIATURE ROSES FOR FLORIDA

Miniature roses are modern roses with small but perfect blooms. The plants usually stay small; in the ground they can grow up to 3 feet, but they will be smaller in a container. There are climbing and trailing varieties that are especially useful. Some are grafted, and some grow on their own roots. Because they are so low to the ground, they are susceptible to spider mites, so watch and treat as needed.

'Beauty Secret'	1965
'Fairhope'	1989
'Fancy Pants'	1987
'Figurine'	1992
'Green Ice'	1971
'Herbie'	1987
'Hot Tamale'	1994
'Irresistible'	1989
'Jet Trail'	1964
'Judy Fischer'	1968
'June Laver'	1989
'Kristin'	1993
'Lavender Jewel'	1978
'Linville'	1989
'Lipstick 'n' Lace'	1995
'Magic Carrousel'	1972
'Minnie Pearl'	1982
'Miss Flippins'	1996
'Mother's Love'	1989
'Over the Rainbow'	1972
'Pierrine'	1988
'Popcorn'	1973
'Rainbow's End'	1984
'Red Beauty'	1981
'Simplex'	1961
'Starina'	1965
'Stars 'n' Stripes'	1976
'Tangerine Twist'	1996
'Tennessee'	1988
'X-Rated'	1995
'Yellow Doll'	1962

BERMUDA MYSTERY ROSES

Dr. Malcolm Manners of Florida Southern College imported these roses into the United States in 1988, and they served their federal quarantine in his garden. They are all so old that they have lost their names and dates, and some of the classifications are uncertain. All of them grew in Bermuda, an even more difficult climate than Florida, and survived with little care. 'Bellfield' is perhaps the real 'Slater's Crimson China', the ancestor of all modern red roses, long believed to be extinct. Here they are, old roses with new names. Those with "Bermuda" as part of the name are different from roses (of other categories) that have the same name otherwise.

'Bellfield'	China
'Bermuda Anna Olivier'	Tea
'Bermuda Catherine Mermet'	Tea
'Bermuda Kathleen'	Tea
'Bermuda Perle des Jardins'	Tea
'Brightside Cream'	Noisette
'Carnation'	China
'Emmy Gray'	China
'Maitland White'	Noisette or China
'Smith's Parish'	Tea
'Somcy'	Tea
'Spice'	Tea
'St. David'	China
'Trinity'	Tea
'Vincent Godsiff'	China

EXTRA LONG-LASTING ROSES FOR BOUQUETS

The selections in the following list are known to last a long time compared to other roses. Cut stems at a 45-degree angle back to a five-leaved leaflet (on the stem). It is best not to take a stem that is too long because you need to leave plenty of foliage on the bush to give the plant energy for future blooms. Always leave at least two five-leaflet leaves on the stem that remains on the plant to ensure future flowers.

Ted Stevens, author of *Roses under the Sun: A Guide for Raising Roses in Florida*, shares these tips: "A rose has several basic structures, and when and how to cut depend on the structures. The sepals, the little green points that hold the bud, must be down when cutting the rose, or the bud will not open. The fragrance will be lost if you cut too late, and the bloom won't open if you cut too soon."

'Alec's Red'	Hybrid Tea	1970
'Anne Harkness'	Floribunda	1980
'Blue Moon'	Hybrid Tea	1964
'Bonica'	Shrub	1981
'Double Delight'	Hybrid Tea	1977
'Elina'	Hybrid Tea	1985
'Fragrant Cloud'	Hybrid Tea	1963
'Hannah Gordon'	Floribunda	1983
Iceberg'	Floribunda	1958
'Korresia (Sunsprite)'	Floribunda	1974

'Marchesa Boccella'	Hybrid Perpetual	1842
'Mrs. Dudley Cross'	Tea	1907
'Pascali'	Hybrid Tea	1963
'Paul Neyron'	Hybrid Perpetual	1869
'Peace'	Hybrid Tea	1945
'Polar Star (Polarstern)'	Hybrid Tea	1992
'Precious Platinum'	Hybrid Tea	1974
'Pristine'	Hybrid Tea	1978
'Queen Elizabeth'	Grandiflora	1955
'Sexy Rexy'	Floribunda	1984
'Sombreuil'	Climbing Tea	1850
'Souvenir de la Malmaison'	Bourbon	1843
'Starina'	Miniature	1965
'Touch of Class'	Hybrid Tea	1984

 "One of my favorite red roses for cutting is 'Uncle Joe'. If you grow it right, you can cut 3- and 4-foot stems with big flowers even in the summer. It's not a terrific bloomer, but it will repeat with good-quality bloom. It never opens completely. To me, it is one of the best for stems, foliage, and flower." —Dr. Rubert Prevatt, professor, Florida Southern College; ARS lifetime judge and consulting rosarian.

JOE FREEMAN'S FAVORITE ROSES

We asked Joe Freeman, the chief horticulturist at Cypress Gardens, if he had any favorite roses. The following list is his reply. Joe says the first thing he looks for is resistance to pests and diseases. After that, flower color, fragrance, and growth habit come into play. "I prefer the heritage type [antique] roses, but I also enjoy some of the David Austin hybrids and the Bermuda mystery roses. These are wonderful landscape roses but may also serve well as cut flowers. I also check a variety's rating with the American Rose Society, but still always double check with local rosarians on a rose's positives and negatives."

'Abraham Darby'	David Austin Shrub	1990
'Belinda's Dream'	Shrub	1988
'Carefree Beauty'	Floribunda	1977
Chestnut rose (*Rosa roxburghii*)	Species	Pre-1814
'Gold Medal'	Grandiflora	1982
'Heritage'	David Austin Shrub	1984
'Louis Phillipe'	China	1834
'Maitland White'	Noisette	Unknown
'Mr. Lincoln'	Hybrid Tea	1964
'Mutabilis'	China	1894
'Nur Mahal'	Hybrid Musk	1923
'Old Blush'	China	1752
'Othello'	David Austin Shrub	1990
'Pink Pet'	Polyantha	1928
'Prosperity'	Hybrid Musk	1919
'Smith's Parish'	Tea	Unknown
'Sombreuil'	Climbing Tea	1850
'Spice'	Tea	Unknown
'St. David'	China	Unknown

ROSES THAT CLIMB AND RAMBLE

There is nothing so lovely as roses overhead. An arbor or a covered gate can change the whole feeling of a landscape and give an extra, richer dimension to any garden. Such gardens seem to envelop visitors in "rooms" of flowers.

Most of the roses on this list will not reach maturity until their second or third year, after which you will need to prune to keep them neat. They will probably bloom before that, though not as much or as often as when they are thoroughly established. The roses on this list will reach 12 feet or more, so give them plenty of room and solid support. All are repeat bloomers except those with asterisks; they bloom only in the spring.

'America'	Climber	1976
'Alachua Red Climber'	Found	Unknown
'Ballerina'	Hybrid Musk	1937
'Blossomtime'	Climber	1951
'Buff Beauty'	Hybrid Musk	1939
'Cecile Brunner, Climbing'	Climbing Polyantha	1894
'Clair Matin'	Climber	1963
'Cocktail'	Floribunda	1957
'Dortmund'	Kordesii	1955
'Felicia'	Hybrid Musk	1928
'Lamarque'	Noisette	1830
'Marechal Neil'	Climber	1864
'Mermaid'	Hybrid Bracteata	1918
'Pink Perpetue'	Climber	1965
'Prosperity'	Hybrid Musk	1919
'Rev d'Or'	Noisette	1869
'Rosarium Ueteresen'	Climber	1977
'Royal Sunset'	Climber	1960
'Seven Sisters'*	Hybrid Multiflora	1817
'Souvenir de la Malmaison'	Climbing Bourbon	1843
'White Lady Banks' * (*Rosa banksia*)	Species	1807
'Wind Chimes'	Hybrid Musk	1949
'Yellow Lady Banks'* (*Rosa banksia* 'Lutea')	Species	1824

GREAT PILLAR ROSES

These are climbing roses that won't overrun your garden with their vigor. They grow from 7 to 12 feet and can be trained on pillars, fences, trellises, and other supports. Pillar roses are perfect for vertical accent in a small garden or as a less dominant feature in a large garden.

As you wrap or braid the canes around their support, make every effort to train them horizontally. They will produce many more flowers if you do. Canes that grow straight up tend to bloom only at the top.

You will find differences among these selections that only local growers can teach you about, so join or form a rose group in your area or subscribe to their newsletter if you are too far away to get to meetings. For example, 'New Dawn' thrives for grower Valerie Oppenheim in Gainesville, but in the Tampa area rosarian Trish Montesano finds that it is very slow to become established (after a year, it starts to flourish).

'Aloha'	Climbing Hybrid Tea	1949
'Altissimo'	Large-flowered climber	1966
'Alister Stella Grey'	Noisette	1894
'Belinda'	Hybrid Musk	1936
'Buff Beauty'	Hybrid Musk	1939
'Celine Forestier'	Noisette	1858
'Champney Pink Cluster'	Noisette	1811
'Climbing Pinkie'	Climbing Polyantha	1952
'Don Juan'	Large-flowered Climber	1958
'Erfurt'	Hybrid Musk	1939
'Maggie'	Found Bourbon	Unknown
'New Dawn'	Large-flowered Climber	1930
'Pinata'	Climber	1978
'Prosperity'	Hybrid Musk	1919
'Sea Foam'	Shrub	1964
'Sombreuil'	Climbing Tea	1850
'Vanity'	Hybrid Musk	1920

ROSES WITH DISEASE RESISTANCE

Florida summers are notorious for their ideal black spot conditions. It is possible for a rose variety to be highly resistant to such diseases in its youth but lose that resistance with maturity. Of all the roses, however, the following are most likely to resist or withstand rose diseases.

'Altissimo'	Large-flowered Climber	1966
'Ballerina'	Hybrid Musk	1937
'Belinda's Dream'	Shrub	1988
Bermuda mystery roses	See previous list	
'Bonica '82'	Shrub	1981
'Cecile Brunner'	Climbing Polyantha	1881
'Don Juan'	Large-flowered Climber	1958
'Dortmund'	Kordesii	1955
'Iceberg'	Floribunda	1958
'Korresia (Sunsprite)'	Floribunda	1974
'Louis Philippe'	China	1834
'Mary Manners'	Hybrid Rugosa	1970
'Mermaid'	Hybrid Bracteata	1918
'Pascali'	Hybrid Tea	1963
'Pink Pet, Caldwell's Pink'	Found Polyantha	1928
'The Fairy'	Polyantha	1932
Wild or Macartney rose (*Rosa bracteata*)	Species	1793

"All of the Teas and Chinas of any variety tend to be disease resistant, especially to black spot. I would recommend 'Belinda's Dream' more than practically any other rose for its resistance. And all of the Bermuda mystery roses are remarkable for this trait. I grow most of mine on Fortuniana rootstocks. Some are safe on their own roots, but some will start out well and then die out after four or five years, so I don't recommend any for their own rootstocks until I've grown them for ten years that way."
—Dr. Malcolm Manners, professor of citrus and horticulture, Florida Southern College, Lakeland.

ROSES FOR CONTAINERS

With regular watering and proper maintenance, just about any rose can be grown in a container. The following are good selections for pots because they have a nice form and aren't too large.

Roses in pots have some great advantages over those in the ground. First, you have more control of soil and drainage. You can move roses into and out of the spotlight when they are in or out of bloom. And, if you move to a different house, your roses are ready to go along! On the other hand, nature will not cover any neglect in container growing. You must be there to water—and that can be every day in hot, dry weather.

LC: Many rosarians who have swimming pools tell me that the roses growing in pots around the pool are not as troubled by black spot and other foliage diseases, perhaps because of the chlorine evaporating from the pool.

'Anisley Dickson'	Floribunda	1983
'Ballerina'	Hybrid Musk	1937
'Bonica'	Shrub	1981
'Cecile Brunner'	China	1880
'Galaxy'	Miniature	1980
'Green Ice'	Miniature	1971
'Hannah Gordon'	Floribunda	1983
'Kathy'	Miniature	1970
'Lavender Jewel'	Miniature	1978
'Mutabilis'	China	1894
'Peace'	Hybrid Tea	1945
'Perfume Delight'	Hybrid Tea	1973
'Popcorn'	Miniature	1973
'Precious Platinum'	Hybrid Tea	1974
'Sea Foam'	Shrub	1964
'Sexy Rexy'	Floribunda	1984
'Starina'	Miniature	1965
'The Fairy'	Polyantha	1932

"It is a good idea to fertilize container roses often with mild liquid fertilizers such as fish emulsion or liquid seaweed, because it can be difficult to deal with any buildup of solid fertilizer ingredients. If the container is small, you can always change the soil, but if it's large, you may even want to take a soil test if your roses seem to have trouble." —Liz Druitt, author, *The Organic Rose Garden.*

ROSES THAT MAKE GOOD HEDGES

Why have an evergreen hedge when you can have an ever-blooming one? A hedge of roses of all one variety is a stunning landscape feature. Rose hedges with mixed varieties are less formal and have less visual impact, but they are more colorful and fun. Tea and China roses are excellent hedge plants in Florida, as are polyanthas and Hybrid Musks.

While training a rose hedge, prune the plants a little harder the first two or three years, then just keep them shaped as you would any other hedge. Rose bushes tend to grow taller in

Florida than most other places, and some grow taller the farther south they grow in the state. Trimming 6 weeks before the first spring bloom and again in the early fall will create two massive displays a year and a few in-between flushes of bloom.

Low (2 to 4 feet)

'Ballerina'	Hybrid Musk	1937
'China Doll'	Polyantha	1946
'Green Ice'	Miniature	1971
'Keepsake'	Hybrid Tea	1980
'Nastarana'	Noisette	1879
'Penelope'	Hybrid Musk	1924
'Regenberg'	Floribunda	1979
'Stanwell Perpetual'	Scotch	1838
'Starina'	Miniature	1965
'The Fairy'	Polyantha	1932

Medium (4 to 6 feet)

'Belinda'	Hybrid Musk	1936
'Bonica'	Shrub	1981
'Carefree Wonder'	Meidiland	1990
'First Light'	Shrub	1998
'Golden Wings'	Shrub	1956
'Jean Bach Sisley'	China	1889
'La Marne'	Polyantha	1915
'Madame Berleieu'	Tea	1899
'Marie van Houtte'	Tea	1871
'Mary Manners'	Hybrid Rugosa	1970
'Mons. Tillier'	Tea	1891
'Old Blush'	China	1752
'Peace'	Hybrid Tea	1945
'Penelope'	Hybrid Musk	1924
'Precious Platinum'	Hybrid Tea	1974
Rosa rugosa rubra	Species	Unknown

Large (6 to 8 feet)

'Carefree Beauty'	Shrub	1977
'Dortmund'	Kordesii climber	1955
'Mrs. B.R. Cant'	Tea	1901
'Mutabilis'	China	Pre-1894
'Sarah Van Fleet'	Rugosa	1926
'Souvenir de la Malmaison'	Bourbon	1843

 "Many of the antique roses can be made into hedges. 'Old Blush' makes a 6-foot barrier hedge. 'Pink Pet' makes a small hedge good to line a driveway or sidewalk." —Peggy Coven, owner, Old Fashioned Bloomers, Howey-in-the-Hills.

ROSES FOR EXHIBITION

For some growers this is a most important list, for to them showing is as much fun as growing. Anyone interested in exhibiting roses should certainly join a rose society first and visit a show or two with pen in hand to mark personal favorite varieties. The following list includes the favorite exhibition roses of Allen and Virginia Woking, master gardeners who live and grow their roses in Tampa.

'Alec's Red'	Hybrid Tea	1970
'Anisley Dickson'	Floribunda	1983
'Anne Harkness'	Floribunda	1980
'Blue Moon'	Hybrid Tea	1964
'Bride's Dream'	Hybrid Tea	1986
'Christian Dior'	Hybrid Tea	1958
'Color Magic'	Hybrid Tea	1978
'Confidence'	Hybrid Tea	1951
'Crystalline'	Hybrid Tea	1987
'Dearest'	Floribunda	1960
'Desert Peace'	Hybrid Tea	1992
'Double Delight'	Hybrid Tea	1977
'Dublin'	Hybrid Tea	1983
'Elina'	Hybrid Tea	1985
'Elizabeth Taylor'	Hybrid Tea	1985
'Europeana'	Floribunda	1963
'Fairhope'	Miniature	1989
'First Edition'	Floribunda	1976
'Folklore'	Hybrid Tea	1977
'Grace de Monaco'	Hybrid Tea	1956
'Hannah Gordon'	Floribunda	1983
'Hot Tamale'	Miniature	1994
'Iceberg'	Floribunda	1958
'Irresistible'	Miniature	1989
'Jean Kenneally'	Miniature	1984
'Keepsake'	Hybrid Tea	1980
'Kristin'	Miniature	1993
'Lynette'	Hybrid Tea	1985
'Minnie Pearl'	Miniature	1982
'Miss All American Beauty'	Hybrid Tea	1965
'Miss Flippins'	Miniature	1996
'Olympiad'	Hybrid Tea	1982
'Peace'	Hybrid Tea	1945
'Pierrine'	Miniature	1988
'Pink Favorite'	Hybrid Tea	1956
'Playboy'	Floribunda	1976
'Playgirl'	Floribunda	1986
'Precious Platinum'	Hybrid Tea	1974
'Princess Margaret of England'	Hybrid Tea	1968
'Princesse de Monaco'	Hybrid Tea	1981
'Pristine'	Hybrid Tea	1978
'Red Beauty'	Miniature	1981

'Royal Highness'	Hybrid Tea	1962
'Sexy Rexy'	Floribunda	1984
'Sheer Bliss'	Hybrid Tea	1987
'Showbiz'	Floribunda	1981
'Starina'	Miniature	1965
'St. Patrick'	Hybrid Tea	1996
'Touch of Class'	Hybrid Tea	1984
'Uncle Joe'	Hybrid Tea	1972

"'Touch of Class' is the classic example of good form. The judge will be looking for roses with high centers, petals open one-half to two-thirds of the way, good substance, no defects, balance, and proportion. That latter means the stem should be neither too long nor too short for the bloom. Condition them well in tepid water and then keep them in a cooler at 38 to 40 degrees for a few hours to a few days until just before the show. Knowing the cultivar and how quickly it will open is very important. Cover each bud with a baggie so they won't bruise in transit." —Dr. Rubert Prevatt, professor, Florida Southern College; ARS lifetime judge and consulting rosarian.

A SAMPLER OF ROSES BY COLOR

If your first priority is color, use this list to help you select some good Florida roses. Not all the roses on this list are included in the preceding lists.

Red

Red roses, the florist's specialty, seem to fill a deep emotional need for many people. Red is the most popular color of roses with men. They are the classic gift to express every sentiment from true love to deep sympathy. The following list should satisfy all cravings. These varieties are true reds—no dark pinks or questionable mauves—and they are also good garden varieties for Florida. If you are blending them for a precise color pattern, remember that most floral reds, even the most true, often have a touch of either orange or lavender and choose accordingly.

'Alec's Red'	Hybrid Tea	1970
'Altissimo'	Large-flowered Climber	1966
'American Home'	Hybrid Tea	1960
'Beauty Secret'	Miniature	1965
'Christian Dior'	Hybrid Tea	1958
'Chrysler Imperial'	Hybrid Tea	1952
'Cramoisi Superieur'	China	1832
'Don Juan'	Large-flowered Climber	1958
'Dortmund'	Kordesii	1955
'Dublin'	Hybrid Tea	1983
'Dwarfking'	Miniature	1957
'Europeana'	Floribunda	1963
'Fisherman's Friend'	Shrub	1987
'Galax'	Miniature	1980
'Kardinal'	Hybrid Tea	1986
'Kenney's Rose'	Hybrid Tea	1996
'Martha Gonzales'	China	Unknown
'Mr. Lincoln'	Hybrid Tea	1964

Red Roses (*continued*)

'Mother's Value'	Hybrid Tea	1989
'Oklahoma'	Hybrid Tea	1964
'Olympiad'	Hybrid Tea	1982
'Precious Platinum'	Hybrid Tea	1974
'Red Bird'	Hybrid Tea	1957
'Samantha'	Hybrid Tea	1984
'Scarlet Knight, Samurai'	Grandiflora	1968
'Uncle Joe'	Hybrid Tea	1972

Orange to Coral

Orange is one of those colors that gardeners either love or hate; rarely is there any in-between. These include shades of orange that you might define as coral or apricot.

'America'	Climber	1976
'Artistry'	Hybrid Tea	1997
'Just Joey'	Hybrid Tea	1973
'Sonia'	Grandiflora	1973
'Starina'	Miniature	1965
'Tropicana'	Hybrid Tea	1964

Pink or Pink Blend

There are probably more pink roses than any other color. They vary from the faintest pink of 'Champney's Pink Cluster' to the deep rose pink of 'Paul Neyron' and many blends in between. When selecting color, try to see at least a photo and preferably a blooming bush to be sure—even then the pinks can change from day to day on some like 'Mutabilis'. The Chinas tend to get more intense as they mature. This list is merely a starting place.

'Anisley Dickson'	Floribunda	1983
'Belinda'	Hybrid Musk	1936
'Belinda's Dream'	Shrub	1988
'Carefree Wonder'	Meidiland	1990
'Cecile Brunner'	China	1880
'Dearest'	Floribunda	1960
'Champney's Pink Cluster'	Noisette	1811
'First Light'	Shrub	1998
'Hannah Gordon'	Floribunda	1983
'Keepsake'	Hybrid Tea	1980
'Mutabilis'	China	1894
'Old Blush'	China	1752
'Paul Neyron'	Hybrid Perpetual	1869
'Pink Perpetue'	Climber	1965
'Pink Pet'	Polyantha	1928
'Pink Favorite'	Hybrid Tea	1956
'Queen Elizabeth'	Grandiflora	1955
'Regenberg'	Floribunda	1979
'Royal Highness'	Hybrid Tea	1962
'Secret'	Hybrid Tea	1993

'Sexy Rexy'	Floribunda	1984
'Stanwell Perpetual'	Scotch	1838
'Sunset Celebration'	Hybrid Tea	1998

White or White Blend

White roses, no matter if they include a touch of yellow, red, or pink, will fit into any garden color scheme. They tend to be more delicate in the vase, but that very delicacy makes them most special.

'Ducher'	China	1869
'Fortuniana'	Misc. OGR	1850
'Iceberg'	Floribunda	1958
'Lamarque'	Noisette	1830
'Mary Manners'	Hybrid Rugosa	1970
'Nastarana'	Noisette	1879
'Pascali'	Hybrid Tea	1963
'Polar Star (Polarstern)'	Hybrid Tea	1992
'Prosperity'	Hybrid Musk	1919
'Sea Foam'	Shrub	1964
'Simplex'	Miniature	1961
'Sombreuil'	Climbing Tea	1850
'Souvenir de la Malmaison'	Bourbon	1843
'White Masterpiece'	Hybrid Tea	1969
'White Lady Banks' (*Rosa banksia*)	Species	1807
Wild or Macartney rose (*Rosa bracteata*)	Species	1793

Yellow or Yellow Blend

For those who want to blend colors to a certain plan, here are a few good yellows for Florida. Add your own favorites as you find them.

'Anne Harkness'	Floribunda	1980
'Buff Beauty'	Shrub	1922
'Celine Forestier'	Noisette	1858
'Desert Peace'	Hybrid Tea	1992
'Elina'	Hybrid Tea	1985
'Fortune's Double Yellow'	Misc. OGR	1845
'Golden Wings'	Shrub	1956
'Graham Thomas'	Shrub	1983
'Isabella Sprunt'	Tea	1855
'Lemarque'	Noisette	1830
'Marchal Neil'	Noisette	1864
'Mermaid'	Hybrid Bracteata	1918
'Midas Touch'	Floribunda	1992
'Mrs. Dudley Cross'	Tea	1907
'Peace'	Hybrid Tea	1945
'Penelope'	Hybrid Musk	1924
'Reve d'Or'	Noisette	1869
'Sun Flare'	Floribunda	1981
'Sunsprite (Korresia)'	Floribunda	1974
'Yellow Lady Banks' (*Rosa banksiae* 'Lutea')	Species	1824

Special Colors

A few roses have unusual color combinations, and sometimes colors change as the rose ages. This list will get you started if you are looking for roses that offer an extraordinary mix.

'Angel Face'	Floribunda	Pink/lavender	1969
'Anna Oliver'	Tea	Cream/buff/pale pink	1872
'Brigadoon'	Hybrid Tea	White/coral/pink	1992
'Double Delight'	Hybrid Tea	White/ruby edge	1977
'Mutabilis'	China	Yellow/pink/crimson	Pre-1896
'Perle d'Or'	Polyantha	Apricot/pink	1884
'Pinata'	Climber	Yellow/scarlet	1978
'Red Gold'	Floribunda	Yellow/edged in red	1971
'Folklore'	Hybrid Tea	Orange/pink/yellow	1977
'Stars 'n' Stripes'	Miniature	Crimson/white stripes	1976

PERENNIALS

Most of us who leave traditional northern gardens think at first that there aren't many perennials in Florida because some of our old favorites like bearded iris and peonies don't grow here. But it will take us decades to discover all the native and other treasures that thrive here. Many perennials from other regions and countries grow well here, and many of our native "weeds" make spectacular garden flowers. Even native grasses such as sea oats and blue-eyed grass are becoming sought-after items for gardens. "Perennials are just starting to come of age here. We're going to be seeing and using many more of them because of the water situation," says Richard White, a landscape contractor in Brandon.

In relatively "seasonless" Florida, the ever-changing nature of perennials provides month-to-month interest that gardeners can anticipate and relish. "Perennials should be a part of every Florida landscape," says Sydney Park Brown, Extension Agent in Hillsborough County (Tampa). "Their diverse textures and flowers enrich a garden in ways that shrubbery cannot, and the activity of the butterflies and hummingbirds they attract brings movement and excitement to a yard."

The lists in this chapter also include bulbs and ornamental grasses that we treat as perennials. Many of the plants listed as perennials in central and south Florida will grow as annuals in north Florida until frost. There isn't room to make any list complete, so pencil in your own additions as you discover them.

Special thanks to Sue Watkins of Tallahassee Nurseries for her review of these lists, and to Russell Adams of Gainesville Tree Farm for his guidance through the amazing maze of gingers. Sue believes that so many plants are new to the marketplace that it is nearly impossible for one person to know them all, let alone list them. So use these lists as a start.

SELECTING AND GROWING PERENNIALS IN FLORIDA

Most perennials live for many years, so you will want to plan carefully when selecting and planting them. Some people keep them in pots and move the pots around for a few weeks to see where the plants seem happiest before planting. Fortunately, even after planting, most perennials are still relatively easy to move if you should make a mistake. Exceptions include perennials that can spread beyond control and those with a very large root or bulb such as crinum lilies and four-o'clocks.

POINTERS FOR SELECTING PERENNIALS

- *Choose plants that are adapted to the site*—that is, plants that tolerate sun for sunny spots, and shade-tolerant plants for shady spots. The same is true for a plant's need for moisture. Group those that need lots of water away from those that don't like too much.
- *Choose so that you will have something blooming in each season.*
- *Select plants for an interesting range of heights, colors, and textures.* Artful combinations come with time and experience. Visit other gardens to learn about plants and get ideas for combinations, and open your mind to new possibilities. Magazines are a good source of inspiration, but check carefully on plants you see in pictures. You may have to make Florida substitutions.
- *Learn as much about each plant as you can.* Good sources are the Extension Service, books (especially ones written for Florida), local plant societies, master gardeners, local TV or radio programs, garden centers, and public gardens. Often the key to success is choosing a particular named selection. Good examples of this on our lists are the hostas and lilies. Many of the new discoveries are made by gardeners who rarely leave any flower garden without a start of something "new" in hand. We recommend some books in the introduction. You can study catalogs, but watch carefully for plants that tolerate the hot, humid climate or endless summer of our zones 8 to 11.

HOW-TO LIST FOR GROWING PERENNIALS SUCCESSFULLY

- *Test the soil for pH and nutrient content.* This will help you know how much (or how little) to fertilize.
- *Buy locally whenever possible, or get divisions from other gardeners.* When plant shopping, ask about specific selections for your locale. Always buy perennials from an accountable source to be sure you get good plants that are properly labeled, and make a record in your garden notebook or on a calendar so when you have a great success, you can get or recommend the same selection. Watch especially for community plant sales like those held at the University of South Florida in Tampa twice every year.
- *Prepare the soil well.* Mix in up to 50 percent composted organic matter, tilling or working it in to a depth of at least 8 inches.
- *Plant at the proper time.* Generally, the best time to plant perennials is in the fall. Although container-grown (not bare-root) plants purchased at a nursery can be set out anytime, planting in fall gives the plants a chance to grow roots before the spring, when furious new growth puts a big demand on the root system. This is especially true in north Florida. In warmer parts of the state, growth may be steadier throughout the year, but the demand on the root system is always greatest in spring and summer because of the heat. Planting ahead of the prime growing season gives plants good time to spread their roots in a new location.
- *Mulch well.* But be sure not to pile mulch up near the stem of the plants.
- *Water as needed, especially until established.* New plants need regular watering, no matter how drought tolerant they will eventually be.
- *Fertilize at planting and again as needed.* Use a controlled-release plant food.
- *Prune plants if needed.* Cutting flowers for bouquets is a natural way to do this.
- *Remove spent blossoms (deadheads) as needed*, especially for daylilies, coreopsis, and others that set seed or bloom for a long time.

Divide perennials that are diminished by crowding. Some perennials such as daylilies and iris don't bloom well if too crowded. Others just need dividing to keep them in bounds or from getting too massive.

"To root difficult cuttings, I sink a 3-inch clay pot with a cork in the hole into a larger, say 8-inch, clay pot full of damp but not soggy sterile builder's sand. Then I use a small electric fish tank aerator, cost about $5, and set it beside the pots with the plastic tubing leading over the top and down into the sand where the air stone is buried. After sticking in the cuttings (12 to 15), I put water in the center pot and let it seep through the clay slowly to the cuttings in the sand, adding more as needed. The aerator plugs in and keeps air moving through the sand. Cover both pots and cuttings with a clear plastic saucer or bag, but leave it loose enough to let in air as needed." —Barry Schwartz, plant collector and active member of the Aroid Club of Tampa, Lutz.

PERENNIALS WITH VERTICAL, SPIKE FLOWERS

Mixing flowers with contrasting line and form can add as much interest to the garden as the different shapes and textures of foliage. The vertical spikes of flowers are often, but not always, on the tallest plants. They lead the eye upward to the taller plants or trees, the vista, or the glorious Florida skies. Many also make excellent cut flowers because they are almost a bouquet on a single stem.

Fragrant callisia (*Callisia fragrans*)	S
Costus (*Costus* spp.)	N, C, S
Blue ginger (*Dichorisandra thyrsiflora*)	C, S
Joe-Pye weed (*Eupatorium purpureum*)	N
Gladiolus hybrids	N, C, S
Lobster claw (*Heliconia* spp.)	C, S
Jacobinia (*Justicia* spp.)	N
Gayfeather or blazing star (*Liatris spicata*)	N, C, S
Cardinal flower (*Lobelia cardinalis*)	N, C, S
Cat whiskers (*Orthosiphon stamineus*)	C, S
Nun's orchid (*Phaius tankervilliae*)	C, S
False dragonhead (*Physostegia virginiana*)	N, C, S
Tuberose (*Polianthes tuberosa*)	N, C, S
Salvia (*Salvia coccinea, S. leucantha, S. longispicata × farenace, S. madrensis, S. uligonosa*)	N, C, S
Goldenrod (*Solidago* spp.)	N, C, S
Upright verbena (*Verbena bonariensis*)	N, C, S
Veronica (*Veronica spicata, V. longifolia*)	N, C
Pinecone ginger (*Zingiber zerumbet*)	N, C, S

"The lush, informal style of the cottage garden, so popular with English Victorians during the Industrial Revolution, is coming into style again even in Florida. Cottage gardens get their charm from the unique color and plant combinations and make an ideal break from plain green lawns and boring hedges." —Jon George, landscape designer and owner, The Cottage Gardener, Gainesville.

PERENNIALS FOR THE SHADE

It is important to notice how much the shade and sun patterns change with the seasons, since the sun comes at a different angle in winter. And because trees grow so quickly here, shade spreads farther into the sunny areas every year. Luckily, many plants that like full sun elsewhere appreciate shade for part of the day, especially midafternoon, in Florida. Plant the winter bloomers near the deciduous trees and shrubs. Start your plants in what you think is the most likely place. Move them while they are small if they don't thrive. If they do, take cuttings or divisions to new and sunnier locations should the shade deepen. If you are faced with a yard entirely shaded, check the other chapters for more lists of plants for shade.

Spiny bear's-breech (*Acanthus spinosissimus*)	N
Achimenes (*Achimenes* spp.)	N
Lily-of-the-Nile (*Agapanthus africanus*)	N, C, S
Bugleweed (*Ajuga reptans*)	N, C, S
Variegated alpinia (*Alpinia zerumbet variegata*)	N, C, S
Bluestar (*Amsonia tabernaemontana*)	N
Japanese anemone (*Anemone* hybrids)	N
Angelonia (*Angelonia angustifolia*)	C, S
Native columbine (*Aquilegia canadensis*)	N, C
Astilbes (*Astilbe* spp.)	N
Ganges primrose (*Asystasia gangetica*)	C, S
Philippine violet (*Barleria cristata*)	N, C, S
Begonias (*Begonia* spp.)	C, S
Chinese ground orchid (*Bletilla striata*)	N, C, S
Caladiums (*Caladium* spp. and hybrids)	C, S
Northern sea oats (*Chasmanthium latifolium*)	N, C, S
Clerodendron (*Clerodendron paniculata*)	N, C, S
Kaffir lily (*Clivia miniata*)	S
Crossandra (*Crossandra infundibuliformis*)	C, S
Fern-leaf bleeding heart (*Dicentra eximia*)	N, C
Bleeding heart (*Dicentra spectabilis*)	N
Sweet woodruff (*Galium odoratum*)	N
Blood lily (*Haemanthus multiflorus*)	N, C, S
Ginger (*Hedychium* spp., *Costus* spp.)	N, C, S
Hostas (*Hosta* spp.)	N, C
Polka dot plant (*Hypoestes phyllostachya*)	C, S
Indigo (*Indigofera decora*)	N, C, S
Shrimp plant (*Justicia brandegeana*)	N
Jacobinia (*Justicia carnea*)	N
Peacock ginger (*Kaempferia* spp.)	N, C, S
Cardinal flower (*Lobelia cardinalis*)	N, C, S
Big blue lobelia (*Lobelia siphilitica*)	N
Creeping Jenny (*Lysimachia* 'Aurea', *L.* 'Eco Dark Satin')	N, C
Four-o'clock (*Mirabilis jalapa*)	N, C, S
Walking iris (*Neomerica* spp.)	C, S
Cardinal's spear (*Odontonema strictum*)	N, C, S
Cat whiskers (*Orthosiphon stamineus*)	C, S
Cardinal's guard (*Pachystachys coccinea*)	C, S
Nun's orchid (*Phaius tankervilliae*)	C, S

Cardinal
flower

Blue phlox (*Phlox divaricata*)	N, C
Salvia (*Salvia guaranitica, S. madrensis, S. vanhouttii*)	N, C, S
Strawberry geranium (*Saxifraga stolonifera*)	N, C, S
Purple queen, purple heart (*Setcreasea pallida*)	N, C, S
Strobilanthes (*Strobilanthes dyeranus*)	N, C, S
Spiderwort (*Tradescantia ohiensis*)	N, C, S
Toad lily (*Tricyrtis* spp.)	N

PERENNIALS WITH VARIEGATED OR COLORED FOLIAGE

Florida offers a rich array of perennials with variegated or colored foliage, from groundcovers such as ajuga and wandering Jew to tall and shrublike plants. Many are houseplants that can grow happily outside in the nearly frost-free habitat of south Florida. Use these as accents.

Century plant (*Agave americana*)	N, C, S
Chinese evergreen (*Aglaonema* spp.)	S
Bugleweed (*Ajuga reptans*)	N, C, S
Joseph's coat (*Amaranthus tricolor*)	C, S
Zebra plant (*Aphelandra squarrosa*)	C, S
Cast-iron plant (*Aspidistra elatior* 'Milky Way')	N, C, S
Begonias (*Begonia*, red-leafed types B. 'Rex', B. 'Iron Cross')	C, S
Caladium (*Caladium* spp.)	C, S
Calathea (*Calathea* spp.)	C, S
Canna (*Canna* 'Stuttgartt')	N, C, S
Spider plant (*Chlorophytum comosum*)	C, S
Black leafed taro (*Colocasia esculenta* 'Illustris')	C, S
Ti plant (*Cordyline terminalis*)	C, S
Dumb cane (*Dieffenbachia* spp. and hybrids)	S
Dracaena (*Dracaena* spp.)	C, S
Nerve plant (*Fittonia varschaffeitii*)	S
False roselle (*Hibiscus acetosella*)	N, C
Hostas (*Hosta* spp.)	N, C
Polka-dot plant (*Hypoestes phyllostachya*)	C, S
Blood leaf (*Iresine lindennii*)	C, S
Cardinal flower (*Lobelia cardinalis* 'Dark Crusade')	N
Golden creeping Jenny (*Lysimachia nummularia* 'aurea')	N
Prayer plant (*Maranta* spp.)	C, S
Ornamental banana (*Musa* spp.)	C, S
Peperomia (*Peperomia glabella, P. obtusifolia*)	C, S
Plectranthus (*Plectranthus* spp.)	C, S
Oyster plant (*Rhoeo spathacea*)	C, S
Strawberry geranium (*Saxifraga stolonifera*)	N, C
Purple queen or purple heart (*Setcreasea pallida* 'Purple queen')	N, C, S
Persian shield (*Strobilanthes dyeranus*)	N, C
Nephthytis (*Syngonium podophyllum*)	C, S
Wandering Jew (*Zebrina pendula*)	C, S
Pinecone ginger (*Zingiber zerumbet* 'Variegata')	C, S
Penstemon (*Penstemon* spp. 'Husker Red')	N

PERENNIALS NATIVE TO FLORIDA

Native plants are gaining in popularity as folks discover how many of our indigenous plants can get by with little water or other care. Interestingly, a few of our most popular native perennials, such as purple coneflower, butterfly weed, and blanket flower, have long been common in the nursery trade. However, today's emphasis on water conservation (coupled with advancements in the science of plant propagation) make it possible for us to also grow many other lesser-known natives in our gardens. In the wild, these plants may have showy blossoms or some other desirable characteristic that first catches the attention of a native-plant enthusiast. Although "wild," these natives are usually just as worthy as well-known exotics (imported species) such as jacobinia and caladiums. In the garden, native plants often abound in improved size and show because garden conditions are often better than those in the wild.

An interesting garden will mix both natives and exotics in a wise use. If given a place in your yard similar to the conditions where they thrive in the wild, most of these natives will require little maintenance, though they will do even better with occasional water and fertilizer. A few of the plants listed below are not original to the state but were introduced long ago and have made themselves at home by naturalizing. We have tried not to include any that have naturalized to the point of becoming noxious weeds.

Wild century plant (*Agave neglecta*)	S
Lazy daisy (*Aphanostephus skirrhobasis*)	N, C, S
Green dragon (*Arisaema dracontium*)	N, C
Jack-in-the-pulpit (*Arisaema triphyllum*)	N
Swamp milkweed (*Asclepias incarnata*)	N, C, S
Butterfly weed (*Asclepias tuberosa*)	N, C, S
Climbing aster (*Aster carolinianus*)	N, C, S
Sea oxeye daisy (*Borrichia frutescens*)	N, C, S
Golden canna (*Canna flaccida*)	N, C, S
Lanceleaf tickseed (*Coreopsis lanceolata*)	N, C, S
Swamp coreopsis (*Coreopsis nudata*)	N
Swamp lily (*Crinum americanum*)	N, C, S
Twinflower (*Dyschoriste oblongafolia*)	N, C, S
Purple coneflower (*Echinacea purpurea*)	N, C
Blue ageratum (*Eupatorium incarnatum*)	N
Blanket flower (*Gaillardia pulchella*)	N, C, S
Firebush (*Hamelia patens*)	N
Sneezeweed (*Helenium autumnale*)	N, C
Sunflower (*Helianthus angustifolius*)	N, C, S
Beach sunflower (*Helianthus debilis*)	N, C, S
Swamp sunflower (*Helianthus simulans*)	N
Texas star (*Hibiscus coccineus*)	N, C
Rose mallow, swamp mallow (*Hibiscus moscheutos*)	N, C, S
Spider lily (*Hymenocallis crassifolia*)	N, C
Blue flag iris (*Iris hexagona*)	N, C, S
Yellow flag (*Iris pseudacorus*)	N, C
Lantana (*Lantana camara*)	N, C, S
Blazing star (*Liatris spicata*)	N, C, S
Catesby lily (*Lilium catesbaei*)	N, C, S
Cardinal flower (*Lobelia cardinalis*)	N, C, S

Sneezeweed

Lupine (*Lupinus diffusus*)	N, C, S
Beebalm (*Monarda fistulosa*)	N, C
Dotted horsemint (*Monarda punctata*)	N, C
Blue phlox (*Phlox divaricata*)	N, C
False dragon's head (*Physostegia virginiana*)	N, C
Meadow beauty (*Rhexia* spp.)	N, C, S
Orange coneflower (*Rudbeckia fulgida*)	N, C
Black-eyed Susan (*Rudbeckia hirta*)	N, C, S
Marsh pinks (*Sabatia dodecandra*)	N, C
Azure sage (*Salvia azurea*)	N, C, S
Tropical sage (*Salvia coccinea*)	N, C, S
Sea purslane (*Sesuvium portulacastrum*)	N, C, S
Goldenrod (*Solidago* spp.)	N, C, S
Stoke's aster (*Stokesia laevis*)	N, C, S
Spiderwort (*Tradescantia oniensis*)	N, C, S
Vervain (*Verbena bonariensis*)	N
Beach verbena (*Verbena maritima*)	N, C, S
Tampa vervain (*Verbena tampensis, Glandularia tampensis*)	N, C, S
Ironweed (*Vernonia angustifolia*)	N, C
Florida violet (*Viola floridana*)	N, C, S
Bear grass (*Yucca filamentosa*)	N, C, S
Atamasco lily (*Zephyranthes atamasco*)	N, C, S

LILIES FOR FLORIDA

Lilies benefit from the same fertilizer as hostas and also semishade, ideally in the afternoon. Bruce Cavey, manager of the Plant Shoppe in Gainesville, plants them in pots sunk into the ground because of problems with squirrels, moles, and voles, and also surrounds the bulbs (in the ground) with sharp gravel and pottery shards for extra protection. He feeds them monthly as well to replenish energy for next year's blooms and leaves them in the ground until they need dividing. Some growers in central and south Florida succeed with lilies by digging and storing the bulbs through the summer and replanting in the fall for spring bloom.

Pineapple lily (*Eucomis* spp.)	N, C, S
Leopard lily (*Lachenalia* spp.)	N, C, S
Gold band (*Lilium aureum* 'Gold Band')	N
Madonna lily (*Lilium candidum*)	N, C
Pine lily (*Lilium catesbaei*)	N, C, S
Formosa lily (*Lilium formosanum*)	N
Asiatic lily (*Lilium* hybrids 'Enchantment', 'Connecticut King', 'Sorbet', 'Apollo', 'Corina')	N
Tiger lily (*Lilium lancifolium, L. tigrinum*)	N, C
Easter lily (*Lilium longiflorum*)	N
Philippine lily (*Lilium philippinensis*)	N, C
Regal lily (*Lilium regale*)	N, C, S
Rubrum (*Lilium peciosum rubrum*)	N
Toad lily (*Tricyrtis* spp.)	N, C

Lily

ORNAMENTAL GRASSES FOR FLORIDA

Unlike lawn grasses, ornamental grasses are perennials that have the landscape qualities of a shrub or groundcover. Widely used in Europe for decades, they are just beginning to become widely grown here. Only a few, such as the well-known pampas grass, have been popular here very long. However, gardeners are using ornamental grasses more and more because they are reliable and tolerant of drought. Many are also tolerant of salt.

These grasses vary from a foot tall to 10 feet tall. Some of the giant ones make excellent screens, while the low ones may be used as groundcover. All are an accent when used singlely. Because of their ability to tolerate drought, they are a good choice for large containers in full sun.

All of the grasses will need to be cut back in late winter to remove old, tattered leaves. For the most dense grasses, such as pampas grass, you'll make the job easier with a brush cutter attachment to a string trimmer.

Here are a few of the best grasses for Florida. The ones marked with an asterisk are native.

Sweet flag (*Acorus gramineus*)	N, C
Big bluestem (*Andropogon gerardii*)	N, C
Carex (*Carex morrowii*)	N
Inland sea oats (*Chasmanthium latifolium*)*	N, C, S
Pampas grass (*Cortaderia selloana*)	N, C, S
Palm grass (*Curculigo capitulata*)	C, S
Lemongrass (*Cymbopogon citratus*)	N, C, S
Clump bamboo (*Fargesia murielae*)	N, C
Juncus rush (*Juncus infusus*)	N, C
Variegated miscanthus (*Miscanthus sinensis variegatus*)	N, C
Zebra grass (*Miscanthus sinensis* 'Zebrinus')	N
Muhly grass (*Muhlenbergia capillaris*)*	N, C, S
Fountain grass (*Pennisetum* spp.)	N, C, S
Ribbon grass (*Phalaris arundinacea* var. *picta*)	N, C
Blue-eyed grass (*Sisyrinchium angustfolium*)*	N, C, S
Lop-sided Indian grass (*Sorghastrum secundum angustfolium*)	N, C, S
Smooth cordgrass (*Spartina alterniflora*)*	N, C
Sand cordgrass (*Spartina patens*)*	N, C
Fakahatchee grass (*Tripsacum dactyloides*)*	N, C, S
Florida gama grass (*Tripsacum floridana*)*	N, C, S
Sea oats (*Uniola paniculata*)*	N, C, S
Vetiver (*Vetiveria zizanoides*)	N, C, S

"Shrubs are defined as woody plants of relatively low height, having several stems arising from the base and lacking a single trunk. I challenge the classic interpretation and suggest using native grasses as shrubs—in particular, muhly grass (*Muhlenbergia capillaris*). An attractive grass with spectacular pink-purple plumes a good part of the year, it has proven to be drought and pest resistant while providing the screening or formal lines often looked for in the use of shrubs." —Kathy Beck, Tampa Parks superintendent.

INVASIVE PERENNIALS

Some plants do so well that they can be invasive, but here again the list is different than it would be in other states. Some of these can be used well in a garden, as long as you know to be ruthless and keep them in bounds. You might want to plant some in a sunken pot to control runners and control others by pulling out all unwanted seedlings.

MB: I find little problem with pulling out the many offspring of Madagascar periwinkle, and if I miss some, they only bloom. But the seedlings of black-eyed Susan vine or balsam pear entangle as they grow and can really make a mess. Yet I've seen the former used very well at Kanapaha Gardens in Gainesville. Be aware that St. Augustine grass is also considered a noxious weed, and I often agree, but it is the most popular Florida lawn grass nonetheless. A weed is a plant out of place, and depending on how you use the plants below, they may be a blessing. But warn others when you share these that they can be a curse if undisciplined. Some that are a terrible threat in south Florida can be harmless in north Florida, where freezes cut them back each year. The ones marked with an asterisk are considered noxious weeds, so you may be kinder not to plant them, depending on where you live.

Bugleweed (*Ajuga reptans*)	N, C, S
Ganges primrose (*Asystasia gangetica*)*	C, S
Madagascar periwinkle (*Catharanthus roseus*)*	C, S
Elephant's ears (*Colocasia antiquorum*)	N, C, S
Montebretia (*Crocosmia × crocosmiiflora*)	N, C, S
Tassel flower (*Emilia javanica*)	N, C, S
Pothos (*Epipremnum aureum*)	C, S
False bird-of-paradise (*Heliconia psittacorum*)	S
False roselle (*Hibiscus acetosella*)	N, C
Air plant, life plant (*Kalanchoe* spp.)	C, S
Matchweed (*Lippia nudiflora*)	N, C, S
Plume poppy (*Macleaya microcarpa*)	N, C
Mint (*Mentha* spp.)	N, C, S
Four-o'clock (*Mirabilis jalapa*)	N, C, S
Balsam pear (*Momordica charantia*)	N, C, S
Sword fern (*Nephrolepis* spp.)	N, C, S
Oxalis (*Oxalis* spp.)	N, C, S
Beach grass (*Panicum amarum*)	N, C, S
False dragonhead (*Physostegia virginiana*)	N, C
Oyster plant (*Rhoeo spathacea*)*	C, S
Mexican petunia (*Ruellia* spp.)	C, S
Monkey plant (*Ruellia makoyana*)	N, C, S
Purple queen, purple heart (*Setcreasea pallida*)	N, C, S
Nephthytis (*Syngonium podophyllum*)	C, S
Jewels of Opar (*Talinum paniculatum*)	N, C, S
Spiderwort (*Tradescantia* spp.)	N, C, S
Puncture vine (*Triloobus terrestris*)	N, C, S
Wandering Jew (*Zebrina pendula*)	C, S

PERENNIALS WITH SILVERY FOLIAGE

Perennials with silver, gray, or blue-gray foliage add volumes of subtle color to a planting and ensure the harmony of bright-colored flowers. Some on this list are great year-round. Other silvers are from arid climates and can suffer in Florida's rainforestlike summer, giving us only eight or nine months of outstanding service. But that is about as much as anyone can ask of a plant. For a better chance of longest beauty, put some in clay pots, give them afternoon shade in summer, excellent drainage, good air circulation, mulch between the soil and the foliage, and some protection from pounding rains as under a porch or carport roof. Many of the silver-leaved perennials are especially sensitive to the heat and humidity in summer and may "melt-out" or rot.

Century plant (*Agave americana*)	N, C, S
Bugleweed (*Ajuga reptans* 'Silver Beauty')	N, C, S
Silver chives, corkscrew chives (*Allium senesces glaucum*)	N, C, S
Artemisia (*Artemisia* spp. A. 'Powis Castle', A. 'Silver King')	N, C
Clove pink (*Dianthus caryophyllus*)	N, C
Curry plant (*Helichrysum* spp.)	N, C, S
English lavender (*Lavandula angustifolia*)	N, C, S
Spanish lavender (*Lavandula dentata candicans*)	N, C, S
Plume poppy (*Macleaya microcarpa*)	N, C
Silver horehound (*Marrumbium incanum*)	N, C, S
Catnip (*Nepeta mussinii* 'Dropmore')	N, C, S
Perovskia (*Perovskia atriplicifolia*)	N
Phlomis (*Phlomis fruticosa*)	N
Aluminum plant (*Pilea cadieri*)	S
Plectranthus (*Plectranthus argentata*)	C, S
Rue (*Ruta graveolens*)	N, C, S
Mexican sage (*Salvia leucantha*)	N, C, S
Garden sage (*Salvia officinalis*)	N, C, S
Clary sage (*Salvia sclarea*)	N
Santolina (*Santolina chamaecyparissus*)	N, C, S
Lamb's ears (*Stachys byzantina*)	N, C, S
Silver-leaved tansy (*Tanacetum vulgare*)	N, C, S
Silver-leaved thyme (*Thymus vulgaris argentaeus*)	N, C, S
Silver germander (*Teucrium fruticans*)	N, C, S

PERENNIALS FOR FULL SUN

Most perennials, even those that like shade, can take the Florida sun through the fall, winter, and early spring while the days are short and high temperatures are short lived. But from April until September the sun is intense, increasingly so the farther south you are in the state. The plants that withstand even summer sun are listed here. Soil conditions affect tolerance to sun; plants can usually take more sun in moist, fertile, humusy, well-drained soil. Raised or mounded beds can improve drainage in the rainy summer when it is crucial.

LC: But, as my friend Glenn Morris says, "There is always a plant out there that will make a liar out of you." So, with that in mind, here are some perennials that will take full sun all day long and grow throughout most of the state. In some cases, a whole group of related species, such as the ornamental salvias, is included because so many will work. While there aren't any specific ornamental grasses listed below, look for them as you shop for sun-loving plants; many are extremely tough in the full, blazing sun.

Butterfly
weed

Yarrow (*Achillea* spp.)	N, C
Wormwood (*Artemisia* spp.)	N, C, S
Butterfly weed (*Asclepias tuberosa*)	N, C, S
False indigo (*Baptisia australis*)	N
Snowbank boltonia (*Boltonia asteroides* 'Snowbank')	N
Canna (*Canna* × *generalis*)	N, C, S
Coreopsis (*Coreopsis* spp.)	N, C
Calliopsis (*Calliopsis grandiflora*)	N, C, S
Crocosmia (*Crocosmia* 'Lucifer')	N, C
Mexican heather (*Cuphea* spp. 'Georgia Scarlet')	N, C, S
Cigar plant, Georgia scarlet (*Cuphea micropetala*)	N, C, S
Golden dewdrop (*Duranta repens*)	N, C, S
Purple coneflower (*Echinacea purpurea*)	N, C, S
Hardy ageratum (*Eupatorium coelestinum*)	N, C, S
Joe-Pye weed (*Eupatorium purpureum*)	N
Gaura (*Gaura lindheimeri*)	N, C
Beach sunflower (*Helianthus debilis*)	N, C, S
Daylily (*Hemerocallis* spp.)	N, C, S
Lantana (*Lantana camara*)	N, C, S
Gayfeather, blazing star (*Liatris spicata*)	N, C, S
Patrinia (*Patrinia scabiosifolia*)	N
Russian sage (*Perovskia atriplicifolia*)	N
Plumbago (*Plumbago auriculata*)	C, S
Goldsturm rudbeckia (*Rudbeckia fulgida* 'Goldsturm')	N, C
Rudbeckia (*Rudbeckia maxima*)	N, C, S
Mexican petunia (*Ruellia brittoniana*)	C, S
Sedum (*Sedum* spp.)	N, C, S
Goldenrod (*Solidago* spp.)	N, C, S
Stoke's aster (*Stokesia laevis*)	N, C, S
Copper canyon daisy (*Tagetes lemonii*)	N, C, S
Society garlic (*Tulbaghia violacea*)	N, C, S
Verbena (*Verbena* spp. and hybrids)	N, C, S
Veronica (*Veronica* 'Goodness Grows')	N, C, S
Adam's needle (*Yucca filamentosa*)	N, C, S

"We especially recommend blanket flower, a semiperennial that is good in coastal areas; black-eyed Susan, which is more of a perennial; and lanceleaf tickseed (*Coreopsis lanceolata*), which is more perennial and likes drier areas." —Gary Henry, landscape architect, Florida Department of Transportation, Tallahassee. Gary has the enviable task of selecting wildflowers to plant along Florida roadsides. You can bet that his choice of plants will include those easiest to establish and maintain.

PERENNIALS WITH FRAGRANT FLOWERS

MB: When my first born was a toddler and we had a greenhouse and flower shop, he greeted all new plants with a stoop and a sniff. I am also especially enamored of flowers that fill the air with perfume, yet there are some I have grown for years without appreciating their wonderful smells because I forget to stoop and sink my nose in the blossom. A few like the snake plant release their scent only in the evening, and some orchids must be open for a few days before you can catch the fragrance. With some plants, like lilies, different varieties have different fragrances. And others flowers are variable; some of us can smell them, and others can't at all.

Abyssinian gladiolus (*Acidanthera bicolor*)	N, C, S
Belladonna lily (*Amaryllis belladonna*)	N
Angel trumpet (*Brugmansia* × *candida*)	N, C
Red valerian (*Centranthus ruber*)	N
Crinum lily (*Crinum* spp. and hybrids)	N, C, S
Pinks (*Dianthus* spp.)	N, C
Amazon lily, eucharis lily (*Eucharis amazonica*)	C, S
Freesia (*Freesia* × *hybrida*)	N, C
Hedychium (*Hedychium* spp.)	C, S
Ginger lily (*Hedychium coronarium*)	N, C, S
Heliotrope (*Heliotropium arborescens*)	C, S
Lemon lily (*Hemerocallis lilioasphodelus*)	N, C
Hostas (*Hosta* 'Honeybells', *H.* 'Royal Standard')	N
Spider lily (*Hymenocallis* spp.)	N, C, S
Ismene (*Hymenocallis narcissiflora*)	N, C, S
English lavender (*Lavandula angustifolia*)	N, C, S
Spanish lavender (*Lavandula dentata*)	N, C, S
Madonna lily (*Lilium candidum*)	N, C
Formosa lily (*Lilium formosanum*)	N
Magic lily (*Lycoris squamigera*)	N, C
Four-o'clock (*Mirabilis jalapa*)	N, C, S
Paper-white narcissus (*Narcissus tazetta*)	N, C
Lotus (*Nelumbo lutea, N. nucifera*)	N, C, S
Evening primrose (*Oenothera* spp.)	N, C, S
Orchid species	N, C, S
Tuberose (*Polianthes tuberosa*)	N, C, S
Snake plant (*Sansevieria* spp.)	C, S
Valerian (*Valeriana officinalis*)	N, C, S
Sweet violet (*Viola odorata*)	N, C, S
Pinecone ginger (*Zingiber zerumbet*)	N, C, S

"Most of the herbs have more subtle fragrances that come from the whole plant, not just the flowers. One of my favorite fragrant flowers is the narcissus, though it is not a herb. They grow wild here, whole yards full around old, abandoned houses, and they spread into the pastures." —Betty O'Toole, O'Toole's Herb Farm, Madison.

DROUGHT-TOLERANT PERENNIALS

Grouping plants according to their need for water is one of the xeriscape principles that really pays off. In fact, just knowing the needs of individual plants will help you know where to hold the hose longer and where to skip over quickly. Many of us are finding that plants like daylilies will do just as well with much less water. All of the following have moderate drought tolerance.

Burn plant (*Aloe* spp.)	C, S
Star begonia (*Begonia heracleifolia*)	N, C, S
Sea oxeye daisy (*Borrichia frutescens*)	N, C, S
Cannas (*Canna* × *generalis*)	N, C, S
Madagascar periwinkle (*Catharanthus roseus*)	C, S
Spider plant (*Chlorophytum comosum*)	N, C, S
Mexican heather (*Cuphea hyssopifolia*)	N, C, S
African iris (*Dietes vegeta*)	N, C, S
Golden dewdrop (*Duranta repens*)	N, C, S
Euryops (*Euryops pectinatus*)	N, C, S
Blue daze (*Evolvulus glomeratus*)	C, S
Gerbera daisy (*Gerbera jamesonii*)	N, C, S
Firebush (*Hamelia patens*)	N, C, S
Beach sunflower (*Helianthus debilis*)	N, C, S
Daylily (*Hemerocallis* spp.)	N, C, S
Morning glory (*Ipomoea* spp.)	N, C, S
Air plant, life plant (*Kalanchoe* spp.)	C, S
Dwarf lantana (*Lantana camara*)	N, C, S
Lavender (*Lavandula* spp.)	N, C, S
Bromeliads (*Bromeliad* spp.)	C, S
Partridge berry (*Mitchella repens*)	N, C, S
Geranium (*Pelargonium* × *hortatum*)	N, C, S
Russian sage (*Perovskia atricipifolia*)	N
Phlox (*Phlox subulata*)	N, C
Plumbago (*Plumbago auriculata*)	N, C, S
Mexican hat (*Ratibida columnifera*)	N, C, S
Mexican petunia (*Ruellia* spp.)	C, S
Strawberry geranium (*Saxifraga stolonifera*)	N, C
Purple queen or purple heart (*Setcreasea pallida*)	N, C, S
Society garlic (*Tulbaghia violacea*)	N, C, S
Sea oats (*Uniola paniculata*)	N, C, S
Wandering Jew (*Zebrina pendula*)	C, S

"In spite of severe water restrictions, anyone in Florida can create a magical garden. . . . Landscapes designed and maintained using xeriscape principles are more attractive, productive, and comfortable than those most Florida home-owners currently have, and, once established, they require less time and money for upkeep than a lawn." — *Xeriscaping for Florida Homes* by Monica Moran Brandies.

PERENNIALS FOR WET SITES

If you happen to have a stream bank, a soggy spot, or a place that floods in hard rains, take advantage and grow some of these plants that like wet feet. Tampa artist John Burke sunk children's wading pools in his yard to grow cattails, models for his copper creations. Be careful about planting cattails or pickerel weed at the edge of a pond, however; they can quickly spread out of control. Also, be aware that some of these plants prefer to stay moist *all* the time, so you may need to water if the soggy spot should begin to dry out in a hot, dry spell. Those that are most tolerant of fluctuations are marked with an asterisk.

Swamp milkweed (*Asclepias incarnata*)*	N, C, S
Cannas (*Canna* spp. and hybrids)*	N, C, S
Water hemlock (*Cicuta maculata*)	N, C, S
Swamp coreopsis (*Coreopsis nudata*)	N
Crinum (*Crinum americanum*)	N, C, S
Joe-Pye weed (*Eupatorium fistulosum*)*	N
Swamp sunflower (*Helianthus simulans*)	N
Texas star (*Hibiscus coccineus*)	N, C, S
Rose mallow, swamp mallow (*Hibiscus moscheutos*)*	N, C, S
Chameleon plant (*Houttuynia cordata*)	N
Spider lily (*Hymenocallis crassifolia*)	N, C
Alligator lily (*Hymenocallis palmeri*)	C, S
Blue flag iris (*Iris hexagona*)	N, C, S
Yellow flag iris (*Iris pseudacorus*)	N, C
Louisiana iris (*Iris* spp.)	N, C, S
Cardinal flower (*Lobelia cardinalis*)*	N, C, S
Pentas (*Pentas lanceolata*)	N, C, S
Pickerel weed (*Pontederia cordata*)	N, C, S
Meadow beauty (*Rhexia virginica, R. mariana*)	N, C, S
Pitcher plant (*Sarracenia* spp.)	N, C, S
Ladies' tress (*Spiranthes odorata*)	N, C, S
Cattail (*Typha latifolia*)	N, C, S
Calla lily (*Zantedeschia* spp.)	N, C
Rain lily (*Zephyranthes atamasco*)	N, C, S

Grasses, Sedges, and Rushes

Sweet flag (*Acorus calamus*)	N, C, S
Japanese sedge (*Carex morrowii*)	N, C
Northern sea oats (*Chasmanthium latifolium*)	N, C, S
Papyrus (*Cyperus* spp.)	N, C, S
Umbrella plant (*Cyperus alternifolius*)	N, C, S
Soft rush (*Juncus* spp.)	N, C, S
Beach grass (*Panicum amarum*)*	N, C, S
Florida gama grass (*Tripsacum floridana*)	N, C, S

TROPICAL BULBS THAT STAY IN THE GROUND

What we call bulbs are actually an assortment of swollen, underground storage roots, which botanically may be corms, rhizomes, or tubers. All serve the same purpose: to store energy to give rise to the next year's growth.

In the garden, the "bulb" enables us to easily dig up the plant when it goes dormant, lifting the bulb like a potato to be stored or transplanted elsewhere. The most well-known true bulbs may be tulips or daffodils; another that looks like a bulb but is actually a tuber is a caladium. Luckily, in Florida, we enjoy a long list of bulbs that would have to be dug each winter in colder climes, but in most of the state, we can just leave them in the ground as perennials.

Garlic

Abyssinian gladiolus (*Acidanthera bicolor*)	N, C, S
Lily-of-the-Nile (*Agapanthus africanus*)	N, C, S
Garlic (*Allium* spp.)	N
Elephant's ear (*Alocasia* spp.)	N, C, S
Inca lily (*Alstromeria pulchella*)	N, C
Caladiums (*Caladium* spp.)	C, S
Taro (*Colocasia esculenta*)	C, S
Crinums (*Crinum* spp. and hybrids)	N, C, S
Montebretia (*Crocosmia × crocosmiiflora*)	N, C, S
African iris (*Dietes vegeta*)	N, C, S
Amazon or eucharis lily (*Eucharis amazonica*)	C, S
Pineapple lily (*Eucomis* spp.)	N, C, S
Freesia (*Freesia × hybrida*)	C, S
Gladiolus hybrids	N, C, S
Gloriosa lily (*Gloriosa rothschildiana*)	N, C, S
Amaryllis (*Hippeastrum* hybrids)	N, C, S
Spider lily (*Hymenocallis* spp.)	N, C, S
Peruvian daffodil (*Hymenocallis narcissiflora*)	N, C, S
Snowflake (*Leucojum aestivum*)	N, C
Lycoris (*Lycoris* spp.)	N, C, S
Tuberose (*Polianthes tuberosa*)	N, C, S
Voodoo lily (*Sauromatum* spp.)	C, S
Harlequin flower (*Sparaxis tricolor*)	N, C, S
Aztec lily (*Sprekelia formossiama*)	N, C, S
Tritonia (*Tritonia crocata*)	N, C, S
Watsonia (*Watsonia* spp.)	N, C, S
Calla lily (*Zantedeschia* spp.)	N, C
Rain lily (*Zephyranthes* spp.)	N, C, S

"The three things I take into consideration in choosing plants are cold hardiness, drought tolerance, and maintenance. If a plant needs more water, I set up the irrigation system to be sure it gets enough. Or I tell a client the oyster plant will need a cleanup every March for winter damage, and if that is a problem, I use something else." —Gary Zierden, Gary's Landscaping, Plant City.

HOSTAS FOR NORTH AND CENTRAL FLORIDA

Hostas are staple perennials of shade gardens throughout most of the country, but in our warm, no-chill climate, many of the varieties just dwindle. It seems that many hostas, like peonies, like a period of cold rest in order to really thrive. However, in gardening, you can usually find an exception to the rule if you look hard enough. Thankfully, one source we know, Bruce Cavey, manager of the Plant Shoppe in Gainesville, has been trying hostas long enough to put together a list of selections that work at least that far south.

Bruce adds that "the green selections are the most vigorous, followed by the yellows, then blues, and last, the yellow-greens." He has installed the following in clients' gardens and grows them in his own garden as well.

H. *elata*	H. 'Ginkgo Tiara'
H. *fortunei* 'Albo-marginata'	H. 'Gold Craig'
H. *fortunei* 'Aureo-marginata'	H. 'Gold Standard'
H. *lanceolata*	H. 'Halcyon Blue'
H. *undulata*	H. 'Honeybells'
H. 'August Moon'	H. 'Royal Standard'
H. 'Frances Williams'	

In addition to Bruce's list, Sue Watkins of Tallahassee Nurseries lists the following. Sue adds that they are slow to mature, which is true of all hostas. You will not see their full size until at least the third year.

H. *elegans*	H. 'Groundmaster'
H. 'Wide Brim'	H. 'Sum & Substance'
H. 'Francee'	H. 'Patriot'

"Hostas will grow as far south as Orlando if they are fertilized monthly with superphosphate or potash, never bonemeal. They will perform better when they can receive a constant chilling period in the winter. After a mild winter they take longer to reappear and are smaller." —Bruce Cavey, manager of the Plant Shoppe, a retail garden center in Greenery Square, Gainesville.

GREAT GINGERS FOR FLORIDA

Gingers are great plants to grow in Florida. Some gingers go dormant in winter, so we don't have to worry about them in case of cold. Others keep growing until and unless it gets too cold and then take a brief rest. They are very reliable and easy to grow. They never need pruning, though the clumps can spread quite far. George Riegler, a gardener in Land o' Lakes, Florida, has a "cardamon" (a Thai or Indian spice that is not a true ginger) that he controls by mowing the spreading edges. You will find dozens of gingers for sale in our state; there was no way we could list them all. Here is a synopsis of the five major groups you are likely to encounter.

Costus are called spiral gingers because they have spiraling leaf stalks. Many of the flowers, like the 'Mauve Dancing Girls', last two to four weeks in arrangements. Plants may range from dwarf to large (15 feet). Most prefer partial sun.

The *Hedychium*, or butterfly gingers, are known for their delicious fragrance; as a group, they are also the most cold hardy, with some hardy as far north as Atlanta. They may be as small as 18 inches (*H. muluense*) or as tall as 7 or more feet ('Elizabeth'). Although perennial in north Florida, they may remain evergreen and bloom continuously in south Florida. They will take full sun if they have plenty of moisture.

The *Kaempferia*, or peacock gingers, make low groundcovers. Many adapt well to container growing. MB: My own favorite is the pinecone ginger. It contains a lanolinlike liquid that I squeeze from the long-lasting cone-shaped flowers every time I pass them for a fragrant, refreshing hand and face lotion. They prefer shade and are dormant in the winter.

The *Cucurma* may remind you of short-stalked banana plants. Called "hidden lilies" because their flowers peer just above a whorl of foliage at the end of a stem, they range in height from 2 to 7 feet and prefer partial to full sun.

Alpinia include species that can reach 15 feet in height. They are often grown for their handsome foliage, which may be deep green or variegated. Some of the more tropical varieties also have showy flowers for cutting. They will grow in partial sun to shade.

Shell ginger (*Alpinia zerumbet*)	N, C, S
Flame ginger (*Costus barbatus*)	C, S
Orange tulip ginger (*Costus curvibracteatus*)	N, C, S
Fiery costus (*Costus cuspidatus*)	N, C, S
Stepladder ginger (*Costus malortieanus*)	C, S
Hidden ginger (*Curcuma petiolata*)	N, C, S
Pride of Burma (*Curcuma roscoeana*)	S
Torch ginger (*Nicolaia elatior*)	C, S
Mauve dancing girls (*Globba winitti*)	N, C, S
Butterfly ginger (*Hedychium coronarium*)	N, C, S
Hedychium 'Elizabeth'	N, C, S
Kalili lily (*Hedychium gardnerianum*)	N, C, S
Hedychium 'Gold Flame'	N, C, S
Epiphytic ginger (*Hedychium hasseltii*)	C, S
Resurrection lily (*Kaempferia pulchra*)	N, C, S
Pinecone ginger (*Zingiber zerumbet*)	N, C, S

Gingerlike Plants

Blue ginger (*Dichorisandra thyrsiflora*)	N, C, S
Thai spice (*Galanga major*)	C, S

Culinary Gingers

Round cardamom (*Alpinia nutans*)	C, S
Curcuma domestica	C, S
Kaempferia galanga	N, C, S
Edible ginger (*Zingiber officinale*)	N, C, S

 "Most gingers prefer partial sunlight, as found under an oak tree or, as we call it, orchid light. They like to be planted in an improved soil and mulched to hold moisture and keep down weeds. We grow over two hundred different types and only promote about eight types for cooking. . . . In different parts of the world many other gingers are used in cooking." —Larry Shatzer, owner, Our Kids Orchids & Nursery, Winter Garden; quoted from an article in *Florida Gardening*.

DOUG GLICK'S FAVORITE DAYLILIES FOR FLORIDA

Florida does not have the wild daylily that blooms in the ditches, but there is no shortage of great cultivars for the garden. Daylilies are easy to grow throughout Florida. Wonderful new cultivars bloom in spring, summer, and fall and are salt and drought tolerant. Some have a subtle fragrance as well as showy flowers. They do as well in full sun as in partial shade. Here are some of the best choices, according to Douglas Glick of Daylily Discounters in Alachua. The ones with an asterisk are fragrant.

Name	Color	Comment
'Condilla'	Gold	Very best double
'Flower Shop'*	Pink	Beautiful, large
'Golden Beacon'*	Yellow-gold	Large flowers
'Irish Elf'	Yellow	Superb border plant, small plant
'Joan Senior'	Near-white	Best for central, north
'Little Gorgeous'	Red	Small-flowered variety
'Malaysian Monarch'	Purple	Very popular large variety
'Midnight Magic'	Black-red	Large variety
'Mykonos'	Near-white	Good for all of Florida
'Pandora's Box'*	Cream w/purple eye	Very popular
'Prelude to Love'	Black-red	Bred in Florida; medium-sized
'Rosie Meyer'	Red	Informal, large daylily
'Seductor'	Red	Our favorite large daylily
'So Excited'	Pink w/red eye	A knockout large daylily
'Sussex Way'*	Yellow	Large-flowered variety
'Tiffany Gold'*	Gold	Superb texture; large
'Yellow Bouquet'*	Double yellow	Reblooms; miniature flowers
'Zara Helma'	Pink w/red eye	Small, great bedding plants

"Growing hints for Florida: Daylilies love compost and Milorganite (or Organix from Dade County). Apply it liberally in the spring with some 10-10-10 fertilizer and in the fall by itself. Soak daylily roots in a solution of Liquid Humus and Soluble Seaweed Powder for a few hours before planting, and you'll grow some happy daylilies." —Douglas Glick, horticulturist, Daylily Discounters, Alachua.

BEGONIAS FOR THE FLORIDA GARDEN

Begonias will thrive, mostly in the shade, in our Florida gardens. There are many local begonia societies where you can learn more about them. Nurseries like Bob Koehler's B & K Tropicals offer over 150 different named varieties. Bob assures us that begonias are perennial anywhere it doesn't frost clear down through the Keys. The canelike, or angel wing, begonias show a great deal of promise for landscape use. Some of them have flower clusters the size of a cantaloupe on each stem all summer long. He highly recommends the following.

'Boomer'
'Green Giant'
'Joe Hayden'
'Marguerite De Cola'

'Pink Rubra'
'Popenoi'
'Sophie Cecile'
'Thomei'

BEGONIAS FOR CONTAINERS

According to Bob, these either haven't been tried in the garden or don't do well in the ground for whatever reason (usually nematodes), but they are very attractive in containers for the patio, porch, or doorstep.

'Avalanche'   'Ginny'
'Beryl'   'Maculata'
'Bunchii'   'Mary Jay'
'Cowardly Lion'   'Morning Sun'
'Dena'   'Ripsaw'

"I have a friend in Jacksonville who plants lots of begonias out in the spring and takes cuttings of anything too big to dig up in the fall. In central Florida a begonia's persistence depends on the weather; a freeze will usually take off the tops, but the plant in most cases will start to regrow almost at once." —Bob Koehler, B & K Tropicals, St. Petersburg.

PERENNIALS FOR ALKALINE SOIL

Many of Florida's grandest gardens are on alkaline fill soil along canals and waterways. The following perennials either prefer or tolerate alkaline soil (pH above 7.0).

Columbine (*Aquilegia canadensis*)	N, C
Artemisia (*Artemisia* spp.)	N, C, S
Ganges primrose (*Asystasia gangetica*)	C, S
Sea oxeye daisy (*Borrichia frutescens*)	N, C, S
Coreopsis (*Coreopsis lanceolata*)	N, C
Crinums (*Crinum* spp. and hybrids)	N, C, S
Pinks (*Dianthus* spp.)	N, C
Bleeding heart (*Dicentra eximia*)	N, C
Purple coneflower (*Echinacea purpurea*)	N, C, S
Beach sunflower (*Helianthus debilis*)	N, C, S
Amaryllis (*Hippeastrum* hybrids)	N, C, S
Morning glory (*Ipomoea* spp.)	N, C, S
Beach elder (*Iva imbricata*)	N, C, S
Kalanchoes (*Kalanchoe* spp.)	C, S
Mexican petunia (*Ruellia* spp.)	C, S
Sea purslane (*Sesuvium portulacastrum*)	N, C, S
Rain lily (*Zephyranthes* spp. and hybrids)	N, C, S

Grasses

Inland sea oats (*Chasmanthium latifolium*)	N, C, S
Beach grass (*Panicum amarum*)	N, C, S
Fountain grass (*Pennisetum* spp.)	N, C, S

PERENNIALS FOR THE BEACH

The beach adds salt spray and saltwater, plus an extra strong dose of wind and sunlight, to special soil problems. Plantings are definitely restricted to tough, salt-tolerant plants, but Florida's seaside gardeners find plenty to make their gardens spectacular. We've been in some that were so impressive we hardly noticed the sea until we'd checked out all the plants. Such gardens take both planning and a certain amount of trial and error. Keep your eyes and notebooks open.

Fern-leaf yarrow (*Achillea filipendulina*)	N, C
Lily-of-the-Nile (*Agapanthus africanus*)	N, C, S
Artemisia (*Artemisia ludoviciana albula* 'Silver King')	N, C
Sea oxeye daisy (*Borrichia frutescens*)	N, C, S
Crinums (*Crinum* spp. and hybrids)	N, C, S
Blanket flower (*Gaillardia pulchella*)	N, C, S
Beach sunflower (*Helianthus debilis*)	N, C, S
Daylily (*Hemerocallis* spp.)	N, C, S
Beach elder (*Iva imbricata*)	N, C, S
Lantanas (*Lantana* spp.)	N, C, S
Dusty miller (*Senecio cineraria*)	N, C, S
Sea purslane (*Sesuvium portulacastrum*)	N, C, S
Society garlic (*Tulbaghia violacea*)	N, C, S
Adam's-needle (*Yucca filamentosa*)	N, C, S

Grasses

Muhly grass (*Muhlenbergia capillaris*)	N, C, S
Beach grass (*Panicum amarum*)	N, C, S
Smooth cordgrass (*Spartina alterniflora*)	N, C
Sand cordgrass (*Spartina patens*)	N, C
Sea oats (*Uniola paniculata*)	N, C, S

LONG-BLOOMING PERENNIALS

One of the most amazing aspects of gardening in Florida is how long some plants stay in bloom. Some bloom almost every day of the year, especially if you are faithful about deadheading. Others alternate flushes of bloom throughout the year with brief rests. Some are seasonal, but their season is much longer than that of many northern perennials. In any case, deadheading will extend the bloom time and increase the abundance and size of the flowers. So will feeding and general good maintenance. You'll find the plants on the following list easy to grow and wonderfully reliable and rewarding.

Blackberry
lily

Abelmoschus (*Abelmoschus manihot*)	C, S
Indian mallow (*Abutilon permolle*)	C, S
Yarrow (*Achillea* spp.)	N, C
Aloe (*Aloe* spp.)	C, S
Angelonia (*Angelonia randiflora*)	N, C, S
Butterfly weed (*Asclepias curassavica*)	N, C, S

Begonias (*Begonia* spp.)	C, S
Blackberry lily (*Belamcanda chinensis*)	N, C
Canna (*Canna* × *generalis*)	N, C, S
Crossandra (*Crossandra infundibuliformis*)	C, S
Manaos beauty (*Centratherum intermedium*)	N, C, S
Becky's daisy (*Chrysanthemum* × *superbum* 'Becky')	N
Crinums (*Crinum* spp. and hybrids)	N, C, S
Mexican heather (*Cuphea* spp.)	N, C, S
African iris (*Dietes vegeta*)	N, C, S
Blue daze (*Evolvulus glomeratus*)	C, S
Gaura (*Gaura lindheimeri*)	N, C
Gerbera daisy (*Gerbera jamesonii*)	N, C, S
Firebush (*Hamelia patens*)	N, C, S
Beach sunflower (*Helianthus debilis*)	N, C, S
Daylily (*Hemerocallis* spp.)	N, C, S
Rose or swamp mallow (*Hibiscus moscheutos* hybrids)	N, C, S
Moonflower (*Ipomoea alba*)	C, S
Jacobinia (*Justicia carnea* vars.)	N, C, S
Air plant, life plant (*Kalanchoe pinnata*)	C, S
Lantanas (*Lantana* spp.)	N, C, S
Beebalm (*Monarda punctata*)	N, C
Cat whiskers (*Orthosiphon stamineus*)	N, C, S
Geranium (*Pelargonium* × *hortatum*)	C, S
Pentas (*Pentas lanceolata*)	N, C, S
Russian sage (*Perovskia* spp.)	N
Garden phlox (*Phlox paniculata*)	N
Mountain mint (*Pycnanthemum incanum*)	N
Oyster plant (*Rhoeo spathacea*)	C, S
Black-eyed Susan (*Rudbeckia fulgida*)	N, C, S
Mexican petunia (*Ruellia brittoniana*)	N, C, S
Salvia (*Salvia greggii, S. guaranitica, S. involucrata, S. leucantha, S. madrensis, S. uliginosa*)	N, C, S
Georgia savory (*Satureia georgiana*)	N, C
Purple fountain (*Scutellaria costaricana*)	C, S
Purple queen or purple heart (*Setcreasea pallida*)	N, C, S
Copper canyon daisy (*Tagetes lemmonii*)	N, C, S
Mexican tarragon (*Tagetes lucida*)	C, S
Princess flower (*Tibouchina urvilleana*)	C, S
Society garlic (*Tulbaghia violacea*)	N, C, S
Veronica (*Veronica alpinia* 'Goodness Grows')	N
Veronica (*Veronica spicata* × 'Sunny Border Blue')	N
Verbena (*Verbena* spp. and hybrids 'Homestead')	N, C, S
Brazilian verbena (*Verbena bonariensis*)	N, C
Australian violet (*Viola hedera*)	N, C, S
Rain lily (*Zephyranthes* spp. and hybrids)	N, C, S

CALADIUMS FOR SUN

Caladiums are perennial in Florida from Orlando south. They are tropical by nature and will rot if they freeze. They are also ruined by nematodes.

Commercial growers here and in Texas put all their caladiums in full sun to produce each year's crop of tubers, and every one survives, though their leaves are not uniformly beautiful. The ones that get very ragged are the ones that do better for home gardens in the shade.

Full sun is a very hot, unwelcome environment in Florida. As Susan Wallace, horticulturist and marketing director for Van Bloem (a wholesale bulb distributor), puts it, "Any caladiums that you grow in the sun will require constant moisture to look good. Commercial growers can get away with it because they are growing their bulbs in peat bogs. Only gardeners with continual irrigation can get the same results. Ideally, these caladiums should get some afternoon shade. You don't quite get the same product in the sun that you do in the shade. Once caladiums flop over (from drying out), they won't stand up again. This happens easily in containers."

Susan recommends that you try to put your "sun" caladiums in a spot where they are shaded by the house or a distant tree from the blazes of the summer afternoon. Their color will be better. "The great thing about caladiums is that you don't have to wait for them to flower like you do bedding plants," she says. "You have color from the time you plant them."

The following are especially recommended for their ability to tolerate more sun than other selections.

Lance or strap-leaf
'Caloosahatchee'
'Lady of Fatima'
'Lance Wharton'
'Pink Gem'
'Red Frill'
'Rosalie'
'White Wing'

Heart-shaped leaves
'Aaron'
'Arno Nehrling'
'Blaze'
'Carolyn Wharton'
'Fire Chief'
'Florida Sweetheart'
'John Peed'
'Red Flash'
'Rosebud'
'White Queen'

 "Caladiums will grow in full sun or full shade as long as they have warmth and moisture. The best varieties for full sun are the strap- and lance-leaf varieties. They are lower growing with smaller leaves and as such have less weight to support during heavy rains or extremely intense heat." —Noel Durrance, owner, Caladium World, Sebring.

GIL WHITTON'S LIST OF UNUSUAL BULBS THAT SHOULD BE PLANTED MORE OFTEN

MB: When I first saw the bloom on a reader's voodoo lily after she called to tell me about it, I was so amazed that I just walked around and around it for fifteen minutes before I even started taking pictures. The rest of the plants on this list were also surprises when I discovered them, except for Eucharis lily, which I carried in my wedding bouquet forty years ago. Gil Whitton told me some years ago that there were names he looked for in every book and seldom found, and when he rattled them off, they were all Greek to me. I am happy to report that when he gave me the list again, I had seen them all, grown most, and appreciated them properly. You may have to search to find these, but you'll never forget them once you see them. Most are easy to grow.

Voodoo lily (*Amorphophallus* spp.)	N, C, S	Many species have attractive foliage that disappears in winter, followed by amazing flowers. Needs medium light and lots of water.
Siam summer tulips (*Curcuma* spp.)	C, S	These gingers have small flowers with long lasting white or pink bracts; foliage dies down in winter. They need partial shade and occasional water.
Amazon lily (*Eucharis amazonica*)	C, S	Dark green foliage and fragrant white flowers in deep shade. They like moist, acid soil; bloom spring, summer, and fall.
Blood lily (*Haemanthus* spp.)	N, C, S	Great balls of reddish flowers in summer. Likes acid soil, low light, lots of water during growing season; bulbs must be dry in winter.
Bat flowers (*Tacca* spp.)	C, S	Year-round unusual almost black flowers with long tentacles, decorative foliage. Needs acid soil, medium light, lots of water.

 "My first voodoo lily bloom was 4 feet across, and the bulb grew from baseball size to 40 pounds in about five years. I planted the seeds, and every one germinated, three to four hundred plants." —Gil Whitton, horticultural consultant in Hawthorn who has had a radio call-in show since 1957 in the Tampa-St. Petersburg area.

LOUISIANA IRIS HYBRIDS

Louisiana iris like moist, acid soil and will do very well in or near a bog garden or pond where the soil is always moist. They will also grow on dry land, but the soil should be enriched with a generous amount of cow manure, and the plant should be well mulched. They like full sun but will also do well under a deciduous tree where they get full sun all winter, when they need it most. Different varieties bloom from the end of February through May; a combination of early, midseason, and late varieties will give you the full extent of bloom time.

Keep in mind that, unlike the bearded iris, with which many gardeners from the North are more familiar, the Louisiana iris can stretch 4 to 5 feet in height.

'Black Game Cock'	Dark blue-purple dwarf	Late
'Cajun Dome'	Blood red	Late
'Dixie Deb.'	Yellow	Midseason
'Gulf Coast'	Dark blue rimmed in white	Early
'Gulf Shores'	Metallic blue ruffles	Midseason
'Jerry'	Purple	Midseason
'Kiss'	Watermelon pink	Midseason
'Marie Callout'	Violet-blue	Late
'Professor Ike'	Violet-red	Late
'Rosy Pink'	Lavender-pink ruffles	Midseason
'Wishbone'	Lemon yellow	Midseason to late

 "Nothing can compare to the regal beauty of an iris. From ancient to modern times, iris have been one of the most beloved flowers and used especially to remember loved ones." —Leeann Connelly, owner, Tropical Pond and Garden, Loxahatchee, who is naming her own hybrids to honor Florida policemen killed on duty.

ANNUALS

To most of us, annuals are bedding plants or potted plants we use for seasonal color. However, from a botanical point of view, annuals are plants that complete their lifecycle, that is produce roots, stems, leaves, flowers, and seeds and die, within one year. Some may reseed, but they won't come back again from the same roots the way perennial plants do. Annuals tend to bloom profusely—indeed, to bloom themselves to death.

In Florida, the line between annuals and perennials gets a little blurred when compared to cooler regions of the country. For example, some plants, such as delphinium, that are perennial in northern states must be treated as annuals here since they cannot take our summer heat and humidity. More common are many plants that are annual in northern states but prove perennial here as long as the weather conditions remain favorable.

Even within Florida there are differences. Some plants grow as annuals in north Florida but become perennials in central or south Florida, so some plants are listed in both the annuals and the perennials chapters. And some plant groups, such as the salvias and the sunflowers, include both annual and perennial species.

So start by treating the plants in the following lists as annuals, including some that are considered biennial where fall and spring are separated by a dormant winter. In Florida the foxgloves grow slowly through the fall and winter and then jump into accelerated growth and bloom in the spring without any actual pause, so they seem like annuals. If some of them come back or stay longer for you, decide if their prolonged performance is worth the space they are taking.

Because most annuals have a limited time in your garden, you can continually dip into the catalogs and try new ones and new combinations. Floridians can grow most annuals at some time of the year.

The regional codes in the lists in other chapters of this book have been omitted in this chapter. Since annuals are not expected to live more than a few seasons, a year at the most, the plants listed here will grow in any region if they are planted at the right time.

To Do List for Annuals

This list is a guide for growing annuals. Check off the following, and annuals will reward you with months of constant color for relatively little work and expense. Most of all they are fun and give you an opportunity to try many different combinations. If what you try doesn't work, you have a chance to start anew next year.

- Note what is growing in your area. Pay close attention to specific variety names when available.
- Find out the best time to plant, the season of bloom, color, height, and how much sun the plant needs.
- When reading seed catalogs, keep Florida climate zones and their conditions in mind. Zones 8, 9, and 10 are roughly equivalent to north, central, and south Florida. The Keys are zone 11.
- Buy bedding plants for instant color and quick spread. If you are patient, start with seeds.
- Improve your soil with all the compost or humus you can get.
- Water a new flower bed daily until the plants are established. After two or three weeks, water as needed.
- Mulch with an organic product such as bark or compost to save moisture, improve soil, and discourage weeds.
- Always fertilize hybrid bedding plants. They demand it. Make the job easy by using a controlled-release product that is labeled to last either three, four, five, or nine months. In Florida's climate, you'll need to cut that time by one third.
- Pick flowers often, especially at first, so the plants will spread.
- Remove flowers before they go to seed to encourage more bloom. Deadhead as needed.
- Rip out and replace waning plants before your pride turns to shame.
- Keep trying new kinds, varieties, and combinations.

"Take the guesswork out of choosing the right cultivar. Use proven All-America Selection bedding-plant winners. These cultivars have been tested in trial gardens around the United States and found to be outstanding in most locations. Plan ahead. Look around your area and make a list of the plants that are vigorous in your region of the state. Then incorporate them into your next planting." —Dennis Hopen, bedding-plant trial coordinator, Walt Disney World, Lake Buena Vista.

ANNUALS THAT LIKE FLORIDA SUMMERS

Summer's frequent heavy rains bring a very humid season to Florida gardens. If you couldn't bring yourself to pull out those nasturtiums remaining from the cool season, they'll soon fade and rot on their own. Better to rip them out and replace them with colorful plants that can better withstand our most difficult conditions. Buy the big, 1-gallon pots or transfer the contents of a hanging basket to a large patio pot for instant effect. If you're looking to fill a big bed, you'll need smaller transplants or 4-inch pots for economy. Some plants you can start from seed or from volunteer seedlings you may find already waiting for you to transplant. The old varieties of Madagascar periwinkles that reseed are still reliable, but the newer varieties are having serious problems with rot.

In north Florida you can add the following to this list: heat-tolerant annual dianthus such as 'Ideal Pink' and the 'Telstar' series, heat-tolerant petunias such as the 'Madness' series, and the old-fashioned *Petunia integrifolia*. The key to keeping these plants through summer is regular removal of the blossoms as soon as they fade. Annuals that will often reseed themselves are marked in the following list by an asterisk.

Coleus (*Coleus* hybrids)
Amaranth, Joseph's coat (*Amaranthus tricolor*)
Dutchman's pipe (*Aristolochia* spp.)
Bacopa 'Snowflake'
Caladium (*Caladium* × *hortulanum*)
Madagascar periwinkle, vinca (*Catharanthus rosea*)*
Celosia, cockscomb (*Celosia cristata* 'New Look')*
Flamingo feather (*Celosia spicata* 'Flamingo Feather')
Spider flower (*Cleome hasslerana*)*
Cup and saucer vine (*Cobaea scandens*)
Hyacinth bean (*Dolichos lablab*)*
Blue daze (*Evolvulus glomeratus*)
Globe amaranth (*Gomphrena globosa*)
Sunflower (*Helianthus annuus*)*
Impatiens (*Impatiens wallerana*, New Guinea hybrids)*
Moonflower (*Ipomoea alba*)*
Cypress vine (*Ipomoea quamoclit*)*
Morning glory (*Ipomoea purpurea*)*
Medallion plant (*Melampodium paludosum*)*
Mina (*Mina lobata*)
Purslane, portulaca, or moss rose (*Portulaca* spp.)*
Scarlet sage (*Salvia splendens*)
Scaevola (*Scaevola aemula* 'Blue Wonder')
Marigold (*Tagetes* spp.)*
Clock vine (*Thunbergia* spp.)
Mexican sunflower (*Tithonia rotundifolia*)*
Wishbone flower (*Torenia fournieri*)

 "Remember that some annuals, such as portulaca and morning glory, will close in the rain or at midday. Moonflowers won't open until evening. Plant them in areas where you can enjoy the morning or evening shows." — Mary Smude, owner, A&A Growers, Plant City. Gardeners drive far to see and buy the unusual plants offered here.

LONG-BLOOMING ANNUALS

Some annuals will continue blooming, and blooming, and blooming until you become so tired of them that you are ready to rip them out. Often, these are the plants that can be planted in the cool fall season in central and south Florida but are also tolerant of some heat. In central and south Florida, these flowers continue blooming through winter and into the following spring and summer. At that point, the plants may even continue into a second year; or you may want to replace them because they are tattered, woody, or leggy; they have lost their original vigor; or you're just ready for a change.

Starting with transplants instead of seed will ensure that these plants bloom from the time they are set in the ground until their time is up. They will need regular watering and fertilizing, too, especially the hybrid selections. Always deadhead to encourage more bloom and keep plants looking neat.

In north Florida, plants on this list that are sensitive to frost can be set out in spring and will continue blooming until the first frost in November or December; they are marked with an asterisk.

Zinnia

Ageratum (*Ageratum houstonianum*)*
Snapdragon (*Antirrhinum majus*)
Begonia (*Begonia × semperflorens-cultorum*)*
Madagascar periwinkle or vinca (*Catharanthus rosea*)*
Globe amaranth (*Gomphrena globosa*)*
Impatiens (*Impatiens wallerana*)*
Alyssum (*Lobularia maritima*)
Medallion plant (*Melampodium paludosum*)*
Petunias (*Petunia* hybrids)
Purslane, portulaca, or moss rose (*Portulaca* spp.)*
Scarlet sage (*Salvia splendens*)*
Copper canyon daisy (*Tagetes lemmonii*)
Wishbone flower (*Torenia fournieri*)
Nasturtium (*Tropaeolum majus*)
Viola (*Viola cornuta*)
Pansy (*Viola × wittrockiana*)
Zinnia (*Zinnia angustifolia*)*

"For best bloom, choose plants that are stocky and bushy and then cut them back soon after they start putting out new growth. Don't get impatient for that first bloom, and if there is one, cut if off. This is to encourage the plant to fill out before it begins blooming. Also amend the soil with up to 50 percent peat, compost, or other humus along with the natural soil. And fertilize often." —Richard White, landscape contractor, Brandon.

ANNUALS FOR SHADE

MB: Because we garden year-round, we must be aware that the patterns of sun and shade can vary greatly from season to season. For example, one fall I picked a spot for winter annuals that never got a shadow in the summer, then found it didn't get much sun at all in winter when the days were shorter and the angle of the sun lower. Your landscape will change as young trees grow, too. Because trees grow so quickly here, a sunny spot can become a shady one in just a few years. The following annuals will reward you with color, but don't expect them to grow in the dark. Coleus, impatiens, and caladium are the great standbys for summer color in the shade; impatiens can bloom all year as long as there is no frost.

During dry weather, when watering is necessary, shady areas often need less watering unless they are packed with tree roots. The deep shade of a magnolia or a low deck will call for mulch or a shade-loving leafy groundcover such as ivy.

Begonia (*Begonia* × *semperflorens-cultorum*)
Browallia (*Browallia speciosa*)
Caladium (*Caladium* × *hortulanum*)
Spider flower (*Cleome hasslerana*)
Coleus (*Coleus* hybrids)
Amazon lily (*Eucharis grandiflora*)
Impatiens (*Impatiens wallerana*)
Lobelia (*Lobelia erinus*)
Flowering tobacco (*Nicotiana alata*)
Primrose (*Primula* hybrids)
Scarlet sage (*Salvia splendens*)
Black-eyed Susan vine (*Thunbergia alata*)
Wishbone flower (*Torenia fournieri*)
Johnny jump-up (*Viola tricolor*)

SUPER EASY FLOWERS FROM SEED

These annuals are easy to start from seed because they sprout and grow quickly and bloom within several weeks, and most of the seeds are big enough to handle easily. Small ones can be sown from an empty seasoning or spice shaker. These annuals are great for kids, and you can get dozens of plants from a single seed packet, often for less than a dollar. You can also save seeds from year to year. Some will self sow and come back again on their own. Such volunteers can get lost in other plantings so be ready to transplant them if you wish. Some may die out in dry times. Search your soil for free starts of those marked with an asterisk because they will often reseed themselves each year.

Ornamental cabbage (*Brassica oleracea*)
Cornflower, bachelor's button (*Centaurea cyanus*)
Cleome (*Cleome hasslerana*)*
Calliopsis (*Calliopsis grandiflora*)*
Cosmos (*Cosmos bipinnatus*)*
Klondike cosmos (*Cosmos sulphureus*)*
Hyacinth bean (*Dolichos lablab*)
Snow-on-the-mountain (*Euphorbia marginata*)

Globe amaranth (*Gomphrena globosa*)*
Sunflower (*Helianthus annuus*)
Balsam (*Impatiens balsamia*)
Morning glory (*Ipomoea* spp.)
Moonflower (*Ipomoea alba*)*
Sweet pea (*Lathyrus odoratus*)
Sweet alyssum (*Lobularia maritima*)
Medallion plant (*Melampodium paludosum*)*
Mina (*Mina lobata*)
Four-o'clock (*Mirabilis jalapa*)*
Nicotiana (*Nicotiana alata*)
Shirley poppy (*Papaver rhoeas*)
Scarlet runner bean (*Phaseolus coccineus*)
Drummond phlox (*Phlox drummondii*)
Gloriosa daisy (*Rudbeckia hirta*)
Marigold (*Tagetes* spp.)*
Black-eyed Susan vine (*Thunbergia alata*)*
Mexican sunflower (*Tithonia rotundifolia*)*
Nasturtium (*Tropaeolum majus*)*
Zinnia (*Zinnia elegans*)*

Sunflower

SUN-LOVING COLEUS

Many of us first met coleus as shade-loving plants. Indeed, we thought they needed shade to succeed. But a dip into history shows that they probably originated in Java, an island of Indonesia, where they grew in both sun and shade. In the 1990s new sun-loving strains were added to and mixed with heirloom plants for brilliant new cultivars, most of them are free from the lankiness and tendency to scorch of the earlier hybrids. These true tropical perennials are now available as cultivars that mature so slowly they bloom only after a year or two and continue to look good, as some of the old shade-loving ones did not even after a short period of bloom. They are mostly propagated vegetatively. Ask at your nursery or get a catalog from a specialist for some of the following. Try some of those you already have in the sun and see how they do. Also be prepared to look for coleus under their new genus name *Solenostemon*.

'Alabama Sunset'
'Burgundy Sun'
'Coppertone'
'Cranberry Salad'
'Freckles'
'Gay's Delight'
'Hurricane Series'
'Japanese Giant'
'Kona Red'

'Olympic Torch'
'Pink Parfait'
'Plum Parfait'
'Red Ruffles'
'Rustic Orange'
'Solar Shade'
'Solar Sunrise'
'Thumbellina'

"The best attributes of these are: easy to propagate, tolerate both full sun or shade, colorful throughout the year, and few flowers produced." —Allan Armitage, professor of horticulture, University of Georgia, Athens.

TALL ANNUALS

Most of us put the tallest plants to the back of the flower border or in the center if the planting is to be seen from all around. But Trish Montesano, landscaper from Riverview, likes to tuck smaller plants behind taller ones and then let a path or a few stepping stones lead into the bed to pleasant surprises. Plants with low foliage such as foxglove can also hide behind others—as long as they get enough sunlight until they send up their taller blooms. Some of the plants that are tall and long lasting in other climates can be more fleeting in Florida's climate. Those are marked here with an asterisk.

	Height in feet
Hollyhock (*Alcea rosea*)*	3–6
Tassel flower (*Amaranthus caudatus*)	2–3
Amaranth, Joseph's coat (*Amaranthus tricolor*)	3–4
Snapdragon (*Antirrhinum majus*)	2–3
Angel-wing begonia (*Begonia* spp.)	2–3
Cosmos (*Cosmos bipinnatus*)	3–4
Flamingo feather (*Celosia spicata* 'Flamingo Feather')	3–3
Cornflower, bachelor's button (*Centaurea cyanus*)*	2–3
Cleome (*Cleome hasslerana*)	3–4
Larkspur (*Consolida ambigua* or *Delphinium ajacis*)	2–3
Coreopsis, tickseed (*Coreopsis tinctoria*)	2–3
Delphiniums (*Delphinium* spp.)*	2–4
Foxglove (*Digitalis* spp.)	3–4
Sunflower (*Helianthus annuus*)	4+
Strawflower (*Helichrysum bracteatum*)	2–3
Hibiscus (*Hibiscus* 'Red Shield')	3–4
Mallow (*Malva sylvestris* 'Zebrina')	3–4+
Shoofly plant (*Nicandra physalodes*)	3–4+
Flowering tobacco (*Nicotiana sylvestris*)*	2–3
Red fountain grass (*Pennisetum setaceum* 'Rubrum')	3–4
Beefsteak plant (*Perilla frutescens*)	2–3
Castor bean (*Ricinus communis*)	4–5+
Scarlet sage (*Salvia splendens*)	2–3
Marigold (*Tagetes* spp.)*	2–3
African marigold (*Tagetes erecta*)	2–3
Mexican sunflower (*Tithonia rotundifolia*)*	4+

THE TRUTH ABOUT DEADHEADING

Because the object of an annual's life (from the plant's point of view) is to produce seed, we can persuade them into continual bloom by removing dead flowers before they go to seed. This way, the plants will continue producing flowers in an effort to set seed. Deadheading also goes far toward keeping the plant looking neat.

Cut or pick blooms as they wither
Abelmoschus (*Abelmoschus manihot*)
Snapdragon (*Antirrhinum majus*)

Calendula, pot marigold (*Calendula officinalis*)
Calliopsis (*Coreopsis tinctoria*)
Cleome (*Cleome hasslerana*)
Cosmos (*Cosmos bipinnatus*)
Klondike cosmos (*Cosmos ulphureus*)
Pinks (*Dianthus chinensis*)
Blanket flower (*Gaillardia pulchella*)
Sunflowers, branching types (*Helianthus annuus*)
Geranium (*Pelargonium crispum*)
Petunias (*Petunia* hybrids)
Primrose (*Primula* hybrids)
Black-eyed Susan (*Rudbeckia hirta*)
Scarlet sage (*Salvia splendens*)
Marigold (*Tagetes* spp.)
African marigold (*Tagetes erecta*)
Copper canyon daisy (*Tagetes limonia*)
Mexican sunflower (*Tithonia rotundifolia*)
Zinnia (*Zinnia elegans*)

Shear to remove masses of seedpods every few weeks
Ageratum (*Ageratum houstonianum*)
Cosmos (*Cosmos bipinnatus, C. sulphureus*)
Coreopsis, tickseed (*Coreopsis tinctoria*)
Toadflax, miniature snapdragon (*Linaria maroccana*)
Sweet alyssum (*Lobularia maritima*)
Purslane, portulaca, or moss rose (*Portulaca* spp.)
Copper canyon daisy (*Tagetes limonia*)
Wishbone flower (*Torenia fournieri*)
Pansy (*Viola* × *wittrockiana*)
Narrowleaf zinnia (*Zinnea linearis*)

Pick flowers at their peak and hang to dry
Celosia, cockscomb (*Celosia cristata*)
Globe amaranth (*Gomphrena globosa*)
Strawflower (*Helichrysum bracteatum*)
Statice or sea lavender (*Limonium sinuatum*)
Bells of Ireland (*Moluccella laevis*)

Remove blooms as soon as they appear (they detract from foliage effect)
Copperleaf (*Acalypha wilkesiana*)
Coleus (*Coleus* hybrids)
Beefsteak plant (*Perilla frutescens*)

"Some people might wonder about marigolds, but they aren't easy for me. They just don't hold up well. I also omit annual salvias (scarlet sage) because most folks don't pinch off the old blooms, and they need that to stay fresh and compact." —Rhoda Boone, owner, Dothan Nurseries, Dothan, Alabama.

ANNUALS FOR FRAGRANCE

You may detect a slight fragrance in many annuals if you bury your nose in their flowers, but the ones listed below have scents that reach out to you. Their alluring perfume floats across the yard when the air is warm. Plant them—especially moonflowers and petunias, which are most fragrant at night—near places where you sit outdoors, and always have some near the front door. (All petunias aren't fragrant, so sniff and compare before you buy.)

Yarrow (*Achillea* spp.)
Calendula, pot marigold (*Calendula officinalis*)
Pinks (*Dianthus* spp.)
Sweet William (*Dianthus barbatus*)
Heliotrope (*Heliotropium arborescens*)
Night-blooming cereus (*Hylocereus undatus*)
Moonflower (*Ipomoea alba*)
Sweet pea (*Lathyrus odoratus*)
Alyssum (*Lobularia miniata*)
Stock (*Matthiola incana*)
Paper-white narcissus (*Narcissus tazetta*)
Flowering tobacco (*Nicotiana sylvestris*)
Basil (*Ocimum* spp.)
Geranium (*Pelargonium* spp.)
Petunias (*Petunia* spp. and hybrids)
Copper canyon daisy (*Tagetes lemmonii*)
Nasturtium (*Tropaeolum majus*)

Basil

  *"Scented geraniums and pots seem to be made for each other. A great benefit of growing geraniums in containers is being able to take them in for protection from frosts in the winter and from drenching rains in the summer. Then they are ready to go out again when the weather improves."* —Carleen Long, grower, All Seasons Nursery (wholesale only), Seffner.

ANNUALS FOR CUT FLOWERS

MB: Another wonder of Florida gardening is being able to pick cut flowers 365 days a year. Even after a frost, pansies, violas, and other cold-hardy flowers remain. I made bouquets for my father's and my daughter's weddings almost completely with flowers from my yard. Betty Barr Mackey and I wrote a book called *A Cutting Garden for Florida*. This list could be pages long, but here are a few of Betty's favorites.

Ageratum (*Ageratum houstonianum*)
Bishop's flower (*Ammi majus*)
Snapdragon (*Antirrhinum majus*)
Ornamental pepper (*Capsicum annuum*)
Celosia, cockscomb (*Celosia cristata*)
Cornflower, bachelor's button (*Centaurea cyanus*)

Cleome (*Cleome hasslerana*)
Coleus (*Coleus* spp.)
Larkspur (*Consolida ambigua*)
Cosmos (*Cosmos bipinnatus*)
Klondike cosmos (*Cosmos sulphureus*)
Dahlias (*Dahlia* hybrids)
Dianthus (*Dianthus* spp.)
Emilia (*Emilia javanica*)
Globe amaranth (*Gomphrena globosa*)
Sunflower (*Helianthus annuus*)
Strawflower (*Helichrysum bracteatum*)
Candytuft (*Iberis umbellata*)
Sweet pea (*Lathyrus odoratus*)
Statice, sea lavender (*Limonium sinuatum*)
Toadflax, miniature snapdragon (*Linaria maroccana*)
Stock (*Matthiola incana*)
Medallion plant (*Melampodium paludosum*)
Flowering tobacco (*Nicotiana sylvestris*)
Love-in-a-mist (*Nigella damascena*)
Shirley poppy (*Papaver rhoeas*)
Petunias (*Petunia* spp. and hybrids)
Drummond phlox (*Phlox drummondii*)
Gloriosa daisy (*Rudbeckia* spp.)
Scarlet sage (*Salvia splendens*)
Silenes (*Silene* spp.)
Marigolds (*Tagetes* spp.)
Copper canyon daisy (*Tagetes lemmonii*)
Tithonia (*Tithonia rotundifolia*)
Wishbone flower (*Torenia fournieri*)
Blue lace flower (*Trachymene coerulea*)
Nasturtium (*Tropaeolum majus*)
Viola (*Viola cornuta*)
Pansy (*Viola × wittrockiana*)
Narrowleaf zinnia (*Zinnia angustifolia*)
Zinnia (*Zinnia elegans*)

Coleus

"Home gardeners don't need to be so concerned about how long the flowers will last because we have a whole garden that will need deadheading anyway. Most flowers last about as long in a vase as in the garden, perhaps a little longer because they do not get pollinated indoors and are protected from excessive heat, sun, wind, and rain." —Betty Barr Mackey, gardener, publisher, co-author of *A Cutting Garden for Florida*.

ANNUALS WITH COLORFUL FOLIAGE

Plants with leaves of red, silver, or pink or colorful combinations can be even more striking in a garden because that foliage color is more constant and more voluminous than flowers. They also, especially the silver ones like dusty miller, tend to help a mix of colors blend with more harmony. The amount of sun and shade can make a difference in how and what colors appear even in the same plants in the same yard in the case of coleus and Joseph's coat. We included a few tropicals here, although in frost-free areas they are perennials.

Copper plant (*Acalypha wilkesiana*)
Chinese evergreen (*Aglaonema* spp.)
Amaranth, Joseph's coat (*Amaranths tricolor* 'Early Splendor')
Begonias (*Begonia* spp., red-leafed types)
Ornamental kale, cabbage (*Brassica oleracea* var. *acephala*)
Caladiums (*Caladium* hybrids)
Calatheas (*Calathea* spp.)
Celosia, cockscomb (*Celosia cristata* 'Wine Sparkler')
Coleus (*Coleus* spp.)
Cuban oregano (*Coleus amboinicus*)
Snow-on-the-mountain (*Euphorbia marginata*)
Hibiscus (*Hibiscus* 'Red Shield')
Wax plant (*Hoya carnosa*)
Polka-dot plant (*Hypoestes phyllostachya* 'White Splash', 'Pink Red Splash')
Prayer plant (*Maranta* spp.)
Basil (*Ocimum* 'Dark Opal', 'Purple Ruffles')
Beefsteak plant (*Perilla frutescens*)
Swedish ivy (*Plectranthus madasgariensis*)
Oyster plant (*Rhoeo spathacea*)
Dusty miller (*Senecio cineraria*)
Wandering Jew (*Zebrina pendula*)

ANNUAL VINES

Annual vines grow almost like the pumpkin vine in *Cinderella*—right before your eyes. Kids love them because there is so little waiting. Most can be started from seed packets and are an inexpensive way to add nearly instant color to trellises, fences, arbors, or porches. Or take a tip from Mother Nature and let the annual ones grow over shrubs or up trees as long as they can be kept under control.

MB: I once had a pine tree that bloomed at night with moonflowers. It was hard on the tree, but I figured it was worth the risk. Some of the vines listed here will freeze to the ground but usually come back either from seeds or from the roots; those are marked with an asterisk. Those with two asterisks can be weeds and will need some control.

Cup-and-saucer (*Cobaea scandens*)
Hyacinth bean (*Dolichos lablab*)
Japanese hop bean (*Humulus japonicus*)
Moonflower (*Ipomoea alba*)*
Variegated sweet potato (*Ipomoea batatas* 'Tricolor')
Morning glory (*Ipomoea purpurea*)
Cypress vine (*Ipomoea quamoclit*)*

Cardinal climber (*Ipomoea × multifida*)
Sweet pea (*Lathyrus odoratus*)
Luffa gourd, Chinese okra (*Luffa* spp.)
Mina (*Mina lobata*)
Balsam pear (*Momordica charantia*)**
Scarlet runner bean (*Phaseolus coccineus*)
Black-eyed Susan vine (*Thunbergia alata*)**
Nasturtium (*Tropaeolum majus*)*
Canary creeper (*Tropaeolum peregrinum*)

"If there is one thing I have learned, it is to experiment with the flowers you love. Don't always believe it can't be done because someone says so. Buy a pack of seeds and try. It may take two or three tries before you are successful. There will be plants that may never work in our unique climate; move on from those and concentrate on all the hundreds that do, and it will make your gardening much more rewarding and fun." —Trish Montesano, owner, Sweet Annie's Antique Roses, Riverview.

ANNUALS FOR THE BEACH

Though waterfront property is doubly valuable and desirable, extra planning, planting, and skill are needed to keep those gorgeous gardens colorful. Bob Hartwig, landscape architect, says, "The only annual for color right on the beach is blanket flower. Mix it with the perennials that offer interesting foliage color and texture." Plants on this list are low and compact, with sturdy stems and waxy or heavy leaves. Still, they will do best where they have some protection from the wind and spray—behind a low wall, slope, or hedge.

Ageratum (*Ageratum houstonianum*)
Wax begonia (*Begonia × semperflorens-cultorum*)
Ornamental cabbage (*Brassica oleracea* var. *acephala*)
Calendula, pot marigold (*Calendula officinalis*)
Blanket flower (*Gaillardia pulchella*)
Gazania (*Gazania rigens*)
Cypress vine (*Ipomoea quamoclit*)
Alyssum (*Lobularia maritima*)
Mina (*Mina lobata*)
Ivy geranium (*Pelargonium peltatum*)
Fancy geranium (*Pelargonium × domesticum*)
Drummond phlox (*Phlox drummondii*)
Purslane, portulaca, or moss rose (*Portulaca oleracea*, cultivars)
Verbenas (*Verbena* hybrids)

"There is a whole new palette of containers that can be used, free standing, in beds, or even on pedestals. They let gardeners on the beach give the annuals a better soil mix. Use compost, peat, and other moisture-holding materials. Locate these in the shelter of a building or wall or taller planting to buffer them from the wind. For summer only you can use the tropicals like bougainvillea, crotons, ixora, and hibiscus. In fall throw them away and start over in north Florida. These are not as fragile and offer some different colors." —Bob Hartwig, landscape architect, Hartwig & Associates, Jacksonville.

Disney's Outstanding Bedding Plants

With thanks to Heather Will-Browne, director of the Walt Disney World bedding plant trials, we offer this list of the varieties found superior among the many used for the constant color displays in all the theme parks. The column labeled "Height" indicates the height that the plants grew while in the Disney trial garden. The column labeled "Days Tested" indicates the days the plants were in bloom from the time Disney gardeners set out mature, greenhouse-grown transplants in the test bed until the plants were removed because they had just passed their peak. Plantings are in the sun unless otherwise stated. Disney finds impatiens do very well in full sun through the winter and up until the beginning of June; during the summer they definitely need shade.

Winter Trial

Name	Color	Height	Days Tested
Chrysanthemum × morifolium 'Glowing Lynn'	Butterscotch, bronze center	17"	100
Chrysanthemum × morifolium 'Orion'	Spoon-tipped quill, golden yellow	18"	120
Chrysanthemum × morifolium 'Spotlight'	White, creamy champagne center	14"	90
Dianthus chinensis × barbatus		17"	124
'Ideal Crimson'	Crimson		
'Ideal Pearl'	Soft pale rose, pink edge	12"	118
'Ideal Violet'	Violet	10"	118
Dianthus × hybridus 'Rainbow Loveliness'	White, lavender, rose, carmine	23"	104
Pelargonium × hortatum 'Maverick Star'	Light rose, dark rose center	20"	181
Snapdragon (Antirrhinum spp.) 'Cherry Chimes'	Bright neon rose	9"	115
Viola cultivar 'Blue Elf'	Dark purple	6"	91

For Shade

Name	Color	Height	Days Tested
Chrysanthemum			
'Laurie'	Dark, golden yellow	20"	105
'Mindy'	Dark, golden yellow	14"	105
'Autumn Kimberly'	Reddish-mauve	19"	105

Impatiens 'Fiesta Series'	Rose, red, pink, mixed	16"	92
Primula 'Libra Blue'	Blue	9"	37
'Liberty Mix'	Mixed	10"	37

Summer Trial

Name	Color	Height	Days Tested
Periwinkle (*Catharanthus roseus*) 'Pacifica White'	White	12"	78
Cockscomb (*Celosia cristata*) 'Prestige Scarlet'	Red	16"	60
Cockscomb (*Celosia globosa*) 'Wine Sparkler'	Red	15"	60
Cosmos bipinnatus 'Versailles Carmine'	Red	44"	57
Impatiens linearifolia 'Patriot Orange'	Orange	12"	67
Pelargonium floribunda 'Julia'	Light salmon	15"	84
Pelargonium × hortatum 'Showcase Bright Red'	Red	14"	109
Pelargonium × hortatum 'Showcase Red'	Green foliage	12"	110
Salvia farinacea 'Sea Breeze'	Blue and white	20"	84
Salvia splendens 'Cleopatra Red'	Red	13"	58
Verbena × hybrida 'Tapien Blue'	Dark purple	5"	244
'Tapien Pink'	Rose pink	8"	244

For Shade

Name	Color	Height	Days Tested
Polka-dot plant (*Hypoestes sanquinolenta*) 'Red Splash Select'	Red and green	15"	80
Impatiens (*Impatiens wallerana*) 'Fiesta Burgundy Rose'	Rose	16"	88

"The wisest words of advice I can give gardeners is to choose the plant for the appropriate season and plant it in the right spot. This seems pretty simple, but it really does take a lot of trial and error." —Heather Will-Browne, horticulture program specialist, Walt Disney World, Lake Buena Vista.

ANNUALS FOR ALKALINE SOILS

LC: Having grown up in the pine flatwoods of north Florida, where the soil is acid, I know nothing about gardening in alkaline soils other than my memory of my uncle's place in Miami and the chalky, white marl ground he had to blast to make a planting hole. My uncle was the ultimate do-it-yourselfer. He built his own house and planted 3 acres of mango trees around it. A deep rocky pit behind the house was a reminder of an abandoned dream—a do-it-yourself swimming pool. At the time, the pit was a great setting for a kid's imaginary games, little knowing that decades later I would be drawing from those memories as my only experience with soil that's "the pits." So to put together this list for you, I defer to someone whose experience is far greater than mine: Scott Ogden. Scott lives and gardens in Texas and has compiled an excellent text, *Gardening Success with Difficult Soils: Limestone, Alkaline Clay, and Caliche*. To learn more about growing plants in soils with high pH, I recommend his book.

For Fall Planting
Cornflower, bachelor's button (*Centaurea cyanus*)
Larkspur (*Consolida* spp.)
Calliopsis (*Coreopsis tinctoria*)
California poppy (*Eschscholzia californica*)
Lisianthus (*Eustoma grandiflorum*)
Blanket flower (*Gaillardia pulchella*)
Lobelia (*Lobelia erinus*)
Alyssum (*Lobularia maritima*)
Stock (*Matthiola incana*)
Love-in-a-mist (*Nigella damascena*)
Drummond phlox (*Phlox drummondii*)

For Spring Planting
Cleome (*Cleome hasslerana*)
Cosmos (*Cosmos bipinnatus*)
Klondike cosmos (*Cosmos sulphureus*)
Dahlberg daisy (*Dyssodia tenuiloba*)
Globe amaranth (*Gomphrena globosa*)
Sunflower (*Helianthus annuus*)
Medallion plant (*Melampodium paludosum*)
Gloriosa daisy (*Rudbeckia hirta* 'Gloriosa Daisy')
Mexican sunflower (*Tithonia rotundifolia*)
Narrowleaf zinnia (*Zinnia angustifolia*)
Zinnia (*Zinnia elegans*)

Calliopsis

 "The harsh, dry conditions typical of limestone soils in summer are too brutal for many moisture-loving plants to endure. . . . Such annuals reverse the season: They germinate in fall, grow through the winter months, flower in spring and go dormant in summer." —Scott Ogden, from *Gardening Success with Difficult Soils: Limestone, Alkaline Clay, and Caliche.*

RESEEDING ANNUAL WILDFLOWERS

MB: I have heard people say they didn't know there were any wildflowers in Florida. "Where do they think the name 'Florida' came from?" asks Gary Henry, landscape architect with the Florida Department of Transportation. Many of the plantings by the DOT on less traveled roads are especially glorious in the spring, but there is some bloom all year long. "These are most certainly flowers that we can use in the garden as well," says Henry.

But naturalizing as we do on the roadsides is not so common in gardens in Florida because we seldom leave an area alone long enough. Gary Henry explains, "Home gardeners tend to give wildflower beds too much TLC. They work them too much, and the seeds end up buried too deep in the home garden. Once they die down, if people get in there and rework the area, what they are actually doing is disturbing the germinating seedlings."

Nevertheless, these plants can bloom in our gardens for a glorious season. Then if we want to plant other flowers in the same spot for other seasons, we'd do best to gather the seeds of these for planting again at the appropriate time. All of the following are native to Florida and will grow and spread wherever we give them the proper conditions.

Beardtongue

Beach mistflower (*Ageratum littorale*)
Butterfly weed, milkweed (*Asclepias* spp.)
Mistflower (*Conoclinium coelestinum*)
Coreopsis, tickseed (*Coreopsis tinctoria*)
Blanket flower (*Gaillardia pulchella*)
Beach sunflower (*Helianthus debilis*)
Beardtongue (*Penstemon laevagatis*)
Drummond phlox (*Phlox drummondii*)
Mexican petunia (*Ruellia caroliniensis*)
Texas sage (*Salvia coccinea*)
Lyre-leaf sage (*Salvia lyrata*)
Silver sage (*Salvia riparia*)

 "The Department of Transportation publishes a booklet called *Wildflowers in Florida* that covers what to plant, where to plant, how to plant, and how to gather seed. It is available for $1.50 from the Maps and Publications Office, 605 Suwannee Street, MS 12, Tallahassee, FL 32399-0450, or call 850-414-4050. We also have a program where anybody can buy wildflower seed, one pound or more, and donate it to the DOT, and they will match it with an equal amount and plant it in your area. This is explained in the booklet with a list of suppliers. The seed costs $18 to $500. Don't send the money to the DOT, or it could go in the big hole." — Gary Henry, landscape architect, Florida Department of Transportation, Tallahassee.

FAVORITE COMBINATIONS FROM DISNEY

The key to a truly artful flower bed is knowing how to combine plants so that they work well together. Besides the obvious importance of choosing colors that harmonize, we gardeners must also select species that are compatible in their need for sun and water, as well as plants with complementary growth habits.

Says Heather Will-Browne, horticulture program specialist at Walt Disney World, "If you realize you cannot devote a lot of time or energy to maintenance, I recommend the following bedding plant combinations in your summer garden. Planting combinations is a great trick. If for some reason one cultivar doesn't do well, the other one can compensate for it. In our central Florida landscapes, many of the bedding plants used are perennials that behave as annuals in our climate. They are unable to survive a full year, but in the right season they can give quite a show."

Shade
Caladiums mixed with impatiens

Partial Shade/Sun
Violas with alyssum

Sun
Red salvia with yellow marigolds
Dusty miller with red salvia
Pink coneflower, blue browallia, and 'Strawberry Fields' globe amaranth
Yellow coreopsis, blue salvia, and red plumed celosia
Salmon nicotiana with lavender globe amaranth
White cosmos, coral *Salvia coccinea*, and lavender globe amaranth
Crossandra with blue salvia
Pentas with angelonia (perennial in C, S)
Lantana with Madagascar periwinkle
Dianthus with dwarf blue delphinium 'Dwarf Blue Butterflies'

A SAMPLER OF ANNUALS BY COLOR

MB: Most of us have flower beds with a variety of colors. I try to keep the yellows and oranges to one side of the garden and the pinks and purples to another. My red flowers go in either mix, depending on the shade.

White or blue flowers (and plants with colored foliage) may be used to bring unity and continuity to a bed with many mixed (and clashing) colors. White and pale pastels are visible at night under the moon or night lighting. Some of us solve the problem of mix-and-no-match by moving plants around. My friend Yvonne Jarrett says, "My plants have to be able to live on the shovel."

If your color scheme is precise, it is best to buy transplants in bloom or start with seeds of a selection with which you are familiar.

In the lists below, we have categorized a number of annuals according to their predominant color. Some, such as pansies, are mentioned more than once because they are available in an assortment of colors.

White Flowers
Snapdragon (*Antirrhinum majus*)
Wax begonia (Begonia × *semperflorens-cultorum*)
Cosmos (*Cosmos bipinnatus* 'Purity', 'Sonata', ' T & M')
Madagascar periwinkle, vinca (*Catharanthus rosea*)
Larkspur (*Consolida ambigua*)
Baby's breath (*Gypsophila elegans*)
Impatiens (*Impatiens wallerana*)
Moonflower (*Ipomoea alba*)
Statice, sea lavender (*Limonium sinuatum*)
Alyssum (*Lobularia maritima*)
Flowering tobacco (*Nicotiana alata*)
Geranium (*Pelargonium* spp.)
Petunias (*Petunia* spp. and hybrids)
Pansy (*Viola* × *wittrockiana*)
Narrowleaf zinnia (*Zinnia angustifolia*)
Zinnia (*Zinnia elegans*)

Baby's breath

Green Flowers
Love lies bleeding (*Amaranths caudatus* 'Viridis')
Bells of Ireland (*Moluccella laevis*)
Flowering tobacco (*Nicotiana alata, N. langsdorffii, N. alata* 'Lime Green')
Zinnia (*Zinnia elegans* 'Envy')

Blue Flowers
Ageratum (*Ageratum houstonianum*)
Asters (*Aster* spp.)
Cornflower, bachelor's button (*Centaurea cyanus*)
Larkspur (*Consolida ambigua*)
Delphiniums (*Delphinium* hybrids)
Blue daze (*Evolvulus glomeratus*)
Morning glory (*Ipomoea tricolor, I.* 'Heavenly Blue')
Statice, sea lavender (*Limonium sinuatum*)
Lobelia (*Lobularia maritima*)
Forget-me-not (*Myosotis sylvatica*)
Petunias (*Petunia* spp. and hybrids)
Wishbone flower (*Torenia fournieri*)
Verbenas (*Verbena* spp. and hybrids)
Pansy (*Viola* × *wittrockiana*)

Pink Flowers
Hollyhock (*Alcea rosea*)
Asters (*Aster* spp.)
Begonia (Begonia × *semperflorens-cultorumt*)
Celosia, cockscomb (*Celosia cristata*)
Dahlias (*Dahlia* hybrids)
Pinks (*Dianthus chinensis*)
Sweet William (*Dianthus barbatus*)
Lisianthus (*Eustoma grandiflora*)

Pink Flowers (*continued*)

Baby's breath (*Gypsophila elegans*)
Impatiens (*Impatiens wallerana*, New Guinea hybrids)
Petunias (*Petunia* hybrids)
Drummond phlox (*Phlox drummondii*)
Wishbone flower (*Torenia fournieri*)
Verbenas (*Verbena* spp.)
Zinnia (*Zinnia elegans*)

Purple or Lavender Flowers
Hollyhock (*Alcea rosea*)
Asters (*Aster* spp.)
Browallias (*Browallia* spp.)
Larkspur (*Consolida ambigua*)
Dahlias (*Dahlia* hybrids)
Delphiniums (*Delphinium* hybrids)
Foxglove (*Digitalis* spp.)
Lisianthus (*Eustoma grandiflora*)
Globe amaranth (*Gomphrena globosa*)
Impatiens (*Impatiens wallerana*, New Guinea hybrids)
Morning glory (*Ipomoea* spp.)
Shoofly (*Nicandra physalodes*)
Petunias (*Petunia* hybrids)
Verbenas (*Verbena* spp.)
Pansy (*Viola* × *wittrockiana*)
Zinnias (*Zinnia* spp.)

Red Flowers
Hollyhock (*Alcea rosea*)
Snapdragon (*Antirrhinum majus*)
Asters (*Aster* spp.)
Wax begonia (*Begonia* × *semperflorens-cultorum*)
Celosia, cockscomb (*Celosia cristata*)
Klondike cosmos (*Cosmos sulphureus*)
Dahlias (*Dahlia* hybrids)
Blanket flower (*Gaillardia pulchella*)
Gazanias (*Gazania* spp.)
Globe amaranth (*Gomphrena globosa*)
Impatiens (*Impatiens wallerana*, New Guinea hybrids)
Balsam (*Impatiens Balsamia*)
Kalanchoes (*Kalanchoe* spp.)
Statice, sea lavender (*Limonium sinuatum*)
Lobelia (*Lobularia maritima*)
Flowering tobacco (*Nicotiana alata*)
Geranium (*Pelargonium* spp.)
Petunias (*Petunia* spp. and hybrids)
Purslane, portulaca, or moss rose (*Portulaca* spp.)
Scarlet sage (*Salvia splendens*)

Verbenas (*Verbena* spp.)
Zinnias (*Zinnia* spp.)

Yellow Flowers
Hollyhock (*Alcea rosea*)
Snapdragon (*Antirrhinum majus*)
Pot marigold (*Calendula officinalis*)
Celosia, cockscomb (*Celosia cristata*)
Calliopsis (*Coreopsis tinctoria*)
Klondike cosmos (*Cosmos sulphureus*)
Crossandra (*Crossandra infundibuliformis*)
Dahlias (*Dahlia* hybrids)
Dahlberg daisy (*Dyssodia tenuiloba*)
Gazanias (*Gazania* spp.)
Sunflower (*Helianthus annuus*)
Strawflower (*Helichrysum bracteatum*)
Kalanchoes (*Kalanchoe* spp.)
Medallion plant (*Melopodium paludosum*)
Purslane, portulaca, or moss rose (*Portulaca* spp.)
Marigolds (*Tagetes* spp.)
Nasturtium (*Tropaeolum majus*)
Pansy (*Viola* × *wittrockiana*)
Zinnias (*Zinnia* spp.)

Salmon or Orange Flowers
Begonia (*Begonia* × *semperflorens-cultorum*)
Calendula, pot marigold (*Calendula officinalis*)
Celosia, cockscomb (*Celosia cristata*)
Crossandra (*Crossandra infundibuliformis*)
Dahlias (*Dahlia* hybrids)
Gazanias (*Gazania* spp.)
Strawflower (*Helichrysum bracteatum*)
Impatiens (*Impatiens wallerana*, New Guinea hybrids)
Kalanchoes (*Kalanchoe* spp.)
Purslane, portulaca, or moss rose (*Portulaca* spp.)
Marigolds (*Tagetes* spp.)
Mexican sunflower (*Tithonia rotundifolia*)
Pansy (*Viola* × *wittrockiana*)
Narrowleaf zinnia (*Zinnia angustifolia*)
Zinnia (*Zinnia elegans*)

EDIBLE LANDSCAPING

In Florida it is not at all difficult to pick fruits and vegetables every day of the year. Even in north Florida, lettuce, collards, and Brussels sprouts live through a freeze.

MB: We combine fruits from the north with fruits from the tropics, so whether the winter is warm or cold, we are sure to have something. We use fruit trees for shade and for framing the landscape, fruiting shrubs for our foundation plantings, strawberries and sprawling herbs for groundcovers, and other herbs for cut flowers, and know well that we live in the next best place to paradise. What is more, we have, as my friend Bob Baker says, "more fun growing these things than God ought to allow."

LC: I was first introduced to gardening by following my father and his brothers around the vegetable garden, and the word *garden* was synonymous with food production. One of my fondest memories is of digging sweet potatoes, for you never know what size or shape they will be. Living in Florida allows one to harvest 365 days a year.

TO DO LIST FOR GROWING VEGETABLES, FRUITS, AND HERBS

MB: My friend the late Armando Mendez picked fresh fruit every day of the year. He had a rather small yard and some lovely flowers besides his fruit, and he also had a small section of lawn. I asked him which took the most work, the fruit or the grass, and he answered without hesitation, "The grass." If you aren't growing even a small portion of your own food, start today.

- List the vegetables, fruits, and herbs you and your family like best and use them first in your landscaping. Taste new ones when you get the chance. Don't judge too quickly. Many tropical fruits like mango and carambola have a slightly different flavor from every tree.
- Visit local public gardens and watch how fruits, vegetables, and herbs grow there.
- Study charts and variety lists from the Cooperative Extension Office first, so you'll plant the best kind at the best time. The Cooperative Extension Service is one of the best sources of information about varieties of fruits and vegetables that are suited to our climate.

- Select your sunniest sites; amazing production is possible even in partial shade.
- Enrich your soil. Add some humus to the entire bed and till or spade it in. Then add a little more to each planting hole.
- Mulch well (except for citrus, which is prone to root rot).
- Fertilize at planting time and again as needed.
- Water as needed, deeply every two weeks for established citrus.
- Pick and enjoy. Crops tend to be smaller but longer lasting here, so you can enjoy a fresh harvest longer.
- Know that you are doing something positive for yourself and your community. Home-grown food tastes better, needs no packaging or transportation, and is usually grown with far fewer pollutants than commercially grown produce. (It also takes less water than grass.)

 "It may not sound like a big deal for one family to grow two fruit trees, three tomato plants, a patch of strawberries, and a hedge of blueberries—but if you multiply the land they would occupy (about .25 acre) by 20 million households, the result would be a half a million acres of producing soil and a tremendous amount of food. And if each person designing a yard began to incorporate conservation measures, professionals would inevitably respond with more responsible designs and products." —Rosalind Creasy, from *The Complete Book of Edible Landscaping.*

HERBACEOUS FRUITS

The fruits on this list are smaller and can mix and mingle with flowers or vegetables or even fit in the front of a shrub border. MB: I mix all mine together in a happy hodgepodge that is certainly beautiful to my eye. Other members of the family find the fruit beautiful when it reaches the table. The best way to get rhubarb is still to visit northern relatives during their growing season—I seldom come home, by plane or car, without a grocery bag full of rhubarb for the freezer—but it is nice to grow a bit here as a winter annual for old time's sake.

Grown as Perennials

Pineapple (*Ananas comosus*)	C, S
Mysore raspberry (*Rubus albescens*)	C, S
Blackberry (*Rubus* 'Brazos')	N, C, S
Blackberry (*Rubus* 'Flordagrand', 'Oklawaha')	C, S
Raspberry (*Rubus idaeus* 'Dormared')	N

Grown as Annuals (fall through spring)

Strawberry (*Fragaria* × *ananassa*)	N, C, S
Rhubarb (*Rheum rhabarbarum*)	N, C, S

 "A new project by Dr. Bob Knight at the University of Florida Research Station at Homestead is showing that northern raspberries that fruit on new wood can be grown as annuals from prechilled canes planted in early spring. You have to buy new canes each year from a mail-order catalog. After the original canes fruit in April or May and die off, a second crop will come from the suckers and bear a crop in July or August, and they bear enough to be exciting even commercial interest. After the chill wears off, they will not bear much again. Researchers are also working to develop a Mysore cross with northern varieties to get a cultivar that would bear perennially." —Gene Joyner, county Extension Agent, West Palm Beach.

CITRUS FOR FLORIDA

Orange trees are almost synonymous with Florida. Many homes are built in old groves. The trees, with their glossy evergreen leaves, are small and well shaped by nature. When they bloom, they fill the neighborhood with wonderful fragrance. Fruits hang on the trees for out-of-hand eating for months at a time, and with careful planning you can have oranges for ten months of the year. With all that, you'd think citrus growing would be difficult. Not so. It is easy. Even in north Florida there are great varieties that thrive in protected garden spots or large containers so they can be moved inside for the short winter.

You can grow citrus like the huge pummelo or the strange-looking Buddha's hand, which most people have never even heard of, as well as red navels and blood oranges and huge lemons. Persian limes are large, seedless, and more cold hardy than key limes. Meiwa kumquats are sweet enough to eat rind and all and are cold hardy to 20 degrees F. Pummelos produce huge, sweet grapefruitlike fruit. Satsuma tangerines are very cold hardy. Some Rare Fruit Council members have thirty to sixty different kinds of citrus growing in their yards.

Listed below are some of the best for the home gardener. Plant personal favorites first and check out season of maturity so you'll be sure to be there and hungry when they are ready to pick.

Calamondin	N, C, S	Oct–April	Perfect size for growing in pots
Dancy tangerine	C, S	Dec–Jan	Zipper peel
Meiwa kumquat	N, C, S	Oct–April	Eat rind and all; cold hardy to 20–25 degrees
Meyer lemon	C, S	Nov–April	Largest lemon; bears year-round
Minneola tangelo	C, S	Dec–Feb	Large, bell-shaped; superb flavor
Murcott honey tangerine	C, S	Jan–March	One of the sweetest citrus
Persian lime	S	Year-round	Large, seedless; hardier than key lime
Pummelo	C, S	Nov–April	Huge fruit like sweet grapefruit
Ruby grapefruit	C, S	Nov–May	Seedless; intensely red flesh
Satsuma tangerine	N, C, S	Sept–Oct	Most cold-hardy citrus
Valencia orange	C, S	March–June	The last orange to mature

"Grow your own fruits and veggies so you know what's sprayed on them— preferably nothing."—Charlie and Kathy Crowley, Crowley's Rare Tropical Fruit, Sarasota.

FRUITS FROM VINES

Vines work well in the landscape for instant shade, color, and food. Many of them, such as the passionflowers, have beautiful flowers as well. The Rangoon creeper, *Quisqualis* spp., opens a few white flowers in the morning. By noon they are pink, and by dusk they are the same rich maroon as yesterday's.

MB: Some of these vines need strong support and can be rampant. My friend Charles Novak has one answer. His passionfruit grows up an oak tree, and he just picks up the fruits as they drop. He also gets kiwi to fruit, but most of us find it grows fine vines with few flowers and no fruit. Gene Joyner, West Palm Beach extension agent, says the farther north in Florida you are and the more chilling hours you have, the better the chance for kiwi fruit. The Rangoon creeper is a nut, and squirrels do get most of mine, but someday they may give me a share. Meanwhile, it is worth growing for me just for the flowers.

While muscadines are the best grapes to eat fresh in Florida, a few bunch grapes are used for wine making. Do not be tempted to order European or other bunch grapes from mail-order catalogs that serve the rest of the country, however, because bunch grapes will not thrive here unless they have been developed for our conditions. The wine grape cultivars bred for Florida include 'Stover', 'Orlando Seedless', and 'Suwanee'. Check with your local master gardeners or County Extension Office for a complete list of these hybrids and how to grow them.

Kiwi (*Actinidia chinensis*)	N, C, S
Monstera (*Monstera deliciosa*)	S
Passionflower (*Passiflora* spp.)	N, C, S
Rangoon creeper (*Quisqualis indica*)	C, S
Muscadine grapes (*Vitis rotundifolia*)	N, C, S
Table and wine grapes (*Vitis* spp.)	N, C, S

"One of the best and easiest to grow of all fruit for the average home owner is the Muscadine grape . . . a native to the southeastern section of the USA and Florida. Many varieties are resistant to Pierce's disease, which makes the growing of most European or northern bunch grapes impossible in Florida." —Lewis Maxwell, author of *Florida Fruits, Florida Vegetables,* and *Florida Flowers.*

STRAWBERRIES

The commercial strawberry capital of the world is around Plant City in central Florida, where they get plants every fall from Canada and treat them like annuals in raised beds. The pick-your-owns will fill the freezer if you live close, but you can grow your own and pick daily from November to June. These are usually 'Sweet Charlie' (early), 'Oso Grande', and 'Rosa Linda' (later).

'Alpine'	Can be grown from seeds or runners; holds berries off the ground
'Dover'	Firm, deep red color; average flavor
'Florida 90'	Medium-sized; deep red; pointed; soft; excellent taste
'Florida Belle'	Large, wedge-shaped with occasional pale top
'Rosa Linda'	Late variety
'Sweet Charlie'	Medium-sized berry with very sweet flavor
'Tufts'	Large, flat, wedge-shaped

"Florida fruit enthusiasts have a multitude of options due to excellent new varieties, container growing, freeze protection, and the existence of microclimates. It's possible to grow bananas as far north as Jacksonville, peaches down to Miami and even Homestead, nectarines south of Tampa, lychees in Orlando, and avocados in Gainesville. Where it gets too cold, container growing and freeze protection are always an option." —Josh Nye, sales manager, Chestnut Hill Nursery, Alachua (wholesalers to Home Depot, Lowes, WalMart, and many other chain and independent retail outlets around the state).

DECIDUOUS FRUITS

Most of the fruits we grow in Florida are evergreen and do not like too much cold. We have to work harder to grow the deciduous ones such as those listed here. These usually need some chilling to break dormancy and induce bloom, and getting that cold in Florida is not always a sure thing. So put these in your coolest microclimates. Also consider placement of trees where you want summer shade but winter sun. Just peeling off the leaves of subtropical apples can fool them into thinking they've been through a winter and induce new growth and bloom.

Over the years, the University of Florida has bred selections of many of these that will set fruit with relatively few hours of chilling. Be sure to contact your local county extension office or master gardeners for a list of specific varieties. A good local garden center will stock them, but beware of buying at large chains that are likely to order varieties for all their stores nationwide—chances are that those varieties will not do well in Florida.

Pear

Kiwi (*Actinidia chinensis*)	N, C, S
Persimmon (*Diospyros kaki*)	N, C, S
Fig (*Ficus carica*)	N, C, S
Apple (*Malus pumila*)	N, C
Nectarine (*Persea persica*)	N, C
Peach (*Persea persica*)	N, C, S
Plum (*Prunus salicina* and hybrids)	N, C, S
Pear (*Pyrus communis*)	N, C
Mysore raspberry (*Rubus albescens*)	C, S
Blackberry (*Rubus* spp.)	N, C, S
Blueberry (*Vaccinium* hybrids)	N, C
Grape (*Vitis* spp.)	N, C, S

"Plants are much like people. They have to be fed, watered, and kept from freezing. If you can take care of these basic needs, you will grow all the exotic edibles you can use. You can landscape your home and yard with exotic fruit-producing trees, bushes, and vines." —Marian Van Atta, author, *Growing and Using Exotic Foods*.

FRUITING SHRUBS FOR HEDGES OR SCREENS

These shrubs can be clipped to hedge form if you desire. Just remember that clipping can become very labor intensive. The same shrubs can be allowed to grow to their natural shape in a less formal border or used alone or in smaller groups for screening.

Bamboo (*Bambusa* and *Phyllostachys* noninvasive spp.)	C, S
Sea grape (*Coccoloba uvifera*)	C, S
Quince (*Cydonia oblonga*)	N, C
Surinam cherry (*Eugenia uniflora*)	C, S
Pineapple guava (*Feijoa sellowiana*)	N, C

Dwarf kumquat (*Fortunella* spp.)	C, S
Prickly pear (*Opuntia ficus-indica*)	N, C, S
Pyracantha, firethorn (*Pyracantha* spp.)	N, C, S
Cattley guava (*Psidium littorale*)	N, C
Pomegranate (*Punica granatum*)	C, S
Downy myrtle (*Rhodomyrtus tomentosa*)	C, S
Rose (*Rosa* spp.)	N, C, S
Elderberry (*Sambucus canadensis*)	N, C, S
Blueberry (*Vaccinium* spp.)	N, C, S
Ginger (*Zingiber officinale*)	N, C, S

"Pineapple guavas bear better when various clones are planted together, three to five varieties for cross pollination. The cooler the growing season, the better. Like all fruits, these do best the more sun they have. Fiejoas are salt and drought tolerant and not fussy about feeding. If you have a good variety, you can propagate by cuttings, layering, or grafting." — Dr. Ralph H. Sharpe of Gainesville, for whom the Sharpe blueberry is named.

TREE FRUITS

The size of some fruits depends on where you live. Grumichama is a shrub here in central Florida, sometimes reduced almost to a perennial, but it is a fine tall tree in West Palm Beach. So that is why some plants are on this and the shrub list. The ones with an asterisk are frost tender and should be protected in central Florida or grown in containers in the north; those without are cold hardy.

Atemoya (*Annona cherimol* × *A. squamosa*)*	C, S
Custard apple (*Annona reticulata*)*	S
Jak-fruit (*Artocarpus heterophyllus*)*	S
Star fruit (*Averrhoa carambola*)*	C, S
Mamey sapote (*Calocarpum sapota*)*	C, S
White sapote (*Casimiroa edulis*)	C, S
Black sapote or chocolate-pudding (*Diospyros digyna*)*	S
Grumichama (*Eugenia dombeyi*)*	S
Fig (*Ficus carica*)	N, C, S
Lychee (*Litchi chinensis*)*	C, S
Mango (*Mangifera indica*)*	C, S
Sapodilla (*Manikara zapot; Achras sapota*)*	C, S
Horseradish tree (*Moringa oleifera*)*	C, S
Mulberry (*Morus* spp.)	N, C, S
Banana (*Musa* hybrids)*	N, C, S
Jaboticaba (*Myricaria cauliflora*)*	C, S
Avocado (*Persea americana*)*	C, S
Tamarind (*Tamarindus indica*)	C, S

FRUITS FROM SHRUBS

Shrub-sized fruit plants can be incorporated into many landscapes, no matter how small. A screen of blueberries is a beautiful thing, and planting the blueberries together makes it easier to cover them with netting for protection from birds. MB: Many of us at the Rare Fruit Council International trade information and plants at meetings. Some members in the Tampa chapter have over two hundred different fruits in their yards and greenhouses. I have only forty-some, my favorites situated between the front door and the mailbox—I get teased about going to check my mail several times a day. Many Florida fruits need a bit of picking every day, so put them on or close to a handy path.

The ones with an asterisk should be protected from frost, but many will come back from the roots if frozen to the ground.

Custard apple, cherimoya (*Annona* spp.)*	C, S
Soursop (*Annona muricata*)*	C, S
Sugar apple (*Annona squamosa*)*	C, S
Papaya (*Carica papaya*)*	C, S
Quince (*Cydonia oblonga*)	N, C
Black sapote, chocolate-pudding (*Diospyros digyna*)*	C, S
Tropical apricot (*Dovyalis hebecarpa* × *abyssinica*)*	C, S
Cherry-of-the-Rio-Grande (*Eugenia aggregata*)*	C, S
Grumichama (*Eugenia dombeyi*)*	C, S
Surinam cherry (*Eugenia uniflora*)*	C, S
Pineapple guava (*Feijoa sellowiana*)	N, C, S
Fig (*Ficus carica*)	N, C, S
Florida cranberry, roselle (*Hibiscus sabdariffa*)*	N, C, S
Barbados cherry (*Malpighia punicifolia*)*	C, S
Jaboticaba (*Myricaria cauliflora*)*	C, S
Prickly pear (*Opuntia ficus-indica*)	N, C, S
Guava (*Psidium guajava*)*	C, S
Cattley, strawberry guava (*Psidium littorale*)	C, S
Pomegranate (*Punica granatum*)	N, C, S
Mysore raspberry (*Rubus albescens*)	C, S
Blackberry (*Rubus* hybrid)	N, C, S
Elderberry (*Sambucus canadensis*)	N, C, S
Miracle fruit (*Synsepalum dulcificum*)*	C, S
Blueberry (*Vaccinium* hybrids)	N, C, S

 There are several chapters of the Rare Fruit Council International (RFCI) throughout Florida. Members share information and plants at meetings and sales, provide tasting tables, and in some cases tend demonstration gardens. Watch the garden page of your local newspaper or call your county Cooperative Extension Service for the details of the group nearest you and go to a meeting or a sale as a guest. Or write to the founding organization: Rare Fruit Council International, Box 56194, Miami, FL 33256, for information.

EASY-TO-GROW FOODS YOU CAN'T OFTEN BUY

Charles Novak, president of the Tampa Chapter of the Rare Fruit Council International, grows over two hundred different fruits in his yard and greenhouse in Plant City. And he is always trying new ones. Here is his list of fun foods that anyone in the right part of Florida can grow, but many have never seen or tasted.

Monkey puzzle (*Araucaria araucana*)   N, C, S
Large, bristly evergreen trees. Female trees produce large pods containing numerous seeds that, when boiled, taste similar to chestnuts.

Pawpaw (*Asimina triloba*)   N, C
An overlooked native fruit with flesh that tastes like sweet custard. Seven species are native to Florida; paw paws sometimes grow wild along highways.

Tea (*Camellia sinensis*)   N, C
Tea is in the same genus as the camellia and produces a similar white-flowered, evergreen shrub.

Pummelo (*Citrus grandis*)   C, S
If you have room for only one citrus tree, this would be my recommendation. Delicious fruits, similar to sweet grapefruit but with a thick rind, may weigh up to 20 pounds. Flesh varies from white to deep red.

Loquat (*Eriobotrya japonica*)   N, C, S
Quality varies from tree to tree. Loquats grafted from known good trees can produce large, tasty fruit up to 2 inches long.

Macadamia nuts (*Macadamia integrifolia*)   C, S
Yes, you can grow macadamia nuts in Florida. Among the world's hardest shelled, use a vise-type nut cracker or a ratchet pipe cutter.

Jaboticaba (*Myricaria cauliflora*)   C, S
Delicious purplish-black fruit, resembling grapes, grows right along the trunk of this evergreen tree.

Downy myrtle (*Rhodomyrtus tomentosa*)   C, S
Rose-pink to light purple flowers, about 1 inch across, are followed by tasty, attractive fruit.

Mysore raspberry (*Rubus albescens*)   C, S
A tropical raspberry—one of the few that will grow and produce in Florida. The fruit is worth risking the many thorns.

Miracle fruit (*Synsepalum dulcificum*)   C, S
After eating the pulp of one of these small fruits, sour foods such as grapefruit and lemons have a sweet flavor. The effect lasts for about an hour.

CHARLIE ANDREWS' HERB RATINGS

LC: I called Charlie Andrews of Hammock Hollow Herb Farm in Cross Creek to ask for his list of the "top ten easiest herbs to grow in Florida." He laughed and said, "Well, I might be able to give you one: basil!" Isn't that encouraging? Don't close the book, though. I was able to coax a few more from Charlie, under the condition they appear in the order given below. Don't miss the cultural notes that follow. Those marked with an asterisk are warm-season annuals. The rest should be planted in October throughout the state. (Except lemongrass, which will be easier to find for sale in spring.)

Charlie's Top Pick
Basil, over 200 varieties (*Ocimum* spp.)*   N, C, S

No. 2 Picks
Cilantro, coriander (*Coriandrum sativum*)   N, C, S
Culantro (*Eryngium foetidum*)*   N, C, S

Others That Charlie Likes
Garlic chives (*Allium tuberosum*)   N, C, S
Chives (*Allium schoenoprasum*)   N, C
Lemongrass (*Cymbopogon citratus*)   N, C, S
Mexican oregano (*Lippia* or *Phyla graveolens*)   N, C, S
Mint (*Mentha* spp.)   N, C, S
Parsley (*Petroselinum crispum*)   N, C, S
French thyme (*Thymus vulgaris*)   N, C, S

These Need Some Work
Dill (*Anethum graveolens*)   N, C, S
Fennel (*Foeniculum vulgare*)   N, C, S

Only for Containers
Rosemary (*Rosmarinus officinalis*)   N, C, S
Garden sage (*Salvia officinalis*)   N, C, S

CULTURAL NOTES FROM CHARLIE

- Over two hundred varieties of basil give gardeners a lot of choices. Basil likes the heat and has very few insects that bother it. It's definitely the easiest herb. Except for basil and cilantro, which are warm-season plants, we start all our herbs in October, when the weather is cooler and drier.
- If you don't recognize cilantro, it's a perennial native to the Caribbean that is similar to coriander. Those with Cuban ties may recognize it as the herb sometimes used in *frijoles negros* (black beans). It is different from the Mexican coriander.
- We have lots of trouble with sage and rosemary. They don't like wet feet. They do much better in a container. If you want a lot of variety in herbs, you will have to do a lot of container growing. The plants dry out faster, and there is excellent drainage, so you avoid disease. Thyme does well in spring and fall. French thyme is best.

- Lemongrass is one we cut down to about 6 inches above the ground and cover with mulch for winter in north Florida.
- Chives need careful watching because, once the weeds come up through the little leaves, they are impossible to clean out.

TWO OR MORE NEEDED FOR POLLINATION

Many of our Florida fruits, almost all of the citrus, are self-pollinating. But some need two different varieties for cross pollination, and these must bloom at the same time. If a neighbor who's close enough (approximately within view) has one, that may do the job. Others, like kiwi and papaya, have male and female flowers on different plants, and you must have one of each (though a few varieties of each have both sexes on the same plant and are therefore self-fertilizing). Blueberries need very specific varieties paired together because varieties tend to bloom at different times. (See "Blueberries" on page xx) Where space is a problem, the two or three necessary plants can be set in the same hole for what looks like a multi-trunked tree, except that only part of it has fruit.

Kiwi (*Actinidia chinensis* 'Tomuri', 'Vincent')	N, C, S
Pawpaw (*Asimina triloba*)	N, C
Papaya (*Carica papaya*)	C, S
Pecan (*Carya illinoensis*)	N, C, S
Chestnut (*Castanea* spp.)	N, C
Tangerine (*Citrus* spp. 'Sunburst', 'Robinson', 'Orlando', 'Minneola')	C, S
Persimmon (*Diospyros kaki*)	N, C, S
Pineapple guava (*Feijoa sellowiana*)	N, C, S
Walnut (*Juglans* spp.)	N, C, S
Apple (*Malus pumila* 'Anna', 'Dorsett', 'Tropic Sweet')	N, C
Mulberry (*Morus albus*)	N, C, S
Avocado (*Persea americana*)	C, S
Nectarine (*Prunus persica* var. *nucipersica*)	N, C
Peach (*Prunus persica*)	N, C, S
Plum (*Prunus* spp. 'Early Bruce', 'Mariposa')	N, C, S
Pear (*Pyrus* spp. 'Flordahome', 'Pineapple')	N, C
Rose, for hips (*Rosa* spp.)	N, C, S
Highbush blueberry (*Vaccinium ashei*)	C
Rabbiteye blueberry (*Vaccinium corymbosum*)	N, C
Grape (*Vitis* spp. 'Fry', 'Jumbo')	N, C, S
Jujube (*Ziziphus jujuba*)	N, C, S

"Most people have trouble getting kiwi to fruit, but it can be done. The main reason most kiwi vines do not produce fruit is that they do not get the required chilling hours. Some vines need only fifty chilling hours to produce fruit. To obtain low-chilling-hour vines, buy only from reputable nurseries familiar with Florida conditions." — Charles Novak, president, Tampa Chapter, Rare Fruit Council International. (See "Low-Chill Fruits for Florida" on pages 164–65.)

BEST TROPICAL FRUITS FOR SOUTH FLORIDA

Chris Rollins, director of the Redlands Fruit and Spice Park in Homestead, offers the following list. The Redlands Fruit and Spice Park has undergone extensive renovation since Hurricane Andrew. If you live or visit near, be sure to spend some time there; it is open daily from 10 A.M. to 5 P.M. Write or call for special classes and activities (reservations required): 24081 SW 187th Avenue, Homestead, FL 33030, 305-247-5727.

Ilama (*Annona diversifolia*)   S
Best-tasting annona, but a shy producer. 'Emory' is a good variety. Seeds need drying.

Jak-fruit (*Artocarpus heterophyllus*)   S
Self-pollinated by wind and difficult to graft. Some as large as 2½ pounds.

White sapote (*Casimiroa edulis*)   S
Frost tender—freezes at 24 degrees F. Best varieties are 'Homestead' and 'Redland'.

Night-blooming cereus (*Cereus guatamalensis*)   S
Watermelon/strawberry-flavored fruit follow beautiful blooms. [MB: Mine has not yet set fruit.]

Pummelo (*Citrus grandis*)   C, S
Fruit is best when allowed to *blet*, or mellow, for four weeks after picking. Keeps well. Best variety is 'Hirado Butan'.

Jaboticaba (*Myricaria cauliflora*)   C, S
May take up to ten years to produce a fruit-bearing tree from seed. The fruit is so good, you may want to buy a large tree.

Abiu (*Pouteria caimito*)   S
Two trees needed for pollination; may take three to four years from seed to fruit.

Red mombin (*Spondias purpurea*)   S
Shrubby tree to 25 feet; in freezes, it will die back to ground and come back.

Cotopritz (*Talisia esculenta, T. oliformis*)   S
Produces male and female trees; need one of each for good pollination and fruiting.

Thai jujube (*Zizyphus thailandia* 'Kong Thai', 'Kong Sali', 'Bombay')   S
Better than Indian or Chinese varieties; these very thorny plants love maintenance.

BEST TOMATOES FOR FLORIDA

Here again, choosing the right variety can make the difference between failure and success. The following hybrids have earned letters attesting to their resistance to verticillium wilt (V), fusarium wilt (F), Race A and Race 2 fusarium wilt (FF), nematodes (N), tobacco mosaic (T), and *Alternaria alternata*—crown wilt— (A). The open-pollinated and heirloom varieties have no official ratings, but they have shown natural resistance or they would not have been around so many years. Grow all of these in fall or spring. Frost does in all tomatoes, and summer does in most except for some cherry tomatoes. Yet good yields are possible the rest of the time—twice as much as northern states enjoy.

Hybrids		**Open-Pollinated Heirlooms**	
'Better Boy'	V, F, N	'Hayslip'	V, FF
'Big Beef'	V, FF, N, T, A		
'Celebrity'	V, FF, N, T, A	**Heirlooms**	
'First Prize'	V, FF, N, T	'Black Prince'	
'Heatwave'	V, FF, A	'Green Zebra'	
'Lemon Boy'	V, F, N	'Cherokee Purple'	
'Solar Set'	V, FF		
'Sweet Chelsea'	V, F, N, T		
'Viva Italia'	V, FF, N, A		

"Tomato growing can be a bit of a challenge in Florida. Our heat and humidity cause increased problems, especially with fusarium wilt and nematodes. The varieties listed above either have the needed resistance or they set their fruit so well and so early that the fruit can mature before the problems overtake the plant." —Linda Sapp, owner, Tomato Growers Supply Company, Fort Myers.

EASY VEGETABLES

MB: Moving to Florida resulted in the best eggplant I'd ever grown the first year we were here. Peanuts keep reseeding in my garden, and I'm always glad to see them as soil builders if nothing else. That some are so easy is surprising. If I can find celery plants in the fall, I put them near the rain barrel, have plenty of leaves and stalks all winter and spring, and freeze or dry the bulk before summer rots it away. Planting at the right time and enriching the soil are the two main keys to success.

To help with timing, we have listed these plants according to whether they grow in the cool season or the warm season. Hint: Okra is easy once it is started, but the seed can be stubborn about germinating. Soak it overnight before planting and never plant it until the soil is good and warm (70 degrees minimum).

Cool Season	**Warm Season**
Celery (*Apium graveolens*)	Okra (*Abelmoschus esculentus*)
Mustard (*Brassica juncea*)	Peanut (*Arachis hypogaea*)
Cabbage, cole crops (*Brassica oleracea*)	Sweet potato (*Ipomoea batatas*)
Collard (*Brassica oleracea*)	Cherry tomato (*Lycopersicon esculentum*)
Kohlrabi (*Brassica oleracea*)	Snap beans (*Phaseolus vulgaris*)
Turnip (*Brassica rapa*)	Chayote (*Sechium edule*)
Leaf lettuce (*Lactuca sativa*)	Eggplant (*Solanum melongena*)

"With all the disease and insect problems we have, picking the right variety is of first importance for preventing pests. The other thing is to get varieties that will tolerate our heat or our time of the year. Your county Extension Service has lists available free." —Tom MacCubbin, author, *Florida Home Grown: Landscaping* and *Florida Home Grown 2: The Edible Landscape.*

BLUEBERRIES

We've given blueberries a list of their own because most of them need a specific other variety—one that will bloom at the same time—to pollinate them and assure a good crop. These are somewhat self-fertilizing, but the difference in production between a few berries and many is well worth planting two or more of the compatible varieties together. They can go in the same pot or hole. Plant only highbush varieties in central and south Florida; these produce very large, sweet, early ripening fruit. Rabbiteye hybrids do best in north Florida.

Highbush blueberries N, C, S	Rabbiteye hybrids N
plant any two or more together:	*plant any two or more together:*
'Flordablue'	'Blue Belle'
'Gulf Coast'	'Bonita'
'Marimba'	'Brightblue'
'Misty'	'Climax'
'Sharpe Blue'	'Premier'
	'Southland'
	'Tifblue'
plant any two or more together:	*plant together:*
'Bluegem'	'Aliceblue'
'Delite'	'Beckyblue'
'Woodard'	

"Since blueberries need a very acid soil, pH 4.0–5.2, most growers now keep them in gallon pots of straight pine bark and feed them three times a year with either azalea and rhododendron food or water-soluble acid fertilizer. I put two different plants in the same pot. You can grow them right in that mix for ten years without repotting. Just add more pine bark as it decomposes." —George Hoagland, owner, Dee's Trees, Seffner.

BACKYARD BANANAS

MB: I just about jumped up and down when I first saw a banana tree with fruit within a mile of my new Florida home. We had three cold winters before we got our first ripe bananas, but we've had some every year since, usually twelve to twenty bunches of the best-tasting bananas you can imagine. Home-grown bananas have as superior a flavor as homegrown green beans. Our neighbors Bob and Sherry Baker grow more than thirty kinds in an average-size back yard. The related plantains can be cooked green as well as eaten ripe.

In the June-July 1997 issue of *Florida Gardening* magazine, Johnny Papaya Burns of Sarasota issued a warning about certain banana varieties. "Panama Disease Race Two is a particularly virulent banana disease that could eventually threaten the commercial industry, causing bananas to become rare and expensive. It has been found in the 'Apple', 'Ice Cream', 'Golden Pillow', and 'Orinoco' varieties. For this reason, the dissemination of these varieties is to be discouraged," wrote Burns.

Listed below are some varieties you can try.

'Brazilian'	Tall; excellent wind tolerance
'Double or Mahoi'	Rare, sweet; may bear two bunches per stalk
'Dwarf Cavendish'	At only 5 to 7 feet, a good container plant; sweet

'Giant Cavendish'	Commercial variety; 14-16 feet tall; nematode susceptible
'Goldfinger'	Fruits in nine to twelve months; disease resistant
'Gran Nain'	Dwarf; huge bunches of delicious fruit; cold and wind hardy
'Jamaican Red'	Tall; red fruit with orange pulp; excellent
'Kru'	One of the most delicious; light red fruit; angular shape
'Mysore'	Lady-finger type; small, sweet fruit in large heads; vigorous
'Nino'	Excellent; small fruit and bunches; disease resistant
'Pysang Raja'	Hardy, tall; wonderful flavor; pinkish-orange pulp
'Rajapuri'	Hardiest and toughest; medium-sized fruit and bunches
'Valery'	Commercial banana; semi-dwarf with large heads; hardy

"Bananas are one of the simplest plants to grow, and they give such a tropical effect that they can brighten even the dreariest day. The plants are so green and leafy and flow with the wind. People as far north as the Carolinas bring theirs in every winter and get some fruit the second year. Bananas give you fruit in one year here in south Florida. Children love to grow them. After Hurricane Andrew they were one of the first plants to return and cheer us up." —Katie and Don Chafin, Going Bananas Nursery, Homestead.

PERENNIAL EDIBLE HERBS

Don't let the lists of short-lived herbs discourage you, because many more herbs will last for several years here. Most are evergreen. A few will disappear for a time and then reappear from new seedlings. A few will die back in a freeze but return from the roots. Parsley, which is technically a biennial, will often live for two years, but the foliage is most tender and succulent only during its first season. The older the plant gets, the more tough even the new growth seems to be. Take cuttings of the ones with an asterisk before a freeze, and if the freeze is severe or long lasting, you'll be ready if you have to start over.

Anise hyssop (*Agastache foeniculum*)	N, C, S
Chives (*Allium schoenoprasum*)	N, C
Garlic chives (*Allium tuberosum*)	N, C, S
Horseradish (*Armoracia rusticana*)	N, C, S
Chicory (*Chicorium intybus*)	N, C, S
Cuban oregano (*Coleus amboinicus*)*	N, C, S
Lemongrass (*Cymbopogon citratus*)	C, S
Cardamom (*Elettaria cardamomum*)	N, C, S
Fennel (*Foeniculum vulgare*)	N, C, S
Horehound (*Marrumbium vulgare*)	N, C, S
Mint (*Mentha* spp.)	N, C, S
Beebalm (*Monarda punctata*, M. *austromontana*)	N, C
Watercress (*Nasturtium officinale*)	N, C, S
Oregano (*Origanum* spp.)	N, C, S
Scented geranium (*Pelargonium* spp.)*	N
Rosemary (*Rosmarinus officinalis*)	N, C, S
Sorrel (*Rumex scutatus*)	N, C, S
Comfrey (*Symphytum officinale*)	N, C, S
Parsley (*Petroselinum crispum*)	N, C, S
Ginger (*Zingiber officinale*)	N, C, S

Chicory

LOW-CHILL FRUITS FOR FLORIDA

Low-chill varieties allow Floridians to grow some fruits that need cold weather. Most of these varieties have been bred by the University of Florida or by other breeding programs in the Deep South. Chilling hours are accumulated when the temperature stays below 45 degrees on a fairly constant basis. Averages vary from fifty to 150 hours in south Florida, through 150 to 350 hours in the center of the state, 350 to 650 in the north. Select plants with tags that indicate chill hours and growing zones. MB: My area near Tampa has an average of 250 chilling hours. Except in the far north and southern tip of Florida, homeowners can have some of both low-chill and subtropical fruit. Then no matter if the winter is warm or cold, there will always be a crop of fruit.

Apple N, C, S
  'Anna' Plant with 'Tropic Sweet' or 'Dorsett' for good pollination
  'Dorsett Golden' Plant with 'Anna' or 'Tropic Sweet' for good pollination
  'Tropic Sweet' No-acid variety; requires least chilling of all apples

Asparagus N, C
  'Mary Washington' Fair performer in N and C from crowns or seeds; stalks grow large and woody quickly in the warm weather
  'UC 157' Developed for the South and Southwest; produces twice the yield of common types

Blackberry N, C, S
  'Arapaho' Thornless; produces large berries in June of first year on erect canes
  'Brazos' Fruits in mid-April on thorny vining canes that need trellising or staking
  'Navaho' Thornless; will produce in June of first year

Nectarine N, C
  'Sun Home' Red- and green-leaved tree produces sweet fruit
  'Sun Mist' Newer variety
  'Sun Racer' Large, excellent fruit quality
  'Sun Red' Good quality, solid fruit

Peaches N, C, S
  'Flordaglo' White flesh and unique flavor; extremely low chill requirements
  'Florida Prince' Most widely planted variety; excellent quality fruit
  'Tropic Sweet' New variety for central Florida
  'UF Gold' Has non-melting flesh gene; fruit keeps well on tree, fine color and flavor

Pear
  'Baldwin' Late-fruiting for fresh eating or canning N
  'Flordahome' Late-producing fruit for eating fresh or canning; needs pollinator N, C, S
  'Hood' Early fruit for eating fresh or canning; good pollinator for 'Pineapple' N, C
  'Kieffer' Late canning variety N
  'Pineapple' Early canning variety; needs pollinator N, C, S

Plums   N, C
 'Gulf Gold'   Yellow skin; very sweet; ripens over long period
 'Gulf Ruby'   Purple skin, red flesh; needs pollinator

Raspberry
 'Dormared'   Grow as an annual   N, C, S
 'Fallgold'   Similar to 'Heritage' but ripens golden yellow; annual   N, C, S
 'Heritage'   Commercial quality; grow as annual; extremely heavy bearer
                    N, C, S
 Mysore raspberry   Tropical raspberry for Florida   C, S
 (*Rubus albescens*)

Rhubarb   N, C, S
 'Cherry Red'   Plant seeds or roots any time in north Florida for perennial
 'Victoria'   growth; plant from August to October in C and S and treat as
                    an annual; does best where winters are cold

 "I have three kinds of blackberries. 'Brazos' is excellent here, ripen from late April through May, and spread by runners in sun or partial shade. Thornless bushes, 'Navaho' and 'Arapaho', ripen through June and into July. From about forty plants, I sold 150 pints last May. I plant them where I can mow grass on both sides and thus be sure that they won't become a bramble patch. This also makes it easier to pick. In the sun, you get more berries, but they aren't quite as large. One customer bought a peach tree while it was still dormant last spring and harvested twenty-nine peaches the very first season." —George Hoagland, owner, Dee's Trees, Seffner.

TENDER WINTER VEGETABLES

These will freeze, so be prepared to cover them. In south and central Florida, we can usually grow many of these warm-season vegetables throughout winter. Often we have beans and tomatoes almost straight through from fall until spring in Tampa. Other years, there is a pause for winter frost and we start over again right away for a spring crop. The only two that don't do well on the second planting for spring harvest are English peas and potatoes. If they don't make it from the first planting in fall or early winter, then you'll have to wait until the next year.

Peas and potatoes are the only vegetables on this list that you would plant in midwinter (January or early February) in north Florida. The rest will need to wait until after frost is past in spring.

Watermelon (*Citrullus lanatus*)   Lima bean (*Phaseolus vulgaris*)
Cucumber (*Cucumis sativus*)   Snap bean (*Phaseolus vulgaris*)
Cantaloupe (*Cucumis* spp.)   Ground cherry (*Physalis peruviana*)
Pumpkin (*Curcurbita* spp.)   English pea (*Pisum sativum*)
Squash (*Curcurbita* spp.)   Eggplant (*Solanum melongena esculentum*)
Tomato (*Lycopersicon esculentum*)   Potato (*Solanum tuberosum*)

 "Enrich your soil with well-rotted manures. Chicken manure is considered to have the highest quantity of nitrogen. For insect control, use (horticultural, not pool-type) diatomaceous earth, garlic sprays, tobacco stems, ladybugs, praying mantids, and *bacillus thuriengensis*." —Marian Van Atta, *Living off the Land*.

PLANTS ESPECIALLY SENSITIVE TO NEMATODES

Nematodes, both beneficial and destructive, are present in any soil anywhere. MB: Florida is the first place I've lived that nematodes can do in a plant or a planting. Some experts say that you won't have much trouble your first year but you may after that. I found just the opposite to be true. Whole plantings of beans died out for me the first few years, and the bumps on their shriveled roots were not nitrogen nodules—these will rub off—but damage from the root-knot nematodes. As I have enriched the soil, I've had fewer and fewer problems. Nematodes seem to do more damage in sandy soils than rich organic ones. The simplest solution for the plants on this list is to mulch them knee deep.

Another way to minimize nematode damage is to build 3-foot-high raised beds and fill them with a good organic soil mix. Avoid introducing your garden soil into the mix. Tomatoes can be grow in 10-gallon or larger containers if you can keep them watered.

Fig (*Ficus carica*)
Strawberry (*Fragaria* × *ananassa*)
Tomato (*Lycopersicon esculentum*)
Banana (*Musa* spp.)

Snap beans (*Phaseolus vulgaris*)
Winged bean (*Psophocarpus tetragonolobus*)
Rhubarb (*Rheum rhabarbarum*)

COLD-HARDY AND SUPERIOR VARIETIES

"The American Chestnut was the dominant tree species in the eastern hardwood forest until it was almost completely destroyed by a bark fungus accidentally introduced from the Orient in 1904. Within forty years, over 3.5 billion chestnuts were killed from Maine to Georgia and west to the Mississippi, probably the largest botanical disaster in history," says R.D. Wallace, owner of the Chestnut Hill Nursery of Alachua, Florida. In the early 1950s, James Carpentar of Salem, Ohio, discovered a blight-free chestnut. After it resisted test inoculations, he sent bud-wood to Dr. Robert Dunstan in North Carolina who grafted the scions onto chestnut rootstock and cross-pollinated them with three superior USDA-released Chinese chestnuts. The first cross began to bear in 1962. The second generation of these trees was moved to Florida, where today there exists a grove of sixty trees that bear heavily at Chestnut Hill Nursery and have never shown any instance of blight. Chestnuts have timber value at maturity comparable to walnuts. They are also excellent for woodlot, wildlife, and reforestation plantings.

Nurseries like Chestnut Hill work closely with the University of Florida in Gainesville to propagate and publicly distribute the best new fruit varieties for all parts of Florida. Thanks to the efforts of such breeders, Florida gardeners may now enjoy both improved fruit favorites as well as new fruit varieties. Here is a long list of them.

Avocado
'Brogdon'   Hardy to 22 F; large fruit with papery smooth purple skin
'Day'   Hardy to 22 F; large green fruits with great flavor
'Winter Mexican'   Hardy to 18 F; smooth black skin, cold hardiest

Banana
'Gran Nain'   Improved from 'Dwarf Cavendish'; huge bunches of delicious fruit
'Ladyfinger'   Short, very sweet desert bananas on tall, elegant plant
'Rajapuri'   Hardiest variety; stocky, wind-resistant trees

Chestnut

'Dunstan Hybrid'   Large, sweet nuts; completely blight resistant; good as far south as Orlando

Citrus

Calamondin orange   Slightly larger than kumquat; prolific
'Meiwa' kumquats   Round sweet fruit can be eaten rind and all
'Meyer' lemon   Large, sweet fruit; an excellent variety
'Nagami' kumquat   Round, sour fruit is good for jams

Fig

'Alma'   Huge, flavorful fruits
'Brown Turkey'   Most popular variety; everbearing
'Celeste'   Small, sweet fruit; also called sugar fig
'Royal Vineyard'   Very large fruit with excellent flavor

Muscadine grape

Black and bronze muscadines are great for wines, jellies, fresh eating, and landscaping.

'Southern Home Hybrid'   Cross between bunch and muscadine grape; table grape with ornamental leaves; vigorous grower; extremely disease resistant

Table and wine grapes

Table and wine grapes are difficult to grow in central and south Florida, but these disease-resistant varieties are worth a try.

'Blue Lake'   Purple to blue; small, ½"
'Daytona'   Pink table grape; large bunches and berries
'Lake Emerald'   Golden when ripe; ½"–¾"

Kiwi

'Issai'   Self-pollinating and extremely cold hardy; seedless; smooth skin
'Tomuri'   Predominantly male plants; good pollinators for females
'Vincent'   Female strain; familiar grocery-market type fruit

Persimmon

These nonastringent cultivars can be eaten at any stage of ripeness.

'Fuyu'   Fruits November to early December
'Hanagosho'   Fruits mid-October to mid-November
'Izu'   Fruits late September to mid-October
'Suruga'   Fruits November to early December

These mouth-puckering astringent cultivars must be picked only when completely ripe.

'Saijo'   Early winter fruit
'Tanenashi'   Late fall to winter; most popular variety
'Atago'   Late winter

EDIBLE FLOWERS

Some flowers, like nasturtiums, have a distinctive taste that can really pep up a salad. Most are rather bland and make little difference in the taste but all the difference in the world in eye appeal. Use them also as garnishes, frozen in ice cubes for drinks, in fruit salads, candied, or stuffed with soft cheese. Blooms of all culinary herbs are edible. The flowers listed here are also edible, but others not on this list may be unappetizing or even poisonous. As with any edibles, try new types cautiously, in small amounts, in case you are allergic to them or find the taste disagreeable.

Anise hyssop (*Agastache foeniculum*)	N, C, S
Chives (*Allium schoenoprasum*))	N, C
Garlic chives (*Allium tuberosum*)	N, C, S
Snapdragon (*Antirrhinum majus*)	N, C
Borage (*Borago officinalis*)	N, C, S
Calendula (*Calendula officinalis*)	N, C, S
Chrysanthemums (*Chrysanthemum* spp.)	N, C, S
Citrus blossom	N, C, S
Squash, pumpkin (*Curcurbita* spp.)	N, C, S
Carnation, pinks (*Dianthus* spp.)	N, C, S
Pineapple guava (*Feijoa sellowiana*)	N, C, S
Gladiolus (*Gladiolus* hybrids)	N, C, S
Sunflower (*Helianthus annuus*)	N, C, S
Daylily (*Hemerocallis* spp.)	N, C, S
Hibiscus (*Hibiscus* spp.)	C, S
Impatiens (*Impatiens* spp.)	N, C, S
Lavender (*Lavandula* spp.)	N, C, S
Honeysuckle (*Lonicera* spp.)	N, C, S
Mint (*Mentha* spp.)	N, C, S
Geranium (*Pelargonium* spp.)	N, C, S
Purslane (*Portulaca* spp.)	N, C, S
Rose (*Rosa* spp.)	N, C, S
Pineapple sage (*Salvia elegans*)	N, C, S
Elderberry (*Sambucus canadensis*)	N, C, S
Marigold (*Tagetes* spp.)	N, C, S
Nasturtium (*Tropaeolum majus*)	N, C, S
Society garlic (*Tulbaghia violacea*)	N, C, S
Violet, pansy (*Viola* spp.)	N, C, S*

"If you grow your own flowers, you must not use chemicals on your plants. Do not go to your local florist and buy flowers to eat—they aren't organically grown. Your local health food store should have them, or better yet, grow them yourself." —Maryon Marsh, owner, The Misting Shed Herb Nursery, Dover.

HEAT-TOLERANT VEGETABLES

"It's harder to grow vegetables in the subtropics than almost anyplace else," says Marian Van Atta in her book, *Living off the Land*. MB: Since vegetables were what I grew mostly before moving to Florida, I hoped to prove her wrong but wound up comforted by her all-too-true statement. Only on rare occasions do I get the great quantities of beans that were part of every summer up north. But I learned about new planting times and special varieties like Roma beans, and we now can pick something almost every day. I don't really mind giving up the freezing and canning. I still do a little for the sparsest months in the dead of winter or summer, but mostly we just eat what is available.

Okra (*Abelmoschus esculentus*)
Tampala (*Amaranthus gangeticus*)
Peanut (*Arachis hypogaea*)
Sweet banana pepper (*Capsicum* spp.)
Costa Rican pepper (*Capsicum* spp.)
Jalapeno hot pepper (*Capsicum annuum*)
Habanero hot pepper (*Capsicum chinense habenero*)
Pigeon pea (*Cajanus cajan*)
Italian squash (*Cucuzzi caravazzi*)
Calabaza, Cuban pumpkin (*Curcurbita moschata*)
Yam (*Dioscorea alata*)
Jerusalem artichoke, sunchoke (*Helianthus tuberosus*)
Sweet potato (*Ipomoea batatas*)
Luffa, Chinese okra (*Luffa aegyptiaca*)
Cherry tomato (*Lycopersicon esculentum*)
Cassava (*Manihot utilissima*)
Jicama (*Pachyrrhizus erosus*)
Winged bean (*Psophocarpus tetragonolobus*)
Chayote (*Sechium edule*)
Eggplant (*Solanum melongena esculentum*)
New Zealand spinach (*Tetragonia tetragonioides*)
Blackeye, southern peas (*Vigna unguiculata*)

"Calabaza, Cuban or Spanish pumpkin, is remarkably productive and particularly suited to the subtropical and tropical climates of Florida. New varieties have been hybridized at the University of Florida to produce a bushier plant with smaller fruit. Except for the hybrids, most of our plants are open-pollinated, and people can save their own seeds from these from year to year." —Elaine Sarasin, owner, Southern Seeds, Lutz, Florida

BEAUTIFUL VEGETABLES FOR FLOWER BEDS

Some neighborhoods have ordinances against vegetable gardens, meaning a plot laid out in rows. Gardeners get around this easily by mixing their vegetables right in with their flowers or shrubs, and no one could ever complain because they make such a pleasant appearance. Here are some of the most decorative. N, C, or S indicates a plant that can be perennial in those zones.

Red okra (*Abelmoschus esculentus* 'Burgundy')
Amaranthus (*Amaranth* spp.)
Swiss chard (*Beta vulgaris* 'Bright Lights')
Red mustard (*Brassica juncea* 'Red Giant')
Flowering cabbage, kale (*Brassica oleracea acephala*)
Red cabbage (*Brassica oleracea* 'Red Royale')
Chinese cabbage (*Brassica rapa*)
Pepper (*Capsicum* spp.)   N, C, S
Radicchio (*Chicorium intybus*)
Cardoon (*Cynara cardunculus*)
Carrot (*Daucus carota*)
Hyacinth bean (*Dolichos lablab*)
Red lettuce (*Lactuca sativa* 'Red Sails')
Green lettuce (*Lactuca sativa* 'Black Seeded Simpson')
Runner bean (*Phaseolus vulgaris, P. coccineus*)
Purple-leaf eggplant (*Solanum melongena*)   C, S
Arrowhead (*Sagittaria* spp.)   N, C, S
New Zealand spinach (*Tetragonia tetragonioides*)

"Whether in pots or in the ground, plants need good air flow, especially in the summer, to prevent diseases. Good grooming is also important. Trim spent flowers weekly. That's the first place you'll find pests. Trim some of the lower branches to let air in. Keep up with pest patrol and use soap or oil alternately as needed. Every living thing has some pests, and pests on plants are like head colds for people. Neither will die from the nuisance and can still function, but the cold or the pests interrupt life, prevent feeling or growing great, and can lead to more serious problems if ignored. Pests cause a plant stress and make it more prone to diseases." —John Allan, owner, All Seasons Nursery (wholesale herbs), Seffner.

HARDY WINTER VEGETABLES

MB: These could die in a hard freeze, but they haven't for me yet, and Katy at O'Toole's Herb Farm says they often grow all winter even in Madison, Florida, about 20 miles from the Georgia border. More often in the central and southern areas they sulk because of too much warm weather even in the winter, so the time frame is shorter and more uncertain. One great gardener told me I could not grow English peas here (near Tampa), but I have. However, he was partly right. I doubt if I'd ever get a bumper crop. Some, like carrots and the cole crops, are happy from the end of one summer to the start of the next summer. All of these are planted in the fall.

Onion (*Allium cepa*)
Leek (*Allium porrum* 'King Richard')
Celery (*Apium graveolens* var. *dulce*)
Swiss chard (*Beta vulgaris* var. *cicla*)
Beet (*Beta vulgaris*)
Collard (*Brassica oleracea acephala*)
Kale (*Brassica oleracea acephala*)
Broccoli (*Brassica oleracea botrytis*)
Cauliflower (*Brassica oleracea botrytis*)
Cabbage (*Brassica oleracea capitata*)
Brussels sprouts (*Brassica oleracea gemmifera*)
Kohlrabi (*Brassica oleracea gongylodes*)
Turnip (*Brassica rapa*)
Endive (*Chicorium endivia*)
Radicchio (*Chicorium intybus*)
Cardoon (*Cynara cardunculus*)
Carrot (*Daucus carota*)
Arugula (*Eruca sativa*)
Jerusalem artichoke, sunchoke (*Helianthus tuberosus*)
Lettuce (*Lactuca sativa*)
Parsley (*Petroselinum crispum*)
Snap pea (*Pisum sativum* 'Sugar Snap')
English pea (*Pisum sativum*)
Radish (*Raphanus sativus*)
Rhubarb (*Rheum rhabarbarum*)
Spinach (*Spinacea oleracea*)
Corn salad (*Valerianella olitoria*)

Kohlrabi

UNCOMMON VEGETABLES

MB: The farther south you live, the more of these you need to discover. Chayote or green papaya can substitute for squash almost year-round. And while we can't grow the usual Halloween pumpkins at that time of year, the Seminole pumpkins are a great trade-off. The first year I planted them I had extras to take to the RFCI meetings for five months of the summer and became known as the pumpkin lady.

It is worth traveling quite a ways to go on the tour of the farm and gardens at ECHO, Educational Concerns for Hunger Organization, in North Fort Myers. Make a point to attend a free tour any Tuesday, Friday, or Saturday at 10 A.M. (except holidays; groups of ten or more by appointment). Volunteer tour guides will show you all sorts of new crops and methods for sub-tropical gardens. ECHO offers seeds by mail (send $1 for a seed list) and has plants for sale in its Edible Landscape Nursery, open 9 to noon, Monday through Saturday. If you get near exit 26 off I-75, do visit. If you live or stay near there, consider volunteering.

Amaranth (*Amaranthus* spp.)	Leaves eaten as greens; seeds ground into flour
Wax gourd (*Benincasa hispida*)	Similar to summer squash
Quail grass (*Celosia argentea*)	Leaves similar to spinach; thrives in hot weather
Chayote (*Sechium edule*)	Similar to squash or cucumber

Uncommon Vegetables (*continued*)

Italian squash (*Cucuzzi caravazzi*)	Similar to zucchini
Calabaza pumpkin (*Curcurbita moschata*)	Pie pumpkin; better than jack-o'lantern types
Roselle (*Hibiscus sabdariffa*)	Florida cranberry
Horseradish tree (*Moringa olifera*)	Roots used like true horseradish; leaves, blossoms, and pods edible
Prickly pear cactus (*Opuntia* spp.)	Thick leaves prepared like squash
Jicama (*Pachyrrhizus erosus*)	Edible tuber similar to water chestnuts
Winged bean (*Psophocarpus tetragonolobus*)	Leaves similar to spinach; eat young pods like green beans; mature pods for dry beans

SPECIALTY PLANTS

This chapter is a gathering of odds and ends that are important to gardening in Florida but that do not fit neatly into other chapters in this book. Here you will find lists on the following subjects:

- plants that attract butterflies
- plants that attract birds
- plants that deer don't like
- plants for bonsai
- plants for moonlit gardens
- plants for water gardens

TO DO LIST FOR ATTRACTING BUTTERFLIES

MB: In my weekly *Brandon News* column I have interviewed quite a few gardeners whose special interest is butterflies, and they have some of the most colorful and beautiful of all the gardens I've visited. You can hardly keep butterflies out of a garden, but you can greatly increase their numbers in a few weeks or months if you give them what they need.

Lois Weber, bird and butterfly chairperson for District 8 of the Florida Federation of Garden Clubs, and Craig Huegel, manager of the Brooker Creek Preserve in Tarpon Springs, offer the following tips to create a thriving butterfly garden. They also give some personal notes on its enjoyment.

- Wear bright colors, even a bandanna, to attract butterflies to you.
- Observe them first as they feed, which is when they stay still the longest. Then learn to watch for them laying eggs or taking shelter.
- Get a good, simple guide with colored pictures and identify your butterflies by name.
- Choose a wide variety of plants. The size of the garden doesn't matter as much as what plants are in it. But the larger the site and the more plants and kinds of plants it holds, the greater the numbers and varieties of butterflies it will attract.

- Include larval food as well as nectar sources (see the following list).
- Remember that butterflies prefer to feed in sunny, open sites.
- If your yard is often windy as it is on the Atlantic Coast, put your butterfly garden in a corner where the wind is blocked.
- Provide a water source, a shallow saucer filled with damp soil or sand. Or put a stone in your birdbath so the butterflies can land on that.
- Plant host shrubs at strategic places so they can always find a place for shelter and rest. A few flat stones around the garden also give butterflies a place to rest.
- *Never use pesticides to combat garden pests.* Pick off pests by hand or spray them with a hose. If you have something like roses that you'll be spraying often, put them in a separate section of the yard as far removed as possible.

"A 10 x10-foot garden is large enough to attract butterflies if you put in the right plants. I've put in such gardens at schools and seen the butterfly population increase within a week from almost none to ten to fifteen at a time. Planting by color, a group of blue flowers in one area, reds in another, yellows together, etc., draws more butterflies." —Dick Smith, formerly in charge of plants in the Wings of Wonder Butterfly Conservatory, Cypress Gardens; now gives Wonder Workshops and is author of books for teaching children about butterflies in Auburndale.

ANNUALS AND PERENNIALS TO ATTRACT BIRDS

These flowers will attract a variety of birds to your garden while giving you color and fragrance. Those that attract hummingbirds will also often invite butterflies to their flowers. Try to have some of them blooming in every season. Let some of them go to seed, for the seed is what most birds are seeking. Many of these are quite attractive in their seed stage, those especially so are marked with an asterisk.

Annuals That Attract Hummingbirds
Snapdragon (*Antirrhinum majus*)
Cleome (*Cleome hasslerana*)
Sunflower (*Helianthus annuus*)*
Impatiens (*Impatiens* hybrids)
Morning glory (*Ipomoea* spp.)
Scarlet morning glory (*Ipomoea coccinea*)
Cypress vine (*Ipomoea quamoclit*)
Red hot poker (*Kniphofia* spp.)
Four-o'clock (*Mirabilis jalapa*)
Flowering tobacco (*Nicotiana* spp.)
Pentas (*Pentas lanceolata*)
Petunias (*Petunia* spp., especially red or pink)
Drummond phlox (*Phlox drummondii*)
Scarlet sage (*Salvia* spp.)
Nasturtium (*Tropaeolum majus*)
Zinnia (*Zinnia angustifolius* 'White Star')

Annuals That Attract Other Birds
Ageratum (*Ageratum houstonianum*)
Amaranth (*Amaranthus* spp.)*
China aster (*Aster chinensis*)
Calendula (*Calendula officinalis*)
Corn flower, bachelor's button (*Centaurea cyanus*)
Calliopsis (*Coreopsis* spp.)
Cosmos (*Cosmos bipinnatus*)
Klondike cosmos (*Cosmos sulphureus*)
Pinks (*Dianthus* spp.)
Balsam (*Impatiens balsamina*)
Love-in-a-mist (*Nigella damascena*)*
Geranium (*Pelargonium* spp.)
Gloriosa daisy (*Rudbeckia hirta*)*
Marigold (*Tagetes* spp.)
Mexican sunflower (*Tithonia rotundifolia*)
Zinnia (*Zinnia elegans*)

Perennials That Attract Hummingbirds
Columbine (*Aquilegia* spp.) — N, C
Texas star (*Hibiscus coccinea*) — N, C, S
Shrimp plant (*Justicia brandegeana*) — C, S
Cardinal flower (*Lobelia cardinalis*) — N, C, S
Pentas (*Pentas lanceolata*) — C, S
False dragonhead (*Physostegia virginiana*) — N, C
Tropical salvia (*Salvia coccinea*) — N, C, S
Pineapple sage (*Salvia elegans*) — N, C, S
Autumn sage (*Salvia greggii*) — N, C, S
Mexican sage (*Salvia leucantha*) — N, C, S

Perennials That Attract Other Birds
Aloe (*Aloe vera*) — C, S
Milkweed (*Asclepias* spp.) — N, C, S
Shasta daisy (*Chrysanthemum × superbum*) — N, C
Purple coneflower (*Echinacea purpurea*)* — N, C, S
Blanket flower (*Gaillardia pulchella*) — N, C, S
Rose mallow (*Hibiscus moscheutos*) — C, S
Four-o'clock (*Mirabilis jalapa*) — C, S
Fountain grass (*Pennisetum setaceum*)* — N, C, S
Rosemary (*Rosmarinus officinalis*) — N, C, S
Black-eyed Susan (*Rudbeckia* spp.)* — N, C, S
Goldenrod (*Solidago* spp.)* — N, C, S
Ironweed (*Vernonia noveboracensis*) — N, C, S

PLANTS TO FEED BUTTERFLY LARVA

Caterpillars are welcome in the butterfly garden. With the help of a field guide, it doesn't take long to identify many of them as friends. The following plants are favorites of many butterflies for laying eggs, so expect to find some holes in their leaves. Most of these are tough and can survive even if they get eaten to the nub, which usually doesn't happen. Provide as much variety as you can. Craig Huegel gives specific instructions for growing and using many of the natives in his book *Butterfly Gardening with Florida's Native Plants*, available from the Florida Native Plant Society, P.O. Box 680008, Orlando, FL 32868. The plants below that are marked with an asterisk are native or have been naturalized. Annuals are not marked with regions because they will grow in all of Florida in the appropriate season. Some of the natives are not likely to appear at retail nurseries, but we list them because they may already be present on your property.

Annuals
Hollyhock (*Alcea rosea*)
Amaranth (*Amaranthus* spp.)
Dill (*Anethum graveolens*)
Snapdragon (*Antirrhinum majus*)
Mustard (*Brassica* spp.)
Sea rocket (*Cakile lanceolate; C. edentula*)*
Calendula (*Calendula officinalis*)
Cleome (*Cleome hasslerana*)
Fennel (*Foeniculum vulgare*)
Peppergrass (*Lepidium virginicum*)*
Parsley (*Petroselinum crispum*)
Bean (*Phaseolus* spp.)
Radish (*Raphanus sativa*)
Rue (*Ruta graveolens*)
Nasturtium (*Tropaeolum majus*)
Warrea (*Warrea simplicifolia, W. carteri*)*

Dill

Perennials

Wormwood (*Artemisia* spp.)	N, C, S
Butterfly weed, milkweed (*Asclepias* spp.)*	N, C, S
Climbing aster (*Aster caroliniensis*)*	N, C, S
Aster (*Aster dumosus*)*	N, C
Walter's aster (*Aster walteri*)*	N, C
Water hyssop (*Bacopa* spp.)*	N, C, S
Golden canna (*Canna flaccida*)*	N, C, S
Rabbit's bell (*Crotalaria pumila, C. rotundifolia*)	N, C, S
Pink dalea (*Dalea carnea*)*	N, C
Summer farewell (*Dalea pinnata*)*	N, C
Snakeroot (*Eryngium aromaticum*)*	N, C, S
Fennel (*Foeniculum vulgare*)	N, C, S
Beach sunflower (*Helianthus debilis*)	N, C, S
Swamp mallow (*Hibiscus coccineus*)	N, C, S
Florida petunia (*Ruellia* spp.)	N, C, S
Rue (*Ruta graveolens*)	N, C, S
Goldenrod (*Solidago* spp.)	N, C, S

Beach verbena (*Verbena maritima*) — N, C, S
Violet (*Viola* spp.) — N, C, S

Vines
Pipe vine (*Aristolochia* spp.)* — N, C, S
Butterfly pea (*Clitoria mariana*) — N, C, S
Milk pea (*Galactia* spp.) — N, C, S
Hop vine (*Humulus* spp.) — N, C
Passionflower (*Passiflora* spp.)* — N, C, S
Wisteria, Chinese wisteria (*Wisteria sinensis*) — N, C

Shrubs
Serviceberry (*Amelanchier arborea*) — N, C
Leadplant (*Amorpha* spp.)* — N, C
Torchwood (*Amyris elemifera*) — C, S
Paw paw (*Asimina obovata, A. reticulata*)* — N, C, S
Tarflower (*Befaria racemosa*) — N, C, S
Jamaica caper (*Capparis cynophallophora*) — C, S
Bahamas cassia (*Cassia chapmanii*)* — S
New Jersey tea (*Ceanothus americanus*) — N, C
Dogwood (*Cornus* spp.) — N, C
Pineland croton (*Croton linearis*) — S
Golden dewdrop (*Duranta repens*)* — N, C, S
Firebush (*Hamelia patens*)* — C, S
Hibiscus (*Hibiscus* spp.) — C, S
Dwarf lantana (*Lantana ovatifolia*)* — C, S
Texas sage (*Leucophyllum frutescens*) — N, C, S
Privet (*Ligustrum* spp.) — N, C, S
Spicebush (*Lindera benzoin*) — N, C
Wax myrtle (*Myrica cerifera*)* — N, C, S
Mistletoe (*Phoradendron serotinum*) — N, C, S
Plumbago (*Plumbago auriculata*) — C, S
Rhododendron (*Rhododendron* spp.) — N, C
Blueberry (*Vaccinium* spp.) — N, C, S
Viburnum (*Viburnum* spp.) — N, C, S
Spanish bayonet (*Yucca* spp.) — N, C, S
Coontie palm (*Zamia floridana*)* — N, C, S

Trees
Paw paw (*Asimina triloba*)* — N
Redbud (*Cercis canadensis*)* — N, C
Citrus (*Citrus* spp.) — N, C, S
Dogwood (*Cornus* spp.) — N, C
Strangler fig (*Ficus aurea*)* — C, S
Shortleaf fig (*Ficus citrifolia*)* — C, S
Pop ash (*Fraxinus caroliniana*) — N, C, S
Green ash (*Fraxinus pennsylvanica*) — N, C
Sweet bay (*Magnolia virginiana*)* — N, C, S
Red bay, swamp bay, or silk bay (*Persea* spp.)* — N, C, S
Blackbead (*Pithecellobium guadalupense*) — C, S

Trees (*continued*)

Cat's claw (*Pithecellobium unguis-cati*)	C, S
Hop tree (*Ptelea trifoliata*)*	N, C
Laurel oak (*Quercus laurifolia*)*	N, C, S
Live oak (*Quercus virginiana*)*	N, C, S
Willow (*Salix caroliniana*)*	N, C, S
Sassafras (*Sassafras albidum*)*	N, C
Hercules' club (*Zanthoxylum clava-herculis*)*	N, C, S
Wild lime (*Zanthoxylum fagara*)*	S

 "We are located near Butterfly World, so the interest here in butterfly gardening is tremendous. One of my favorite plants for butterflies is the wild lime, a native evergreen shrub or tree with foliage that has a lime aroma when bruised. The wild lime is an excellent host plant. Host plants are necessary for both the adult and larval stages to live on and around, and many butterflies are host specific." —Chris Maler, Alexander's Landscaping and Plant Farm, Davie.

FLOWERS WITH NECTAR FOR ADULT BUTTERFLIES

Hundreds of flowers offer nectar for butterflies, but the ones listed below are some of the most attractive to both butterflies and gardeners. Keep these in mind when adding new plants or rearranging and put the butterfly favorites where their visits will be easy to see and enjoy, such as under a window or near a patio or porch. The natives all grow wild in some parts of the state and can be easy to grow in your garden if you give them similar soil and water conditions. All except the Florida petunia do best in the sun, and since butterflies are active only in the sun, plant it where it will be in the sun for the part of the day you'll most likely be watching. The natives and naturalized plants are marked with an asterisk.

Annuals
Ageratum (*Ageratum houstonianum*)
Asters (*Aster* spp.)
Spider flower (*Cleome hasslerana*)
Calliopsis (*Coreopsis* spp.)
Klondike cosmos (*Cosmos sulphureus*)
Pinks (*Dianthus* spp.)
Gazanias (*Gazania* spp.)
Globe amaranth (*Gomphrena globosa*)*
Blanket flower (*Gaillardia pulchella*)*
Sunflower (*Helianthus* spp.)
Heliotrope (*Heliotropium arborescens*)*
Seaside heliotrope (*Heliotropium curassavicum*)
Impatiens (*Impatiens wallerana*)
Lobelia (*Lobelia erinus*)
Pentas (*Pentas lanceolata*)
Drummond phlox (*Phlox drummondii*)*
Black-eyed Susan (*Rudbeckia hirta*)*
French marigold (*Tagetes patula*)
Mexican sunflower (*Tithonia rotundifolia*)
Moss verbena (*Verbena tenuisecta*)
Zinnias (*Zinnia* spp.)

Perennials

Fernleaf yarrow (*Achillea filipendula*)	N, C, S
Milkweed (*Asclepias* spp.)*	N, C, S
Florida paintbrush (*Carphephorus corymbosus*)*	N, C, S
Red valerian (*Centranthus ruber*)	N, C, S
Oxeye daisy (*Chrysanthemum leucanthemum*)	N, C
Purple coneflower (*Echinacea purpurea*)*	N, C, S
Hardy ageratum (*Eupatorium coelestinum*)*	N, C, S
Joe-pye weed (*Eupatorium purpureum*)*	N
Beach sunflower (*Helianthus debilis*)*	N, C, S
Swamp sunflower (*Helianthus simulans*)*	N, C, S
Daylily (*Hemerocallis* spp.)	N, C, S
Kalanchoes (*Kalanchoe* spp.)	N, C, S
Trailing lantana (*Lantana camara*)	N, C, S
Gayfeather, blazing star (*Liatris* spp.)*	N, C, S
Cardinal flower (*Lobelia cardinalis*)	N, C, S
Bee balm (*Monarda* spp.)*	N, C, S
Pickerel weed (*Pontederia cordata*)*	N, C, S
Florida petunia (*Ruellia caroliniensis*)*	N, C, S
Showy sedum (*Sedum spectabile*)	N
Goldenrod (*Solidago* spp.)*	N, C, S
Stoke's aster (*Stokesia laevis*)*	N, C, S
Vervain (*Verbena* spp.)*	N, C, S
Ironweed (*Vernonia* spp.)*	N, C, S
Salvia (*Salvia* spp., *S. coccinea*)*	N, C, S

Shrubs

Abelia (*Abelia* × *grandiflora*)	N, C
Tarflower (*Befaria racemosa*)*	N, C, S
Butterfly bush (*Buddleia officinalis*)*	N, C
Powderpuff (*Calliandra haematocephala*)	C, S
New Jersey tea (*Ceanothus americanus*)	N, C
Buttonbush (*Cephalanthus occidentalis*)*	N, C, S
Cardinal spear (*Erythrina herbacea*)	N, C, S
Poinsettia (*Euphorbia pulcherrima*)	C, S
Garberia (*Garberia fruticosa*)*	N, C
Firebush (*Hamelia patens*)*	C, S
Hibiscus (*Hibiscus* spp.)	C, S
Lantanas (*Lantana* spp.)*	N, C, S
Privet (*Ligustrum* spp.)	N, C, S
Honeysuckle (*Lonicera* spp.)	N, C, S
Barbados cherry (*Malpighia glabra*)	C, S
Chaya (*Onidoscolus chayamansa*)	N, C, S
Pentas (*Pentas lanceolata*)	C, S
Plumbago (*Plumabo auriculata*)	C, S
Piedmont azalea (*Rhododendron canescens*)*	N, C
Sumac (*Rhus copallina*)	N, C, S
Chaste tree (*Vitex agnus-castus*)	N, C, S

 "The #1 plant for butterflies in my garden is the scarlet milkweed, *Asclepias curassavica*. Every butterfly in the garden visits it either for nectar or larva, and it also attracts hummingbirds." —Lois Weber, bird and butterfly chairperson for District 8 of the Florida Federation of Garden Clubs, Tarpon Springs.

TREES, SHRUBS, AND VINES TO ATTRACT BIRDS

Backyard birdwatching is one of the great rewards of gardening. Birds add movement, song, color, and interest to the garden, and they are nature's best pest patrol, eating great quantities of mosquitoes and other insects that would otherwise make outdoor living most uncomfortable. Planting for the birds can give them a more reliable food source than putting grain in a feeder (but you can do that as well). It is most important to give them a water source and keep it clean and full. Although you will likely find birds in your garden no matter what you plant, certain trees, shrubs, and flowers are favorites of a particular bird species.

Hummingbirds are attracted to tubular flowers for nectar—to many of the same plants that attract butterflies, in fact. They are a special, seasonal treat in Florida gardens. If you plant for them and keep your eyes and ears open, eventually you will see some, though it may take a few years, especially on the peninsula. They are more common in the panhandle.

Trees to Attract Hummingbirds

Mimosa (*Albizia* spp.)	N, C, S
Bottlebrush (*Callistemon* spp.)	N, C, S
Hong Kong orchid (*Bauhinia* × *blakeana*)	C, S
Geiger tree (*Cordia sebestena*)	C, S
Royal poinciana (*Delonix regia*)	S

Trees to Attract Other Birds

Gumbo limbo (*Bursera simaruba*)	S	Parrots, parakeets, others
Satin leaf (*Chrysophyllum oliviforme*)	C, S	Warblers, cardinals, gnat-catchers
Pigeon plum (*Coccoloba diversifolia*)	C, S	Mockingbirds, catbirds, robins, woodpeckers
Short-leaf fig (*Ficus citrifolia*)	C, S	Catbirds, woodpeckers
Blolly (*Guapira discolor*), female	C, S	Fruit-eating birds
Dahoon holly (*Ilex cassine*), female	N, C, S	Cardinals, mockingbirds, cedar waxwings
Wild tamarind (*Lysiloma latisiliqua*)	C, S	Warblers, gnat-catchers, flycatchers
Mulberry (*Morus rubra*)	N, C, S	Fruit-eating birds
Lancewood (*Pseudopanax crassifolius*)	C, S	Fruit-eating birds, thrushes
Slash pine (*Pinus elliottii* var. *densa*)	N, C, S	Doves, blue jays, warblers, owls
Live oak (*Quercus virginiana*)	N, C, S	Woodpeckers, vireos, warblers, bluejay, grackles, owls
Mahogany (*Swietenia mahagoni*)	S	Nest sites for many birds
Paradise tree (*Simaruba glauca*)	S	Fruit-eating birds

Shrubs to Attract Hummingbirds (Asterisk indicates perennial in north Florida)

Butterfly bush (*Buddleia officinalis*)	N, C
Powderpuff (*Calliandra haematocephala*)	C, S
Golden dewdrop (*Duranta repens*)	C, S
Firebush (*Hamelia patens*)	C, S
Hibiscus (*Hibiscus rosa-sinensis*)	C, S
Jacobinia (*Justicia* spp.)*	C, S

Shrimp plant (*Justicia brandegeana*)*   C, S
Lantanas (*Lantana* spp.)*   C, S
Turk's cap mallow (*Malvaviscus arboreus*)*   C, S
Firespike (*Odontonema strictum*)   N, C, S
Golden shrimp plant (*Pachystachys lutea*)   C, S
Pentas (*Pentas lanceolata*)   C, S
Firecracker plant (*Rusellia equisetiformis*)   C, S
Necklace pod (*Sophora tomentosa*)   C, S

Shrubs to Attract Other Birds

Plant	Region	Birds
Marlberry (*Ardisia paniculata*)	N, C, S	Mockingbirds, catbirds, cardinals
Locustberry (*Byrsonima lucida*)	S	Mockingbirds
Beautyberry (*Callicarpa americana*)	N, C, S	Mockingbirds, cardinals, bulbuls, brown thrashers, catbirds
Spicewood (*Calyptranthes pallens*)	S	Fruit-eating birds, shelter for warblers, wrens
Cocoplum (*Chrysobalanus icaco*)	S	Fruit-eating birds
Hibiscus (*Hibiscus rosa-sinensis*)	C, S	Orioles, buntings
Barbados cherry (*Malpighia glabra*)	C, S	Fruit-eating birds
Turk's cap (*Malvaviscus arboreus*)	C, S	Painted buntings
Orange jessamine (*Murraya paniculata*)	N, C, S	Mockingbirds, catbirds, cardinals
Simpson stopper (*Myrcianthes simpsonii*)	C, S	Mockingbirds, catbirds, cardinals
Wild coffee (*Psychotria* spp.)	S	Cardinals, blue jays, catbirds
Sumac (*Rhus copallina*)	N, C	Mockingbirds, cardinals, sparrows
Necklace pod (*Sophora tomentosa*)	C, S	Warblers
Blue porterweed (*Stachytarpheta fruiticosa*)	C, S	Cardinals, sparrows
West Indian lilac (*Tetrazygia bicolor*)	S	Mockingbirds, blue jays, cardinals

Vines to Attract Hummingbirds

Trumpet vine (*Campsis radicans*)   N, C
Purple cestrum (*Cestrum purpureum*)   S
Coral honeysuckle   N, C
   (*Lonicera sempervirens*)
Firethorn (*Pyracantha coccinea*)   N, C, S
Wild grape (*Vitis* spp.)   N, C, S

NIGHT-BLOOMING PLANTS

Evening is a good time to enjoy your garden, especially if you plant flowers that open at night. That gives your garden a different look (and fragrance) for the night than it has by day. Most of the plants on the following list have white or pale yellow blooms that are easy to see at night. Combine them with plants of silvery foliage and a few low-standing lights along a path.

Four-o'clocks and moonflower open at dusk and stay open until morning. Some flowers, like the yucca and the crinum lilies, may stay open for several days. The sansevierias look much the same for several days, but the fragrance at night is heavenly; in the daytime it is absent.

Just as some plants attract butterflies in the daytime, some of those listed here will attract moths to drink the nectar of their night-blooming flowers. Moths also have subtle colors and beauty, especially the colorful cecropia moth, the luminescent green luna moth, and the hawk moth that is so much like a hummingbird.

The one insect that can keep you from enjoying all of this is the mosquito. The breeze from a strong floor fan or several ceiling fans on a patio is often enough to keep the blood suckers away.

Perennials

Crinums (*Crinum* hybrids 'Alamo Village', 'Empress of India')	N, C, S
Butterfly ginger (*Hedychium coronarium*)	N, C, S
Ginger (*Hedychium* spp.)	N, C, S
Spider lily (*Hymenocallis* spp.)	N, C, S
Four-o'clocks (*Mirabilis jalapa*)	N, C, S
Water lily (*Nymphaea* cultivars)	
Missouri primrose (*Oenothera missouriensis*)	N, C, S
Evening primrose (*Oenothera speciosa*)	N, C, S
Baja primrose (*Oenothera stubbi*)	N, C, S
Tuberose (*Polianthes tuberosa* 'Pearl')	N, C, S
Snake plant (*Sansevieria* spp.)	C, S
Rain lily (*Zephyranthes drummondii*, related spp.)	N, C, S

Annuals

Moonvine (*Ipomoea alba*)	C, S
Flowering tobacco (*Nicotiana alata*, *N. sylvestris*)	N, C, S

Shrubs

Angel trumpet (*Brugmansia* spp.)	C, S
Night-blooming jasmine (*Cestrum nocturnum*)	C, S
Night-blooming cereus (*Hylocereus undatus*)	C, S
Confederate jasmine (*Trachelospermum jasminoides*)	N, C, S

TO DO LIST FOR WATER GARDENING

Watering gardening is opening new dimensions of beauty and enjoyment for many gardeners as well as people who have never gardened before. With the improvements in PVC liners and preformed fiberglass, even the most unhandy person can now install a pool in two weekends and maintain it with much less work and expense than most people expect, little more than for a flower border. In return the water sets a mood of enchantment and tranquillity. A fountain can add the sound of trickling or splashing water to your garden scene.

One evening's study of a good catalog or water gardening booklet (see suggestions and sources in the mail-order list at the back of the book) and the help of your distributor will get you started, even if you are completely unfamiliar with the subject. An increasing number of landscapers and garden shops specialize in water gardening. Visit their displays for the information and motivation you need. Then proceed according to the following steps and tips:

- Choose a location for your pool, the focal point of the garden, in the sun and where the fewest leaves will fall into it.
- Plan the design, shape, liner, edging, and surrounding plants.
- Check local building and electrical codes and put safety first.
- Dig the hole and line the pool. Fill the pool halfway with water and let the liner mold the pool to the ground.
- Leave a rim of 3 inches to keep groundwater out. Use rocks, bricks, or paving stones to hide the edge of the liner.
- Fill to the brim. Allow to settle a week before adding fish or plants.
- Add one bunch of oxygenating plants for every 2 square feet of surface area, 50 for a 10 x 10 pool. These will keep the water crystal clean.
- Never use koi in a pond with plants. Goldfish yes, koi no.
- You can plant lilies and lotus in bottom soil, but container planting allows flexibility in depth and position and makes care easier. Plant one lily per pot with a good mix of garden loam and aquatic plant fertilizer.
- Do not use swamp muck, compost, peat moss, or dry manure.
- Plant tropical water lilies upright, hardy ones at an angle against the pot side.
- Welcome frogs or toads or buy some to help control algae and insects.
- Do not overfeed fish. Remove any food left after five to ten minutes.
- Spray plants with a hose often to wash insects into the pool for the fish.
- Never add large amounts of water at once.
- Remove dead foliage and debris and treat for algae only as needed.
- Empty and clean the pool only every several years in the spring.
- Give plants or fish away as they multiply.

GARDEN PLANTS FOR WATER GARDENS

Plants that like wet feet do well next to water gardens, where they often get splashed. The ones below, which may now be growing in other parts of your garden, will live nicely beside or in the shallow margins of garden pools, where water is usually 2-6 inches deep. Just outside the rim of a lined pool, however, the soil can be quite dry unless you make a bog with the leftover liner material. Put this boggy area to the back or side of the pool. Dig the area for the bog garden 14 inches deep and line it as you did the pond. Then fill it with good rich topsoil and cow manure and water as needed, perhaps once a week, to keep the soil moist. Those few plants marked with an asterisk will grow in water but are also drought tolerant.

Leatherfern (*Acrostichum daneifolium*)	N, C, S
*Canna × generalis**	N, C, S
Taro (*Colocasia* spp.)	C, S
Bog lily (*Crinum americanum*)*	N, C, S
Umbrella plant (*Cyperus alternifolius*)*	N, C, S
Dwarf papyrus (*Cyperus isocladua*)*	N, C, S
Giant Egyptian papyrus (*Cyperus papyrus*)*	N, C, S

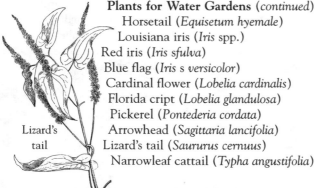

Plants for Water Gardens (*continued*)

Horsetail (*Equisetum hyemale*)	N, C, S
Louisiana iris (*Iris* spp.)	N, C, S
Red iris (*Iris sfulva*)	N, C, S
Blue flag (*Iris s versicolor*)	N, C, S
Cardinal flower (*Lobelia cardinalis*)	N, C
Florida cript (*Lobelia glandulosa*)	N, C, S
Pickerel (*Pontederia cordata*)	N, C, S
Arrowhead (*Sagittaria lancifolia*)	N, C, S
Lizard's tail (*Saururus cernuus*)	N, C, S
Narrowleaf cattail (*Typha angustifolia*)	N, C, S

Lizard's tail

OUTSTANDING TROPICAL WATER LILIES

Although most tropical water lilies can't take frost, they're desirable plants for a water garden because of their fragrance and their spectacular large flowers, which are held well above the water's surface. They come in a wider range of colors than hardy water lilies. Some tropicals bloom during the day, and some bloom at night. All are fragrant, and all are hybrids of the genus Nymphaea. If you live in north Florida, these will be annuals in your pond.

Day Bloomers

'Albert Greenberg'	Rose yellow; will burn in direct sun in S
'Blue Anemone'	Double with up to 75 petals; rare
'Blue Beauty'	Nice
'Dauben'	Pale blue
'Director Moore'	Purple; foliage not so good
'Gene Joyner'	Large violet-blue fades to silver
'General Pershing'	Pink; drop-dead gorgeous
'Helen Nash'	Lavender-pink; mottled purple and green leaves
'Panama Pacific'	Purple; fantastic
'White Delight'	Striking
'Yellow Dazzler'	Good yellow

Night Bloomers

'Antares'	Red
'Emily Grant Hutchings'	Red
'Leeann Connelly'	Pink with white stripes
'Mrs. George C. Hitchcock'	Pink
'Red Flare'	Red
'Wood's White Knight'	White

"Why is water gardening becoming the fastest, most popular aspect of gardening in modern America? Because water is the essence of all life. All life requires water and revolves around water. As a matter of fact, our bodies are made primarily of water, and it is only natural that we would feel this closeness with it. Nothing will relieve tension like sitting next to a waterfall enjoying your goldfish or having them nibble food off of your fingers." — Leeann Connelly, owner, Tropical Pond and Garden, Loxahatchee.

DWARF WATER PLANTS FOR TUB GARDENS

You don't need a big lot for a water garden. You can grow aquatic plants in waterproof containers the size of half whiskey barrels. (If you use a whiskey barrel, line it with plastic first.) Here are some of the best dwarf water lilies and lotus for such a use. Some others will adjust to the amount of space they're given, but these will have the least adjustment to make. All of these will thrive throughout Florida. There is no basic difference in the care of tropical and hardy water lilies, but there is a difference in the planting. The tropicals should be planted vertically in the center of the tub; the hardy ones will grow more horizontally across the tub.

Tropical Water Lilies
'Dauben'	Pale blue; shade tolerant
'Blue Anemone'	Rare double
Nymphaea colorada	Pygmy; medium blue with dark maroon stamens

Hardy Water Lilies
'Baby red'	Most reds burn, but this does not
'Pride of Palm Beach'	Double white with a tinge of pink
'Laydekeri Rosea'	Lavender pink; very small
'Helvola'	Yellow; smallest in the world, 2 to 3 inches
'Chrysantha'	Apricot that deepens to reddish orange

Lotus
'Tulip'	White

"You may want to place your water-garden-in-a-tub in a spot where it will receive a few hours of afternoon shade. Water lilies will bloom better with more sunlight, with the one exception of very small gardens, especially tub gardens. They will actually produce more blossoms if they get a few hours of shade in the hottest part of the day. The reason is water lilies are accustomed to gradual changes in the daily temperature of the water, but when you have a small body of water, especially one above ground, the daily temperature variations substantially increase. If you provide a few hours of shade, this will reduce that greater temperature variation, which causes a mild amount of stress on the plant—enough that it reduces the amount of blooming it would do otherwise." —Charles Thomas, Lilypons Water Gardens, Buckeystown, Maryland.

MAIL-ORDER
SOURCES

Some nurseries charge for their catalogs, and some have a minimum order, so please inquire first. In some cases, the companies below carry more than we've indicated; we mention only those items relevant to this book. Companies vary in size from big operations that offer full-color catalogs to small ones that have only a list of plants or books. Write or leave a message on an answering machine.

B.B. Mackey Books
(garden books, including those by Monica Brandies)
P.O. Box 475
Wayne, PA 19087-0475
610-971-4909

B & K Tropicals
(begonias, hoyas)
5300 48th Terrace North
St. Petersburg, FL 33709
813-522-8691

Brookhill Gardens
(camellias)
1109 Heath Avenue
Lynchburg, VA 24502

W. Atlee Burpee & Co.
(seeds of annuals, vines)
300 Park Avenue
Warminster, PA 18974
800-888-1447

Caladium World
(caladiums, elephant's ears)
P.O. Drawer 629
Sebring, FL 33871-0629
941-385-7661

Canterbury Farm and Nursery
(trees, shrubs, perennials)
Linda Hunter
22351 SW 147th Avenue
Miami, FL 33170

Charles Alford Plants
(ferns and orchids)
1645 9th Street SW
Vero Beach, FL 32962-4314

Martha S. Davies Antique Roses
(antique, Bermuda; no spray roses)
1575 Palm Place South
Bartow, FL 33830
941-533-3073

Daylily Discounters
(daylilies)
One Daylily Place
Alachua, FL 32615
904-462-1539
Web page: www.daylily-discounters.com
E-mail: catalog@daylily-discounters.com

ECHO
(seeds of uncommon vegetables)
17430 Durrance Road
North Fort Myers, FL 33917
941-543-3246
Web page: www.xc.org/echo

The Exotic Plumeria
Alan Bunch
(largest plumeria nursery in Florida)
Seffner, FL 33584
813-685-0146

Florida Gardening **Magazine**
Kathy Nelson, Editor
P.O. Box 500678
Malabar, FL 32950-0678
407-951-4500

Florida Native Plants, Inc.
(native trees, shrubs, vines, groundcovers,
wildflowers)
730 Myakka Road
Sarasota, FL 34240
941-322-1915

Giles Rose Nursery
(roses of all kinds)
2611 Holly Hill Cut-off Road
Davenport, FL 33837
941-422-8102

Going Bananas Nursery
Don and Katie Chafin
(bananas, edible landscaping)
24401 SW 197th Avenue
Homestead, FL 33031
305-247-0397

Great Outdoors Publishing
4747 29th Street North
St. Petersburg, FL 33714
800-869-6609

J.L. Hudson, Seedsman
(seeds of almost anything, catalog $1)
Star Route 2, Box 337
La Honda, CA 94020

The Misting Shed Herb Nursery
(herbs, organically grown)
4818 Pennyroyal Lane
Dover, FL 33527
813-685-1843

Maurice Kong
(Thai jujube, rare and tropical fruit)
14735 NW 48th Terrace
Miami, FL 33185
305-554-1333

Old Fashioned Bloomers
Peggy Coven
(antique roses)
8711 No. 2 Road
Howey-in-the-Hills, FL 34737
352-324-3837

Our Kids Orchids & Nursery
Larry Shatzer
(bananas, citrus, gingers, tropical fruit)
17229 Phil C. Peters Road
Winter Garden, FL 34787
407-877-6883

Park Seed
(seed of annuals and wildflowers, bulbs,
perennials)
Cokesbury Road
Greenwood, SC 29647-0001

The Neem Tree Company
Victoria Parsons
604 Southwood Cove
Brandon, FL 33511
813-689-2616

Winn Soldani's Fancy Hibiscus
(catalog $2, refundable)
1142 SW 1st Avenue
Pompano Beach, FL 33060
800-432-8332
Web page: www.fancy hibiscus.com

Southern Seeds
Elaine Sarrasin
(unusual vegetables, roselle; catalog $2,
refundable)
P.O. Box 803
Lutz, FL 33548
813-948-3419

Thompson & Morgan
(seeds of annuals, perennials)
Box 1208
Jackson, NJ 08527

Tomato Growers Supply Co.
P.O. Box 720
Fort Myers, FL 33902

Tropical Pond and Garden
Leeann Connelly
(water gardening, Louisiana iris)
17888 61st Place North
Loxahatchee, FL 33470
561-791-8994

University of Florida Press
(garden books)
15 NW 15th Street
Gainesville, FL 32611
800-226-3822
Web page: nersp.nerdc.ufl.edu/upf

Marian Van Atta
(garden books and newsletter)
P.O. Box 2131
Melbourne, FL 32902-2131

Wayside Gardens
(perennials, shrubs, roses, vines, trees)
1 Garden Lane
Hodges, SC 29695-0001
800-845-1124

Woodlanders
(native and noteworthy exotic plants)
1128 Colleton Avenue
Aiken, SC 29801
803-648-7522

Water Gardening Information

**Northwest Florida Water Management
District**
Route 1, Box 3100
Havana, FL 32333
904-539-5999

St. Johns River Water Management District
P.O. Box 1429
Palatka, FL 32178-1429
904-329-4540

South Florida Water Management District
P.O. Box 24680
West Palm Beach, FL 33416-4680
407-686-88800

**Southwest Florida Water Management
District**
2379 Broad Street
Brooksville, FL 34609-6899
904-796-7211

**Suwannee River Water Management
District**
Route 3, Box 64
Live Oak, FL 32060
904-362-1001

INDEX